THE DIARY OF SAMUEL PEPYS

THE DIARY OF SAMUEL PEPYS

EDITED AND WITH A PREFACE
BY RICHARD LE GALLIENNE

Introduction by Robert Louis Stevenson

THE MODERN LIBRARY

NEW YORK

2001 Modern Library Edition
Published in the United States by Modern Library, a division of
Random House, Inc., New York,
and simultaneously in Canada by Random House of Canada Limited,
Toronto.

MODERN LIBRARY and colophon are registered trademarks
of Random House, Inc.

LIBRARY OF CONGRESS CATALOGING-IN-PUBLICATION DATA
Pepys, Samuel, 1633–1703.
The diary of Samuel Pepys / edited and with a preface by
Richard Le Gallienne; introduction by Robert Louis Stevenson.—
Modern Library ed.
p. cm.
ISBN 0-679-64221-8 (alk. paper)
1. Pepys, Samuel, 1633-1703—Diaries. 2. Great Britain—Social life
and customs—17th century. 3. Authors, English—Early
modern, 1500-1700—Diaries. 4. Great Britain—Politics and
government—1660-1688. 5. Statesmen—Great Britain—Diaries.
I. Le Gallienne, Richard, 1866–1947. II. Title.
DA447.P4 A4 2001
941.06'6'092—dc21
[B]   00-054817

Modern Library website address:
www.modernlibrary.com

Printed in the United States of America on acid-free paper

2 4 6 8 9 7 5 3 1

Introduction

Robert Louis Stevenson

The Diary

That there should be such a book as *The Diary of Samuel Pepys* is incomparably strange. Pepys, in a corrupt and idle period, played the man in public employments, toiling hard and keeping his honour bright. Much of the little good that is set down to James the Second comes by right to Pepys; and if it were little for a king, it is much for a subordinate. To his clear, capable head was owing somewhat of the greatness of England on the seas. In the exploits of Hawke, Rodney, or Nelson, this dead Mr. Pepys of the Navy Office had some considerable share. He stood well by his business in the appalling plague of 1666. He was loved and respected by some of the best and wisest men in England. He was President of the Royal Society; and when he came to die, people said of his conduct in that solemn hour—thinking it needless to say more—that it was answerable to the greatness of his life. Thus he walked in dignity, guards of soldiers sometimes attending him in his walks, subalterns bowing before his periwig; and when he uttered his thoughts they were suitable to his state and services. On February 8, 1668, we find him writing to Evelyn, his mind bitterly occupied with the late Dutch war, and some thoughts of the different story of the repulse of the Great Armada:

> "SIR,—You will not wonder at the backwardness of my thanks for the present you made me, so many days since, of the Prospect of the Medway, while the Hollander rode master in it, when I have told you that the sight of it hath led me to such reflections on my particular interest, by my employment, in the reproach due to that miscarriage, as have given me little less disquiet than he is fancied to have who found his face in Michael Angelo's hell. The same should serve me also in excuse for my silence in celebrating your mastery shown in the design and draught, did not indignation rather than courtship urge me so far to commend them, as to wish the furniture of our House of Lords changed from the story of '88 to that of '67 [of Evelyn's designing], till the pravity of this were reformed to the temper of that age, wherein God Almighty found his blessings more operative than, I fear, he doth in ours his judgments."

This is a letter honourable to the writer, where the meaning rather than the words is eloquent. Such was the account he gave of himself to his contemporaries; such thoughts he chose to utter, and in such language: giving himself out for a grave and patriotic public servant. We turn to the same date in the Diary by which he is known, after two centuries, to his descendants. The entry begins in the same key with the letter, blaming the "madness of the House of Commons" and "the base proceedings, just the epitome of all our public proceedings in this age, of the House of Lords"; and then, without the least transition, this is how our diarist proceeds: "To the Strand, to my bookseller's, and there bought an idle, rogueish French book, *L'escholle des Filles,* which I have bought in plain binding, avoiding the buying of it better bound, because I resolve, as soon as I have read it, to burn it, that it may not stand in the list of books, nor among them, to disgrace them, if it should be found." Even in our day, when responsibility is so much more clearly apprehended, the man who wrote the letter would be notable; but what about the man, I do not say who bought a roguish book, but who was ashamed of doing so, yet did it, and recorded both the doing and the shame in the pages of his daily journal?

We all, whether we write or speak, must somewhat drape ourselves when we address our fellows; at a given moment we apprehend our character and acts by some particular side; we are merry with one, grave with another, as befits the nature and demands of the relation. Pepys's letter to Evelyn would have little in common with that other one to Mrs. Knipp which he signed by the pseudonym of *Dapper Dicky;* yet each would be suitable to the character of his correspondent. There is no untruth in this, for man, being a Protean animal, swiftly shares and changes with his company and surroundings; and these changes are the better part of his education in the world. To strike a posture once for all, and to march through life like a drum-major, is to be highly disagreeable to others and a fool for oneself into the bargain. To Evelyn and to Knipp we understand the double facing; but to whom was he posing in the Diary, and what, in the name of astonishment, was the nature of the pose? Had he suppressed all mention of the book, or had he bought it, gloried in the act, and cheerfully recorded his glorification, in either case we should have made him out. But no; he is full of precautions to conceal the "disgrace" of the purchase, and yet speeds to chronicle the whole affair in pen and ink. It is a sort of anomaly in human action, which we can exactly parallel from another part of the Diary.

Mrs. Pepys had written a paper of her too just complaints against her husband, and written it in plain and very pungent English. Pepys, in an agony lest the world should come to see it, brutally seizes and destroys the tell-tale document; and then— you disbelieve your eyes—down goes the whole story with unsparing truth and in the cruellest detail. It seems he has no design but to appear respectable, and here he keeps a private book to prove he was not. You are at first faintly reminded of some of the vagaries of the morbid religious diarist; but at a moment's thought the resemblance disappears. The design of Pepys is not at all to edify; it is not from repentance that he chronicles his peccadilloes, for he tells us when he does repent, and, to be just to him, there often follows some improvement. Again, the sins of the religious diarist are of a very formal pattern, and are told with an elaborate whine. But in Pepys you come upon good, substantive misdemeanours; beams in his eye of which he alone remains unconscious; healthy outbreaks of the animal nature, and laughable subterfuges to himself that always command belief and often engage the sympathies.

Pepys was a young man for his age, came slowly to himself in the world, sowed his wild oats late, took late to industry, and preserved till nearly forty the headlong gusto of a boy. So, to come rightly at the spirit in which the Diary was written, we must recall a class of sentiments which with most of us are over and done before the age of twelve. In our tender years we still preserve a freshness of surprise at our prolonged existence; events make an impression out of all proportion to their consequence; we are unspeakably touched by our own past adventures, and look forward to our future personality with sentimental interest. It was something of this, I think, that clung to Pepys. Although not sentimental in the abstract, he was sweetly sentimental about himself. His own past clung about his heart, an evergreen. He was the slave of an association. He could not pass by Islington, where his father used to carry him to cakes and ale, but he must light at the King's Head and eat and drink "for remembrance of the old house sake." He counted it good fortune to lie a night at Epsom to renew his old walks, "where Mrs. Hely and I did use to walk and talk, with whom I had the first sentiments of love and pleasure in a woman's company, discourse and taking her by the hand, she being a pretty woman." He goes about weighing up the *Assurance,* which lay near Woolwich under water, and cries in a parenthesis, "Poor ship, that I have been twice merry in, in Captain Holland's time"; and after revisiting the *Naseby,* now changed into the *Charles,* he confesses "it was a great pleasure to myself to see the ship that I began my good fortune in." The stone that he was cut for he preserved in a case; and to the

Turners he kept alive such gratitude for their assistance that for years, even after he had begun to mount himself into higher zones, he continued to have that family to dinner on the anniversary of the operation. Not Hazlitt nor Rousseau had a more romantic passion for their past, although at times they might express it more romantically; and if Pepys shared with them this childish fondness, did not Rousseau, who left behind him the *Confessions,* or Hazlitt, who wrote the *Liber Amoris,* and loaded his essays with loving personal detail, share with Pepys in his unwearied egotism? For the two things go hand-in-hand; or, to be more exact, it is the first that makes the second either possible or pleasing.

But, to be quite in sympathy with Pepys, we must return once more to the experience of children. I can remember to have written, in the fly-leaf of more than one book, the date and the place where I then was—if, for instance, I was ill in bed or sitting in a certain garden; these were jottings for my future self; if I should chance on such a note in after years, I thought it would cause me a particular thrill to recognise myself across the intervening distance. Indeed, I might come upon them now, and not be moved one title—which shows that I have comparatively failed in life, and grown older than Samuel Pepys. For in the Diary we can find more than one such note of perfect childish egotism; as when he explains that his candle is going out, "which makes me write thus slobberingly"; or as in this incredible particularity, "To my study, where I only wrote thus much of this day's passages to this, and so out again"; or lastly, as here, with more of circumstance: "I staid up till the bellman came by with his bell under my window, *as I was writing of this very line,* and cried, 'Past one of the clock, and a cold, frosty, windy morning.' " Such passages are not to be misunderstood. The appeal to Samuel Pepys years hence is unmistakable. He desires that dear, though unknown, gentleman keenly to realise his predecessor; to remember why a passage was uncleanly written; to recall (let us fancy, with a sigh) the tones of the bellman, the chill of the early, windy morning, and the very line his own romantic self was scribing at the moment. The man, you will perceive, was making reminiscences—a sort of pleasure by ricochet, which

comforts many in distress, and turns some others into sentimental libertines: and the whole book, if you will but look at it
in that way, is seen to be a work of art to Pepys's own address.

Here, then, we have the key to that remarkable attitude preserved by him throughout his Diary, to that unflinching—I had
almost said, that unintelligent—sincerity which makes it a miracle among human books. He was not unconscious of his
errors—far from it; he was often startled into shame, often re-
formed, often made and broke his vows of change. But whether
he did ill or well, he was still his own unequalled self; still that
entrancing *ego* of whom alone he cared to write; and still sure of
his own affectionate indulgence, when the parts should be
changed, and the writer come to read what he had written.
Whatever he did, or said, or thought, or suffered, it was still a
trait of Pepys, a character of his career; and as, to himself, he
was more interesting than Moses or than Alexander, so all
should be faithfully set down. I have called his Diary a work of
art. Now when the artist has found something, word or deed,
exactly proper to a favourite character in play or novel, he will
neither suppress nor diminish it, though the remark be silly or
the act mean. The hesitation of Hamlet, the credulity of Oth-
ello, the baseness of Emma Bovary, or the irregularities of Mr.
Swiveller, caused neither disappointment nor disgust to their
creators. And so with Pepys and his adored protagonist: adored
not blindly, but with trenchant insight and enduring, human
toleration. I have gone over and over the greater part of the
Diary; and the points where, to the most suspicious scrutiny, he
has seemed not perfectly sincere, are so few, so doubtful, and so
petty, that I am ashamed to name them. It may be said that we
all of us write such a diary in airy characters upon our brain;
but I fear there is a distinction to be made; I fear that as we render to our consciousness an account of our daily fortunes and
behaviour, we too often weave a tissue of romantic compli-
ments and dull excuses; and even if Pepys were the ass and
coward that men call him, we must take rank as sillier and more
cowardly than he. The bald truth about oneself, what we are all
too timid to admit when we are not too dull to see it, that was
what he saw clearly and set down unsparingly.

It is improbable that the Diary can have been carried on in the same single spirit in which it was begun. Pepys was not such an ass, but he must have perceived, as he went on, the extraordinary nature of the work he was producing. He was a great reader, and he knew what other books were like. It must, at least, have crossed his mind that someone might ultimately decipher the manuscript, and he himself, with all his pains and pleasures, be resuscitated in some later day; and the thought, although discouraged, must have warmed his heart. He was not such an ass, besides, but he must have been conscious of the deadly explosives, the gun-cotton and the giant powder, he was hoarding in his drawer. Let some contemporary light upon the Journal, and Pepys was plunged for ever in social and political disgrace. We can trace the growth of his terrors by two facts. In 1660, while the Diary was still in its youth, he tells about it, as a matter of course, to a lieutenant in the navy; but in 1669, when it was already near an end, he could have bitten his tongue out, as the saying is, because he had let slip his secret to one so grave and friendly as Sir William Coventry. And from two other facts I think we may infer that he had entertained, even if he had not acquiesced in, the thought of a far-distant publicity. The first is of capital importance: the Diary was not destroyed. The second—that he took unusual precautions to confound the cipher in "rogueish" passages—proves, beyond question, that he was thinking of some other reader besides himself. Perhaps while his friends were admiring the "greatness of his behaviour" at the approach of death, he may have had a twinkling hope of immortality. *Mens cujusque is est quisque,* said his chosen motto; and, as he had stamped his mind with every crook and foible in the pages of the Diary, he might feel that what he left behind him was indeed himself. There is perhaps no other instance so remarkable of the desire of man for publicity and an enduring name. The greatness of his life was open, yet he longed to communicate its smallness also; and, while contemporaries bowed before him, he must buttonhole posterity with the news that his periwig was once alive with nits. But this thought, although I cannot doubt he had it, was neither his first nor his deepest; it did not colour one word that he wrote;

and the Diary, for as long as he kept it, remained what it was when he began, a private pleasure for himself. It was his bosom secret; it added a zest to all his pleasures; he lived in and for it, and might well write these solemn words, when he closed that confidant for ever: "And so I betake myself to that course which is almost as much as to see myself go into the grave; for which, and all the discomforts that will accompany my being blind, the good God prepare me."

A LIBERAL GENIUS

Pepys spent part of a certain winter Sunday, when he had taken physic, composing "a song in praise of a liberal genius (such as I take my own to be) to all studies and pleasures." The song was unsuccessful, but the Diary is, in a sense, the very song that he was seeking; and his portrait by Hales, so admirably reproduced in Mynors Bright's edition, is a confirmation of the Diary. Hales, it would appear, had known his business; and though he put his sitter to a deal of trouble, almost breaking his neck "to have the portrait full of shadows," and draping him in an Indian gown hired expressly for the purpose, he was preoccupied about no merely picturesque effects, but to portray the essence of the man. Whether we read the picture by the Diary or the Diary by the picture, we shall at least agree that Hales was among the number of those who can "surprise the manners in the face." Here we have a mouth pouting, moist with desires; eyes greedy, protuberant, and yet apt for weeping too; a nose great alike in character and dimensions; and altogether a most fleshly, melting countenance. The face is attractive by its promise of reciprocity. I have used the word *greedy*, but the reader must not suppose that he can change it for that closely kindred one of *hungry*, for there is here no aspiration, no waiting for better things, but an animal joy in all that comes. It could never be the face of an artist; it is the face of a *viveur*—kindly, pleased, and pleasing, protected from excess and upheld in contentment by the shifting versatility of his desires. For a single desire is more rightly to be called a lust;

but there is health in a variety, where one may balance and control another.

The whole world, town or country, was to Pepys a garden of Armida. Wherever he went, his steps were winged with the most eager expectation; whatever he did, it was done with the most lively pleasure. An insatiable curiosity in all the shows of the world and all the secrets of knowledge, filled him brimful of the longing to travel, and supported him in the toils of study. Rome was the dream of his life; he was never happier than when he read or talked of the Eternal City. When he was in Holland, he was "with child" to see any strange thing. Meeting some friends and singing with them in a palace near the Hague, his pen fails him to express his passion of delight, "the more so because in a heaven of pleasure and in a strange country." He must go to see all famous executions. He must needs visit the body of a murdered man, defaced "with a broad wound," he says, "that makes my hand now shake to write of it." He learned to dance, and was "like to make a dancer." He learned to sing, and walked about Gray's Inn Fields "humming to myself (which is now my constant practice) the trillo." He learned to play the lute, the flute, the flageolet, and the theorbo, and it was not the fault of his intention if he did not learn the harpsichord or the spinet. He learned to compose songs, and burned to give forth "a scheme and theory of music not yet ever made in the world." When he heard "a fellow whistle like a bird exceeding well," he promised to return another day and give an angel for a lesson in the art. Once, he writes, "I took the Bezan back with me, and with a brave gale and tide reached up that night to the Hope, taking great pleasure in learning the seamen's manner of singing when they sound the depths." If he found himself rusty in his Latin grammar, he must fall to it like a schoolboy. He was a member of Harrington's Club till its dissolution, and of the Royal Society before it had received the name. Boyle's *Hydrostatics* was "of infinite delight" to him, walking in Barnes Elms. We find him comparing Bible concordances, a captious judge of sermons, deep in Descartes and Aristotle. We find him, in a single year, studying timber and the measurement of timber; tar and oil, hemp, and the process of preparing cordage; mathematics and accounting; the hull and the rigging of ships from a model; and "looking and improving himself of the (naval) stores with"—hark to the fellow!—"great delight." His familiar spirit of delight was not the same with Shelley's; but how true it was to him through life! He is only copying something, and behold, he "takes great pleasure to rule the lines, and have the capital words wrote with red ink"; he has only had his coal-cellar emptied and cleaned, and behold, "it do please him exceedingly." A hog's harslett is "a piece of meat he loves." He cannot ride home in my Lord Sandwich's coach, but he must exclaim, with breathless gusto, "his noble, rich coach." When he is bound for a supper party, he anticipates a "glut of pleasure." When he has a new watch, "to see my childishness," says he, "I could not forbear carrying it in my hand and seeing what o'clock it was an hundred times." To go to Vauxhall, he says, and "to hear the nightingales and other birds, hear fiddles, and there a harp and here a Jew's trump, and here laughing, and there fine people walking, is mighty divertising." And the nightingales, I take it, were particularly dear to him; and it was again "with great pleasure" that he paused to hear them as he walked to Woolwich, while the fog was rising and the April sun broke through.

He must always be doing something agreeable, and, by preference, two agreeable things at once. In his house he had a box of carpenter's tools, two dogs, an eagle, a canary, and a blackbird that whistled tunes, lest, even in that full life, he should chance upon an empty moment. If he had to wait for a dish of poached eggs, he must put in the time by playing on the flageolet; if a sermon were dull, he must read in the book of Tobit or divert his mind with sly advances on the nearest women. When he walked, it must be with a book in his pocket to beguile the way in case the nightingales were silent; and even along the streets of London, with so many pretty faces to be spied for and dignitaries to be saluted, his trail was marked by little debts, "for wine, pictures, etc.," the true headmark of a life intolerant of any joyless passage. He had a kind of idealism in pleasure; like the princess in the fairy story, he was conscious of a roseleaf out of place. Dearly as he loved to talk, he could not enjoy nor shine in a conversation when he thought himself unsuitably dressed. Dearly as he loved eating, he "knew not how to eat alone"; pleasure for him must heighten pleasure; and the eye and ear must be flattered like the palate ere he avow himself content. He had no zest in a good dinner when it fell to be eaten "in a bad street and in a periwig-maker's house"; and a collation was spoiled for him by indifferent music. His body was indefatigable, doing him yeoman's service in this breathless chase of pleasures. On April 11, 1662, he mentions that he went to bed "weary, *which I seldom am*"; and already over thirty, he would sit up all night cheerfully to see a comet. But it is never pleasure that exhausts the pleasure-seeker; for in that career, as in all others, it is failure that kills. The man who enjoys so wholly and bears so impatiently the slightest widowhood from joy, is just the man to lose a night's rest over some paltry question of his right to fiddle on the leads, or to be "vexed to the blood" by a solecism in his wife's attire; and we find in consequence that he was always peevish when he was hungry, and that his head "asked mightily" after a dispute. But nothing could divert him from his aim in life; his remedy in care was the same as his delight in prosperity; it was with pleasure, and with pleasure only, that he sought to drive out sorrow; and, whether he was jealous of his wife or skulking from a bailiff, he would equally take refuge in the theatre. There, if the house be full and the company noble, if the songs be tunable, the actors perfect, and the play diverting, this odd hero of the secret Diary, this private self-adorer, will speedily be healed of his distresses.

Equally pleased with a watch, a coach, a piece of meat, a tune upon the fiddle, or a fact in hydrostatics, Pepys was pleased yet more by the beauty, the worth, the mirth, or the mere scenic attitude in life of his fellow-creatures. He shows himself throughout a sterling humanist. Indeed, he who loves himself, not in idle vanity, but with a plenitude of knowledge, is the best equipped of all to love his neighbours. And perhaps it is in this sense that charity may be most properly said to begin at home. It does not matter what quality a person has:

Pepys can appreciate and love him for it. He "fills his eyes" with the beauty of Lady Castlemaine; indeed, he may be said to dote upon the thought of her for years; if a woman be good-looking and not painted, he will walk miles to have another sight of her; and even when a lady by a mischance spat upon his clothes, he was immediately consoled when he had observed that she was pretty. But, on the other hand, he is delighted to see Mrs. Pett upon her knees, and speaks thus of his Aunt James: "a poor, religious, well-meaning, good soul, talking of nothing but God Almighty, and that with so much innocence that mightily pleased me." He is taken with Pen's merriment and loose songs, but not less taken with the sterling worth of Coventry. He is jolly with a drunken sailor, but listens with interest and patience, as he rides the Essex roads, to the story of a Quaker's spiritual trials and convictions. He lends a critical ear to the discourse of kings and royal dukes. He spends an evening at Vauxhall with "Killigrew and young Newport—loose company," says he, "but worth a man's being in for once, to know the nature of it, and their manner of talk and lives." And when a rag-boy lights him home, he examines him about his business and other ways of livelihood for destitute children. This is almost half-way to the beginning of philanthropy; had it only been the fashion, as it is at present, Pepys had perhaps been a man famous for good deeds. And it is through this quality that he rises, at times, superior to his surprising egotism; his interest in the love affairs of others is, indeed, impersonal; he is filled with concern for my Lady Castlemaine, whom he only knows by sight, shares in her very jealousies, joys with her in her successes; and it is not untrue, however strange it seems in his abrupt presentment, that he loved his maid Jane because she was in love with his man Tom.

Let us hear him, for once, at length:

"So the women and W. Hewer and I walked upon the Downes, where a flock of sheep was: and the most pleasant and innocent sight that ever I saw in my life. We found a shepherd and his little boy reading, far from any houses or sight of people, the Bible to him; so I made the boy read to me, which he did with the forced tone that children do usually read, that was mighty pretty; and then I did give him something, and went to the father, and talked with him. He did content himself mightily in my liking his boy's reading, and did bless God for him, the most like one of the old patriarchs that ever I saw in my life, and it brought those thoughts of the old age of the world in my mind for two or three days after. We took notice of his woollen knit stockings of two colours mixed, and of his shoes shod with iron, both at the toe and heels, and with great nails in the soles of his feet, which was mighty pretty; and taking notice of them, 'Why,' says the poor man, 'the downes, you see, are full of stones, and we are faine to shoe ourselves thus; and these,' says he, 'will make the stones fly till they ring before me.' I did give the poor man something, for which he was mighty thankful, and I tried to cast stones with his horne crooke. He values his dog mightily, that would turn a sheep any way which he would have him, when he goes to fold them; told me there was about eighteen score sheep in his flock, and that he hath four shillings a week the year round for keeping of them; and Mrs. Turner, in the common fields here, did gather one of the prettiest nosegays that ever I saw in my life."

And so the story rambles on to the end of that day's pleasuring; with cups of milk, and glowworms, and people walking at sundown with their wives and children, and all the way home Pepys still dreaming "of the old age of the world" and the early innocence of man. This was how he walked through life, his eyes and ears wide open, and his hand, you will observe, not shut; and thus he observed the lives, the speech, and the manners of his fellow-men, with prose fidelity of detail and yet a lingering glamour of romance.

It was "two or three days after" that he extended this passage in the pages of his Journal, and the style has thus the benefit of some reflection. It is generally supposed that, as a writer, Pepys must rank at the bottom of the scale of merit. But a style which is indefatigably lively, telling, and picturesque through six large volumes of everyday experience, which deals with the whole matter of life, and yet is rarely wearisome, which condescends to the most fastidious particulars, and yet sweeps all away in the forthright current of the narrative,—such a style may be ungrammatical, it may be inelegant, it may be one tissue of mistakes, but it can never be devoid of merit. The first and the true function of the writer has been thoroughly performed throughout; and though the manner of his utterance may be childishly awkward, the matter has been transformed and assimilated by his unfeigned interest and delight. The gusto of the man speaks out fierily after all these years. For the difference between Pepys and Shelley, to return to that half-whimsical approximation, is one of quality but not one of degree; in his sphere, Pepys felt as keenly, and his is the true prose of poetry—prose because the spirit of the man was narrow and earthly, but poetry because he was delightedly alive. Hence, in such a passage as this about the Epsom shepherd, the result upon the reader's mind is entire conviction and unmingled pleasure. So, you feel, the thing fell out, not otherwise; and you would no more change it than you would change a sublimity of Shakespeare's, a homely touch of Bunyan's, or a favoured reminiscence of your own.

There never was a man nearer being an artist who yet was not one. The tang was in the family; while he was writing the Journal for our enjoyment in his comely house in Navy Gardens, no fewer than two of his cousins were tramping the fens, kit under arm, to make music to the country girls. But he himself, though he could play so many instruments and pass judgment in so many fields of art, remained an amateur. It is not given to anyone so keenly to enjoy, without some greater power to understand. That he did not like Shakespeare as an artist for the stage may be a fault, but it is not without either parallel or excuse. He certainly admired him as a poet; he was the first beyond mere actors on the rolls of that innumerable army who have got "To be or not to be" by heart. Nor was he content with that; it haunted his mind; he quoted it to himself in the pages of the Diary, and, rushing in where angels fear to tread, he set it to music. Nothing, indeed, is more notable than the heroic quality of the verses that our little sensualist in a periwig chose out to marry with his own mortal strains. Some gust from brave Elizabethan times must have warmed his spirit, as he sat tuning his sublime theorbo. "To be or not to be. Whether 'tis nobler"—"Beauty retire, thou dost my pity move"—"It is decreed, nor shall thy fate, O Rome";—open and dignified in the sound, various and majestic in the sentiment, it was no inapt, as it was certainly no timid, spirit that selected such a range of themes. Of "Gaze not on Swans" I know no more than these four words; yet that also seems to promise well. It was, however, on a probable suspicion, the work of his master, Mr. Berkenshaw—as the drawings that figure at the breaking up of a young ladies' seminary are the work of the professor attached to the establishment. Mr. Berkenshaw was not altogether happy in his pupil. The amateur cannot usually rise into the artist, some leaven of the world still clogging him; and we find Pepys behaving like a pickthank to the man who taught him composition. In relation to the stage, which he so warmly loved and understood, he was not only more hearty, but more generous to others. Thus he encounters Colonel Reames, "a man," says he, "who understands and loves a play as well as I, and I love him for it." And again, when he and his wife had seen a most ridiculous insipid piece, "Glad we were," he writes, "that Betterton had no part in it." It is by such a zeal and loyalty to those who labour for his delight that the amateur grows worthy of the artist. And it should be kept in mind that, not only in art, but in morals, Pepys rejoiced to recognise his betters. There was not one speck of envy in the whole human-hearted egotist.

RESPECTABILITY

When writers inveigh against respectability, in the present degraded meaning of the word, they are usually suspected of a taste for clay pipes and beer cellars; and their performances are thought to hail from the *Owl's Nest* of the comedy. They have something more, however, in their eye than the dulness of a round million dinner parties that sit down yearly in old England. For to do anything because others do it, and not because the thing is good, or kind, or honest in its own right, is to resign all moral control and captaincy upon yourself, and go post-haste to the devil with the greater number. We smile over the ascendency of priests; but I had rather follow a priest than what they call the leaders of society. No life can better than that of Pepys illustrate the dangers of this respectable theory of living. For what can be more untoward than the occurrence, at a critical period and while the habits are still pliable, of such a sweeping transformation as the return of Charles the Second? Round went the whole fleet of England on the other tack; and while a few tall pintas, Milton or Pen, still sailed a lonely course by the stars and their own private compass, the cock-boat, Pepys, must go about with the majority among "the stupid starers and the loud huzzas."

The respectable are not led so much by any desire of applause as by a positive need for countenance. The weaker and the tamer the man, the more will he require this support; and any positive quality relieves him, by just so much, of this dependence. In a dozen ways, Pepys was quite strong enough to please himself without regard for others; but his positive qualities were not co-extensive with the field of conduct; and in many parts of life he followed, with gleeful precision, in the footprints of the contemporary Mrs. Grundy. In morals, particularly, he lived by the countenance of others; felt a slight from another more keenly than a meanness in himself; and then first repented when he was found out. You could talk of religion or morality to such a man; and by the artist side of him, by his lively sympathy and apprehension, he could rise, as it were dramatically, to the significance of what you said. All that matter in religion which has been nicknamed other-worldliness was strictly in his gamut; but a rule of life that should make a man rudely virtuous, following right in good report and ill report, was foolishness and a stumbling-block to Pepys. He was much thrown across the Friends; and nothing can be more instructive than his attitude towards these most interesting people of that age. I have mentioned how he conversed with one as he rode; when he saw some brought from a meeting under arrest, "I would to God," said he, "they would either conform, or be more wise and not be catched"; and to a Quaker in his own office he extended a timid though effectual protection. Meanwhile there was growing up next door to him that beautiful nature, William Pen. It is odd that Pepys condemned him for a fop; odd, though natural enough when you see Pen's portrait, that Pepys was jealous of him with his wife. But the cream of the story is when Pen publishes his *Sandy Foundation Shaken,* and Pepys has it read aloud by his wife. "I find it," he says, "so well writ as, I think, it is too good for him ever to have writ it; and it is a serious sort of book, and *not fit for everybody to read.*" Nothing is more galling to the merely respectable than to be brought in contact with religious ardour. Pepys had his own foundation, sandy enough, but dear to him from practical considerations, and he would read the book with true uneasiness of spirit; for conceive the blow if, by some plaguy accident, this Pen were to convert him! It was a different kind of doctrine that he judged profitable for himself and others. "A good sermon of Mr. Gifford's at our church, upon 'Seek ye first the kingdom of heaven.' A very excellent and persuasive, good and moral sermon. He showed, like a wise man, that righteousness is a surer moral way of being rich than sin and villainy." It is thus that respectable people desire to have their Greathearts address them, telling, in mild accents, how you may make the best of both worlds, and be a moral hero without courage, kindness, or troublesome reflection; and thus the Gospel, cleared of Eastern metaphor, becomes a manual of worldly prudence, and a handybook for Pepys and the successful merchant.

The respectability of Pepys was deeply grained. He has no idea of truth except for the Diary. He has no care that a thing shall be, if it but appear; gives out that he has inherited a good estate, when he has seemingly got nothing but a lawsuit; and is pleased to be thought liberal when he knows he has been mean. He is conscientiously ostentatious. I say conscientiously, with reason. He could never have been taken for a fop, like Pen, but arrayed himself in a manner nicely suitable to his position. For long he hesitated to assume the famous periwig; for a public man should travel gravely with the fashions, not foppishly before, nor dowdily behind, the central movement of his age. For long he durst not keep a carriage; that, in his circumstances, would have been improper; but a time comes, with the growth of his fortune, when the impropriety has shifted to the other side, and he is "ashamed to be seen in a hackney." Pepys talked about being "a Quaker or some very melancholy thing"; for my part, I can imagine nothing so melancholy, because nothing half so silly, as to be concerned about such problems. But so respectability and the duties of society haunt and burden their poor devotees; and what seems at first the very primrose path of life, proves difficult and thorny like the rest. And the time comes to Pepys, as to all the merely respectable, when he must not only order his pleasures, but even clip his virtuous movements, to the public pattern of the age. There was some juggling among officials to avoid direct taxation; and Pepys, with a noble impulse, growing ashamed of this dishonesty, designed to charge himself with £1000; but finding none to set him an example, "nobody of our ablest merchants" with this moderate liking for clean hands, he judged it "not decent"; he feared it would "be thought vain glory"; and, rather than appear singular, cheerfully remained a thief. One able merchant's countenance, and Pepys had dared to do an honest act! Had he found one brave spirit, properly recognised by society, he might have gone far as a disciple. Mrs. Turner, it is true, can fill him full of sordid scandal, and make him believe, against the testimony of his senses, that Pen's venison pasty stank like the devil; but, on the other hand, Sir William Coventry can raise him by a word into another being. Pepys, when he is with Coventry, talks in the vein of an old Roman. What does he care for office or emolument? "Thank God, I have enough of my own," says he, "to buy me a good book and a good fiddle, and I have a good wife." And again, we find this pair projecting an old age when an ungrateful country shall have dismissed them from the field of public service; Coventry living retired in a fine house, and Pepys dropping in, "it may be, to read a chapter of Seneca."

Under this influence, the only good one in his life, Pepys continued zealous, and for the period, pure in his employment. He would not be "bribed to be unjust," he says, though he was "not so squeamish as to refuse a present after," suppose the king to have received no wrong. His new arrangement for the vict-ualling of Tangier, he tells us with honest complacency, will save the king a thousand and gain Pepys three hundred pounds a year,—a statement which exactly fixes the degree of the age's enlightenment. But for his industry and capacity no praise can be too high. It was an unending struggle for the man to stick to his business in such a garden of Armida as he found this life; and the story of his oaths, so often broken, so courageously re-newed, is worthy rather of admiration than the contempt it has received.

Elsewhere, and beyond the sphere of Coventry's influence, we find him losing scruples and daily complying further with the age. When he began the Journal, he was a trifle prim and puritanic; merry enough, to be sure, over his private cups, and still remembering Magdalene ale and his acquaintance with Mrs. Ainsworth of Cambridge. But youth is a hot season with all; when a man smells April and May he is apt at times to stumble; and in spite of a disordered practice, Pepys's theory, the better things that he approved and followed after, we may even say were strict. Where there was "tag, rag, and bobtail, dancing, singing, and drinking," he felt "ashamed, and went away"; and when he slept in church, he prayed God forgive him. In but a little while we find him with some ladies keeping each other awake "from spite," as though not to sleep in church were an obvious hardship; and yet later he calmly passes the time of service, looking about him, with a perspective glass, on all the pretty women. His favourite ejaculation, "Lord!" occurs but once that I have observed in 1660, never in '61, twice in '62, and at least five times in '63; after which the "Lords" may be said to pullulate like herrings, with here and there a solitary "damned," as it were a whale among the shoal. He and his wife, once filled with dudgeon by some innocent freedoms at a mar-riage, are soon content to go pleasuring with my Lord Brouncker's mistress, who was not even, by his own account, the most discreet of mistresses. Tag, rag, and bobtail, dancing, singing, and drinking, become his natural element; actors and actresses and drunken, roaring courtiers are to be found in his society; until the man grew so involved with Saturnalian manners and companions that he was shot almost unconsciously into the grand domestic crash of 1668.

That was the legitimate issue and punishment of years of staggering walk and conversation. The man who has smoked his pipe for half a century in a powder magazine finds himself at last the author and the victim of a hideous disaster. So with our pleasant-minded Pepys and his peccadilloes. All of a sudden, as he still trips dexterously enough among the dangers of a double-faced career, thinking no great evil, humming to himself the trillo, Fate takes the further conduct of that matter from his hands, and brings him face to face with the consequences of his acts. For a man still, after so many years, the lover, although not the constant lover, of his wife,—for a man, besides, who was so greatly careful of appearances,—the revelation of his infidelities was a crushing blow. The tears that he shed, the indignities that he endured, are not to be measured. A vulgar woman, and now justly incensed, Mrs. Pepys spared him no detail of suffering. She was violent, threatening him with the tongs; she was careless of his honour, driving him to insult the mistress whom she had driven him to betray and to discard; worst of all, she was hopelessly inconsequent, in word and thought and deed, now lulling him with reconciliations, and anon flaming forth again with the original anger. Pepys had not used his wife well; he had wearied her with jealousies, even while himself unfaithful; he had grudged her clothes and pleasures, while lavishing both upon himself; he had abused her in words; he had bent his fist at her in anger; he had once blacked her eye; and it is one of the oddest particulars in that odd Diary of his, that, while the injury is referred to once in passing, there is no hint as to the occasion or the manner of the blow. But now, when he is in the wrong, nothing can exceed the long-suffering affection of this impatient husband. While he was still sinning and still undiscovered, he seems not to have known a touch of penitence stronger than what might lead him to take his wife to the theatre, or for an airing, or to give her a new dress, by way of compensation. Once found out, however, and he seems to himself to have lost all claim to decent usage. It is perhaps the strongest instance of his externality. His wife may do what she pleases, and though he may groan, it will never occur to him to blame her; he has no weapon left but tears and the most abject submission. We should perhaps have respected him more had he not given way so utterly—above all, had he refused to write, under his wife's dictation, an insulting letter to his unhappy fellow-culprit, Miss Willet; but somehow I believe we like him better as he was.

The death of his wife, following so shortly after, must have stamped the impression of this episode upon his mind. For the remaining years of his long life we have no Diary to help us, and we have seen already how little stress is to be laid upon the tenor of his correspondence; but what with the recollection of the catastrophe of his married life, what with the natural influence of his advancing years and reputation, it seems not unlikely that the period of gallantry was at an end for Pepys; and it is beyond a doubt that he sat down at last to an honoured and agreeable old age among his books and music, the correspondent of Sir Isaac Newton, and, in one instance at least, the poetical counsellor of Dryden. Through all this period, that Diary which contained the secret memoirs of his life, with all its inconsistencies and escapades, had been religiously preserved; nor, when he came to die, does he appear to have provided for its destruction. So we may conceive him faithful to the end to all his dear and early memories; still mindful of Mrs. Hely in the woods at Epsom; still lighting at Islington for a cup of kindness to the dead; still, if he heard again that air that once so much disturbed him, thrilling at the recollection of the love that bound him to his wife.

Editor's Preface

The diary of Samuel Pepys is like no other book in the world. To those who love humanity and vivid, unconscious writing, it is infinitely delightful and precious, scarcely to be over-valued. One reason, of course, for this is that its writer had no idea of making a book at all. It is plain beyond doubt that he never dreamed of human eyes falling upon his blessedly frank and naked page. The record was a secret between himself and his own soul, not forgetting his God—whom, as will be seen, he is far from forgetting, and whom he invokes on many curious occasions. Most diarists have written with an eye to publication, or, at all events, with the fear before them of posthumous inspection by the family. They have, therefore, more or less posed themselves as they would have others see them. Most of us have kept diaries in our youth. They are for most people merely the pool of Narcissus. With that dwindling sense of our own importance, as contrasted say with the planet Jupiter, which comes with maturity, most of us have abandoned them. With the abdication of the ego, they become tiresome to us, and absurdly self-important. Pepys, however, though certainly not an egoist, in our modern sense of the word, never lost interest in himself or his affairs. That may perhaps be regarded as one of the many signs of that robust health of mind and body with which his diary abounds. But it is a childlike, boyish interest. It is not so much himself that interests him, nor merely the things that happen to himself, but the people about him and the things that are happening to everybody, all the time, to his nation as well as to his acquaintance. It is the world in which he lives that is so immensely interesting to him every minute— never was the world so full of a number of things as to Samuel Pepys, and the gusto with which he plunges into his experiences is good to see. The smallest happy trifle delights him. When he gets a new watch, for instance, he exclaims upon his "old folly and childishness," because "I cannot forbear carrying my watch in my hand in the coach all this afternoon, and seeing what o'clock it is one hundred times." He was then a grown man of thirty-two! Perhaps other grown men of thirty-two have been equally childish—and engagingly human—but, of course, they have kept it to themselves. Without any doubt, too, they have been as human as Pepys in other directions,—and kept that, too, to themselves. In that matter of women, for instance. There have existed, and still continue to exist, and in numbers so far from small as perhaps to constitute a majority of male humanity, men as susceptible to women as Pepys—it is idle to deny it—but these men have kept that amiable weakness, and still continue to keep it, to themselves; just as Pepys thought he was doing, and, for the most part did. "Respectable" readers, of course, hold up their hands at the frank memoranda of amorous dealings with the numerous fair and frail women, from pretty servingmaids—sweet "Nan" or "Deb" or "Sue" or "Doll"—to "merry wives" of loftier station, each one of them flashingly alive before us, often by the mere mention of their names. Those terrible Restoration times! Well, I wonder if the lives of our big business men, and men in public office, as was Pepys, would stand writing any better than his. Indeed, I don't wonder at all. And as for the madness of woman-worship, it is a question if any previous age has surpassed the present in that particular form of dementia. Pepys was well aware of his weakness, and periodically repentant. "Strange slavery that I stand in to beauty," he exclaims, "that I value nothing near it!" This was *à propos* a call upon "Doll, our pretty 'Change woman, for a pair of gloves trimmed with yellow ribbon, to match the petticoate my wife bought yesterday, which cost me 20s; but she is so pretty, that God forgive me! I could not think it too much." "However, musique and women," he admits elsewhere with a sigh, "I cannot but give way to, whatever my business is." "Unrefined" as I suppose some of his amorous encounters are to be regarded, there is no question that they were all inspired by an intense and catholic love of beauty. No one can bring the charge against Pepys that he ever kissed a homely woman. He reproaches himself, on one occasion, for wasting good business time on some unattractive ladies. "She grows mighty homely and looks old," he says, "thence ashamed of myself for this loss of time." Had it only been Lady Castlemaine, the lovely mistress of the King! In Pepys' disinterested, hopeless worship of her, perforce at a distance, seen in a box with Charles II at the theatre, or walking in Hyde Park, or, as once, in dreams of the night, he attains to something like romance. It is enough for him to fill his eyes with her beauty from afar. It is his own phrase over and over again. "Where I glutted myself with looking at her," he says of seeing her once at White Hall. His diary saddens at any hint of her falling out of the King's favour, and whatever she does is right; for "strange it is how for her beauty I am willing to construe all this to the best and to pity her wherein it is to her hurt, though I know well that she is"—well, no better than she should be. The sight of her petticoats on a clothesline at White Hall thrills poor Pepys to the marrow. "And in the Privy Garden," he says, "saw the finest smocks and linen petticoats of my Lady Castlemaine's, laced with Irish lace at the bottom, that ever I saw, and did me good to look upon them."

This weakness for women, that is pretty women, Pepys never, it has to be acknowledged, overcame. It occasioned no little trouble between him and his spirited young French wife, of whom, for all his marital airs of authority, he stood in marked dread, and for whom, in spite of his philandering—again not so different from his fellows—he had a deep affection. The domestic passages in all their homely, old-world simplicity, are among the most attractive in the diary; their constant quarrels and makings-up, their young fun, jaunts and outings together, their delightful "scenes" with their long processions of servants—not yet, for many a long year, known as "help." The picture thus given of an English middleclass household of those days is far from unattractive, with its greater familiarity and gaiety of intercourse and sense of shared family-life; and no book so well as this diary gives one an idea of what was once meant by "Merry England"—an England which died with its "Merry Monarch," and the accession of his dull and sinister brother. Music and drinking made a great part of the merriment. Of both the diary is full, and it will be noticed that, when gentlemen got together in a tavern, they were never long without a song—and good singing, too. Pepys, indeed, as will appear, was a learned virtuoso of music and was himself a good performer on several instruments. The day seldom began, however early, or ended, however late, without a song—in which the pretty "mayde," or the "rascal" boy, were usually able to take part—or without some brief melody on lute or violin. How excellent and charming a practice, and how far removed from the uncivilized tradesman's world we live in to-day!

As for the drinking: here after a brief, but pretty thorough apprenticeship to Bacchus, Pepys is early seen developing a strength of character, which comes rather as a surprise, though it is an earnest of the success his life was to be, and is the more to his credit when one considers the habits and temptations of his time. The diary has not gone very far when we find him abandoning those "mornings" at taverns—draughts of wine, ale, or other malt and spirituous liquors which for our hardy ancestors took the place of breakfast—and "taking the pledge" to himself not to "indulge" for certain stated periods on pain of certain "forfeits" to the poor box, and such like deprivations, methodically arranged between himself and his own diary-keeping soul. He makes similar "vowes" against too many "theatres," and the buying of too many books; and more feebly on that matter of "beauty." For the most part, he keeps these vows—except as regards "beauty"—manfully; but, on occasion, as the reader will discover, he has ways of evading them with an amusing, quite childish casuistry. Wine, however—with the exception of occasional friendly or family bouts few and far between—he practically renounces for good—and again and again, we find him recording his satisfaction in being able to do so, to the great good of his health and his business. "But thanks be to God," we find him saying, early in January, 1661, when he was not yet twenty-eight, "since my leaving drinking of wine, I do find myself much better and do mind my business better and do spend less money and less time lost in idle company." Later, we find him disposing of his well-stocked cellar, and congratulating himself on the monetary equivalent. And it is now time to say that Pepys was by far from being a fool, far indeed from being the mere sot and sensualist which those who only know his diary by hearsay, or by an occasional preposterous quotation, are apt, with absurd injustice, to regard him. He was, on the contrary, a serious-minded business man, and conscientious public servant, clever, shrewd and painstaking, if not brilliant, and honest as men with his opportunities for "presents" and "perquisites" were in those days, far more honest, indeed, than his detractors—just as honest in fact, as business men ever have been, or ever will be. He was, in addition, a scholar and man of taste, a learned musician, as we have seen, a lover of books and pictures, and so far interested in the growing "science" of the day as to be made President of the Royal Society. He left a valuable library to his alma mater, Magdalene College, Cambridge, and he died, having succeeded in his life's aim as is given to few men to do: the admirable aim of making an honoured and comfortable place in the world for himself, his family and his descendants. And this he did mainly with his own hand, his one asset at the beginning being his relationship, as "first cousin one remove" to Sir Edward Montagu, afterwards Earl of Sandwich, the "My Lord" of the diary, who, however, proved throughout something more than kin to him, and his constantly helpful friend and "patron." It was through Lord Sandwich's influence that Pepys began his career in the Navy office as "Clerk of the Acts," a post equivalent to the post of Permanent Under Secretary at present, and in this capacity as in the post of Secretary to the Admiralty to which he later succeeded, Pepys was brought into frequent contact with the Duke of York (afterwards James II), who was Lord High Admiral, and by whom, as by the King himself, he was frequently complimented on his services to the department. That department had never been in worse case, and evidence is unanimous that it was the energy and industry of Pepys in its reorganization that laid the foundations of the British Navy as we know it to-day. Many other posts, with their responsibilities, honours, and "perquisites," were afterward added unto Pepys, all evidence of his efficiency.

Samuel Pepys was born February 23, 1633, and died May 25, 1703. The name Pepys, by the way, has always been pronounced by the family "Peeps." His diary extends over but eight and a half years of his life, the first entry being made on January 1, 1660, the last on May 31, 1669. The cause of its discontinuance, as the reader will find by referring to that last solemn entry, was the rapid failure of his sight. Henceforth, he says, his diary will have to be "kept by my people in long hand, and must therefore be contented to set down no more than is fit for them and all the world to know"—no slight difference for posterity!—adding characteristically, with a last flash of the old spirit, "or, if there be anything, which cannot be much, now my amours to Deb. are past, and my eyes hindering me in almost all other pleasures, I must endeavour to keep a margin in my book open, to add, here and there, a note in short-hand with my own hand."

The diary, in six calf-bound volumes, stamped with Pepys' arms and crest, was deposited, at Pepys' death, with the other bequeathed books, at Magdalene College, Cambridge, and attracted no particular notice, till at the instance of the Master of the College, an undergraduate, the Rev. John Smith, undertook to decipher it, and beginning his work in the spring of 1819, completed it in April, 1822, having worked on it, he tells us, from twelve to fourteen hours a day, for nearly three years. The system of shorthand used by Pepys was that invented by Thomas Shelton, a copy of whose treatise on what he calls

"Tachygraphy" is in the Pepysian Library. The diary was first published in 1825, edited by Lord Braybrooke, and was reviewed by Sir Walter Scott in "The Quarterly Review."

"That curious fellow Pepys," was Scott's way of referring to him, and he certainly had some curious and absurd ideas. With what extreme seriousness he took himself, certainly without humour in regard to his physical existence and well-being, many quaint and outspoken instances which I have had reluctantly to omit from this edition bear amusing witness; but one of the oddest of his whims is mentionable. On March 26, 1658, he had undergone a successful operation for stone in the bladder. Therefore, the reader will find him, on every annual recurrence of that date, giving what he calls his "stonefeast," a dinner to his most intimate friends in memory of the occasion, and as a token of gratitude to Almighty God. Also we find him having a case made in which to keep the stone, which he had solemnly preserved. He had his superstitions, too. He wore a hare's foot as a charm against the colic, and the reader will find some rhyming spells quoted in his text. Certainly Pepys was a "curious fellow," and as a human document the Diary is literally unique. For some readers it will have a still greater value for its historical importance. The Restoration period lives in the Diary as in a magic glass; and Pepys was either a spectator of, or a partaker in, many picturesque and strange happenings. He was on the ship which brought the King into his own again from Holland. How the joy of the occasion lives again in all its flashing colours and tumultuous happy noise! He went through the Great Fire and the Great Plague, saw London burning, and saw the grass growing in the streets. His accounts of both are masterpieces of description, and his conduct during the Plague is deserving of comment, particularly as he has got (that is, given himself) a certain reputation for cowardice. While the Court, the great doctors, and most of his business associates fled the city, he stuck to his guns, and, almost single-handed, carried on the business of the Navy office. In a letter to one of his colleagues, Sir William Coventry, he writes: "The sickness in general thickens round us, and particularly upon our neighborhood. You, sir, took your turn of the sword; I must not, therefore, grudge to take mine of the pestilence." He was the heart-broken witness of the Dutch burning English ships in the Medway. He saw the heads of Cromwell and other regicides exposed on pikes at Temple Bar, and in Westminster Hall, and he often saw and talked with the lazy, kind-hearted, sad and merry King, against whose wish that barbarity was committed.

"And did you once see Shelley plain?" Well, I think Pepys did better, for he saw Nell Gwynne, time and again, in her tiring room at the King's Theatre, "dressing herself and all unready," "very pretty, prettier than I thought," and heard her curse—"how Nell cursed"—"for having so few people in the pit"; and the way she did it seemed to poor, infatuated Pepys quite "pretty."

Well, Pepys saw these and a thousand other gallant and gay, heart-aching and tragic things, which he enables us to see again, as I said before, as in a magic glass; for how good a writer, how exceptionally vivid and various, he is has never been sufficiently acknowledged. From this reference to his destroying the manuscript of an early college romance of his "Love a Cheate," one might gather that he had some sneaking literary ambition, but he never published anything except his valuable "Memoirs of the Navy." Robert Louis Stevenson comes nearest to a just appreciation of his literary gift. Stevenson's essay, indeed, is the fairest estimate of him all round that is known to me. I cannot do better than quote this passage on Pepys' style: "It is generally supposed that as a writer Pepys must rank at the bottom of the scale of merit; but a style which is indefatigably lively, telling and picturesque, through six large volumes of every-day experience, which deals with the whole matter of a life and yet is rarely wearisome, which condescends to the most fastidious particulars and yet sweeps all away in the forth-right current of the narrative, such a style may be ungrammatical, it may be inelegant, it may be one tissue of mistakes, but it cannot be devoid of merit." But this leaves more to be said. "Cannot be devoid of merit!" That is, after all, a somewhat lame conclusion, and it is no such negative praise that a style so brimming over with the colour and sound of life demands. For giving us "the thing seen" absolutely as he saw it, and in its own peculiar atmosphere, no professional writer need patronize Samuel Pepys. Read his account of the burning of London, or his gloriously lugubrious account of the death of his brother Tom, with all the death-bed, and funeral horrors and humours. It is quite Shakesperean in its quality. And not infrequently Pepys attains real beauty of writing, particularly in some of his pictures of trips into the country, filled with country comeliness and mirth, the freshness of fields and lanes and the fragrance of wild flowers; for Pepys' love of beauty was not limited to beauty in women. It is evident that he had a sensitive dreaming eye for beautiful effects in nature too, a sensitiveness not common in his day.

But it is time I left this "curious fellow" to speak for himself, and I will only add that he is not so inadequately represented in the following selections as might be supposed from the fact that the standard edition of the Diary (Mr. H. B. Wheatley's) from which they have been made is in eight volumes and here, therefore, is but an eighth of the whole material. Yet the nature of the Diary is such that nothing characteristic is thereby lost, for in the original there is, of necessity, much repetition of the same, or similar happenings, from day to day. Here the reader has, I believe, all the extraordinary happenings, with sufficient of the ordinary happenings of Pepys' every-day life—not forgetting his almost every-day dalliances—to justify him in feeling that he knows Samuel Pepys and the world he lived in, as thoroughly as though he had read the whole eight volumes—to which, at all events, this volume cannot but prove a seductive invitation.

RICHARD LE GALLIENNE

THE DIARY OF SAMUEL PEPYS

1660

Blessed be God, at the end of the last year I was in very good health, without any sense of my old pain, but upon taking of cold. I lived in Axe Yard, having my wife, and servant Jane, and no more in family than us three. My wife . . . gave me hopes of her being with child, but on the last day of the year . . . [the hope was belied].

The condition of the State was thus; viz. the Rump, after being disturbed by my Lord Lambert, was lately returned to sit again. The officers of the Army all forced to yield. Lawson lies still in the river, and Monk is with his army in Scotland. Only my Lord Lambert is not yet come into the Parliament, nor is it expected that he will without being forced to it. The new Common Council of the City do speak very high; and had sent to Monk their sword-bearer, to acquaint him with their desires for a free and full Parliament, which is at present the desires, and the hopes, and expectation of all. Twenty-two of the old secluded members having been at the House-door the last week to demand entrance, but it was denied them; and it is believed that [neither] they nor the people will be satisfied till the House be filled. My own private condition very handsome, and esteemed rich, but indeed very poor; besides my goods of my house, and my office, which at present is somewhat uncertain. Mr. Downing master of my office.

JANUARY 1st (LORD'S DAY). This morning (we living lately in the garret,) I rose, put on my suit with great skirts, having not lately worn any other clothes but them. Went to Mr. Gunning's chapel at Exeter House, where he made a very good sermon upon these words:—"That in the fulness of time God sent his Son, made of a woman," &c.; showing, that, by "made under the law," is meant his circumcision, which is solemnized this day. Dined at home in the garret, where my wife dressed the remains of a turkey, and in the doing of it she burned her hand. I staid at home all the afternoon, looking over my accounts.

2ND. In the morning before I went forth old East brought me a dozen of bottles of sack, and I gave him a shilling for his pains. Then I went to Mr. Sheply, who was drawing of sack in the wine cellar to send to other places as a gift from my Lord, and told me that my Lord had given him order to give me the dozen of bottles. Thence I went to the Temple to speak with Mr. Calthropp about the £60 due to my Lord, but missed of him, he being abroad.

4TH. Early came Mr. Vanly to me for his half-year's rent, which I had not in the house, but took his man to the office and there paid him. Then I went down into the Hall and to Will's, where Hawly brought a piece of his Cheshire cheese, and we were merry with it. Then into the Hall again, where I met with the Clerk and Quarter Master of my Lord's troop, and took them to the Swan and gave them their morning's draft, they being just come to town. I went to Will's again, where I found them still at cards, and Spicer had won 14s. of Shaw and Vines. Then I spent a little time with G. Vines and Maylard at Vines's at our viols. So home, and from thence to Mr. Hunt's, and sat with them and Mr. Hawly at cards till ten at night, and was much made of by them. Home and so to bed, but much troubled with my nose, which was much swelled.

5TH. I went to my office. Then I went home, and after writing a letter to my Lord and told him the news that Monk and Fairfax were commanded up to town, and that the Prince's lodgings were to be provided for Monk at Whitehall. Then my wife and I, it being a great frost, went to Mrs. Jem's, in expectation to eat a sack-posset, but Mr. Edward not coming it was put off.

15TH. Having been exceedingly disturbed in the night with the barking of a dog of one of our neighbors that I could not sleep for an hour or two, I slept late, and then in the morning took physic, and so staid within all day. At noon my brother John came to me, and I corrected as well as I could his Greek speech to say the Apposition, though I believe he himself was as well able to do it as myself.

16TH. At noon, Harry Ethall came to me and went along with Mr. Maylard by coach as far as Salsbury Court, and there we set him down, and we went to the Clerks, where we came a little too late, but in a closet we had a very good dinner by Mr. Pinkney's courtesy, and after dinner we had pretty good singing, and one, Hazard, sung alone after the old fashion, which was very much cried up, but I did not like it. Thence we went to the Green Dragon, on Lambeth Hill, both the Mr. Pinkney's, Smith, Harrison, Morrice, that sang the bass, Sheply and I, and there we sang of all sorts of things, and I ventured with good success upon things at first sight, and after that I played on my flageolet, and staid there till nine o'clock, very merry and drawn on with one song after another till it came to be so late. After that Sheply, Harrison and myself, we went towards Westminster on foot, and at the Golden Lion, near Charing Cross we went in and drank a pint of wine, and so parted, and thence home, where I found my wife and maid a-washing. I staid up till the bell-man came by with his bell just under my window as I was writing of this very line, and cried, "Past one of the clock, and a cold, frosty, windy morning." I then went to bed, and left my wife and the maid a-washing still.

18TH. All the world is at a loss to think what Monk will do: the City saying that he will be for them, and the Parliament saying he will be for them.

26TH. Home from my office to my Lord's lodgings where my wife had got ready a very fine dinner—viz. a dish of marrow bones; a leg of mutton; a loin of veal; a dish of fowl, three pullets, and two dozen of larks all in a dish; a great tart, a neat's tongue, a dish of anchovies; a dish of prawns and cheese.

30TH. This morning, before I was up, I fell a-singing of my song, "Great, good, and just," &c., and put myself thereby in mind that this was the fatal day, now ten years since, his Majesty died.

FEBRUARY 3RD. Drank my morning draft at Harper's, and was told there that the soldiers were all quiet upon promise of pay. Thence to St. James's Park, and walked there to my place for my flageolet and then played a little, it being a most pleasant morning and sunshine. Went walking all over White Hall, whither General Monk was newly come, and we saw all his forces march by in very good plight and stout officers. Thence to my house where we dined, but with a great deal of patience, for the mutton came in raw, and so we were fain to stay the stewing of it. In the meantime we sat studying a Posy for a ring for her which she is to have at Roger Pepys his wedding. The town and guards are already full of Monk's soldiers.

4TH. In the morning at my lute an hour, and so to my office.

7TH. To the Hall, where in the Palace I saw Monk's soldiers abuse Billing and all the Quakers, that were at a meeting-place there, and indeed the soldiers did use them very roughly and were to blame.

8TH. A little practice on my flageolet, and afterwards walking in my yard to see my stock of pigeons, which begin now with the spring to breed very fast.

9TH. I called at Mr. Harper's, who told me how Monk had this day clapt up many of the Common-council, and that the Parliament had voted that he should pull down their gates and portcullisses, their posts and their chains, which he do intend to do, and do lie in the City all night. I went home and got some allum to my mouth, where I have the beginnings of a cancer, and had also a plaster to my boil underneath my chin.

11TH. This morning I lay long abed, and then to my office, where I read all the morning my Spanish book of Rome. I went then down into the Hall, where I met with Mr. Chetwind, who had not dined no more than myself, and so we went toward London, in our way calling at two or three shops, but could have no dinner. At last, within Temple Bar, we found a pullet ready roasted, and there we dined. Then to his office, where I sat in his study singing, while he was with his man (Mr. Howell's son) looking after his business. Thence we took coach for the City to Guildhall, where the Hall was full of people expecting Monk and Lord Mayor to come thither, and all very joyful. Here we stayed a great while, and at last meeting with a friend of his we went to the 3 Tun tavern and drank half a pint of wine, and not liking the wine we went to an alehouse, where we met with company of this third man's acquaintance, and there we drank a little. Hence I went alone to Guildhall to see whether Monk was come again or no, and met with him coming out of the chamber where he had been with the Mayor and Aldermen, but such a shout I never heard in all my life, crying out, "God bless your Excellence." And indeed I saw many people give the soldiers drink and money, and all along in the streets cried, "God bless them!" and extraordinary good words. In Cheapside there was a great many bonfires, and Bow bells and all the bells in all the churches as we went home were a-ringing. Hence we went homewards, it being about ten o'clock. But the common joy was every where to be seen! The number of bonfires, there being fourteen between St. Dunstan's and Temple Bar, and at Strand Bridge I could at one view tell thirty-one fires. In King-street seven or eight; and all along burning, and roasting, and drinking for rumps. There being rumps tied upon sticks and carried up and down. The butchers at the May Pole in the Strand rang a peal with their knives when they were going to sacrifice their rump. On Ludgate Hill there was one turning of the spit that had a rump tied upon it, and another basting of it. Indeed it was past imagination, both the greatness and the suddenness of it. At one end of the street you would think there was a whole lane of fire, and so hot that we were fain to keep still on the further side merely for heat.

12TH. So to bed, where my wife and I had some high words upon my telling her that I would fling the dog which her brother gave her out of window if he [dirtied] the house any more.

14TH. Called out in the morning by Mr. Moore, whose voice my wife hearing in my dressing-chamber with me, got herself ready, and came down and challenged him for her valentine, this being the day.

16TH. In the morning at my lute. Then came Shaw and Hawly, and I gave them their morning draft at my house. So to my office, where I wrote by the carrier to my Lord and sealed my letter at Will's, and gave it old East to carry it to the carrier's, and to take up a box of china oranges and two little barrels of scallops at my house, which Captain Cuttance sent to me for my Lord.

18TH. A great while at my vial and voice, learning to sing "Fly boy, fly boy," without book. So to my office, where little to do.

21ST. In the morning going out I saw many soldiers going toward Westminster, and was told that they were going to admit the secluded members again. So I to Westminster Hall, and in Chancery Row I saw about twenty of them who had been at White Hall with General Monk, who came hither this morning, and made a speech to them, and recommended to them a Commonwealth, and against Charles Stuart. They came to the House and went in one after another, and at last the Speaker came. Mr. Prin came with an old basket hilt sword on, and had a great many shouts upon his going into the Hall. They sat till noon, and at their coming out Mr. Crew saw me, and bid me come to his house, which I did, and he would have me dine with him, which I did; and he very joyful told me that the House had made General Monk, General of all the Forces in England, Scotland, and Ireland; and that upon Monk's desire, for the service that Lawson had lately done in pulling down the Committee of Safety, he had the command of the Sea for the time being. He advised me to send for my Lord forthwith, and told me that there is no question that, if he will, he may now be employed again; and that the House do intend to do nothing more than to issue writs, and to settle a foundation for a free Parliament. Here out of the window it was a most pleasant sight to see the City from one end to the other with a glory about it, so high was the light of the bonfires, and so thick round the City, and the bells rang everywhere.

23RD. Thursday, my birthday, now twenty-seven years. A pretty fair morning, I rose and after writing a while in my study I went forth.

27TH. So we went to our Inn, and after eating of something, and kissed the daughter of the house, she being very pretty, we took leave, and so that night, the road pretty good, but the weather rainy to Ep[p]ing, where we sat and played a game of cards, and after supper, and some merry talk with a plain bold maid of the house, we went to bed.

MARCH 2ND. Great is the talk of a single person, and that it would now be Charles, George, or Richard again. For the last of which, my Lord St. John is said to speak high. Great also is the dispute now in the House, in whose name the writs shall run for the next Parliament; and it is said that Mr. Prin, in open House, said, "In King Charles's."

3RD. To Westminster Hall, where I found that my Lord was last night voted one of the Generals at Sea, and Monk the other. Up to my office, but did nothing. At noon home to dinner to a sheep's head.

4TH (LORD'S DAY). Before I went to church I sang Orpheus' Hymn to my viall. After that to Mr. Gunning's, an excellent sermon upon charity. Then to my mother to dinner, where my wife and the maid were come. Then to my mother again, and after supper she and I talked very highly about religion, I in defence of the religion I was born in. Then home.

5TH. Early in the morning Mr. Hill comes to string my theorbo, which we were about till past ten o'clock, with a great deal of pleasure. Great hopes of the King's coming again. To bed.

6TH (SHROVE TUESDAY). I called Mr. Sheply and we both went up to my Lord's lodgings at Mr. Crew's, where he bade us to go home again, and get a fire against an hour after. Which we did at White Hall, whither he came, and after talking with him and me about his going to sea, he called me by myself to go along with him into the garden, where he asked me how things were with me, and what he had endeavoured to do with my uncle to get him to do something for me, but he would say nothing too. He likewise bade me look out now at his turn some good place, and he would use all his own, and all the interest of his friends that he had in England, to do me good. And asked me whether I could, without too much inconvenience, go to sea as his secretary, and bid me think of it. He also began to talk things of State, and told me that he should want one in that capacity at sea, that he might trust in, and therefore he would have me to go. He told me also, that he did believe the King would come in, and did discourse with me about it, and about the affection of the people and City, at which I was full glad. After he was gone, I waiting upon him through the garden till he came to the Hall, where I left him and went up to my office, where Mr. Hawly brought one to me, a seaman, that had promised £10 to him if he get him a purser's place, which I think to endeavour to do. My Lord told me, that there was great endeavours to bring in the Protector again; but he told me, too, that he did believe it would not last long if he were brought in; no, nor the King neither (though he seems to think that he will come in), unless he carry himself very soberly and well. Every body now drinks the King's health without any fear, whereas before it was very private that a man dare do it.

9TH. Home and to bed. All night troubled in my thoughts how to order my business upon this great change with me that I could not sleep, and being overheated with drink I made a promise the next morning to drink no strong drink this week, for I find that it makes me sweat and puts me quite out of order.

10TH. In the morning went to my father's, whom I took in his cutting house, and there I told him my resolution to go to sea with my Lord, and consulted with him how to dispose of my wife, and we resolve of letting her be at Mr. Bowyer's. Then by coach home, where I took occasion to tell my wife of my going to sea, who was much troubled at it, and was with some dispute at last willing to continue at Bowyer's in my absence.

11TH (SUNDAY). All the day busy without my band on, putting up my books and things, in order to my going to sea.

12TH. This day the wench rose at two in the morning to wash, and my wife and I lay talking a great while. I by reason of my cold could not tell how to sleep.

14TH. To my Lord, where infinity of applications to him and to me. To my great trouble, my Lord gives me all the papers that was given to him, to put in order and give him an account of them. Here I got half-a-piece of a person of Mr. Wright's recommending to my Lord to be Preacher of the Speaker frigate. This done (where I saw General Monk and methought he seemed a dull heavy man), he and I to Whitehall, where with Luellin we dined at Marsh's. Coming home telling my wife what we had to dinner, she had a mind to some cabbage, and I sent for some and she had it. Went to the Admiralty, where a strange thing how I am already courted by the people.

16TH. No sooner out of bed but troubled with abundance of clients, seamen. Then to Westminster Hall, where I heard how the Parliament had this day dissolved themselves, and did pass very cheerfully through the Hall, and the Speaker without his mace. The whole Hall was joyful thereat, as well as themselves, and now they begin to talk loud of the King. To-night I am told, that yesterday, about five o'clock in the afternoon, one came with a ladder to the Great Exchange, and wiped with a brush the inscription that was upon King Charles, and that there was a great bonfire made in the Exchange, and people called out "God bless King Charles the Second!" From the Hall I went home to bed, very sad in mind to part with my wife, but God's will be done.

17TH. This morning bade adieu in bed to the company of my wife. We rose and I gave my wife some money to serve her for a time, and what papers of consequence I had. After dinner to my own house, where all things were put up into the dining-room and locked up, and my wife took the keys along with her. This day, in the presence of Mr. Moore (who made it) and Mr. Hawly, I did before I went out with my wife, seal my will to her, whereby I give her all that I have in the world, but my books which I give to my brother John, excepting only French books, which my wife is to have.

18TH. I rose early and went to the barber's (Jervas) in Palace Yard and I was trimmed by him, and afterwards drank with him a cup or two of ale, and did begin to hire his man to go with me to sea. Then to my Lord's lodging where I found Captain Williamson and gave him his commission to be Captain of the Harp, and he gave me a piece of gold and 20s. in silver.

19TH. All the discourse now-a-day is, that the King will come again; and for all I see, it is the wishes of all; and all do believe that it will be so. My mind is still much troubled for my poor wife, but I hope that this undertaking will be worth my pains. This day my Lord dined at my Lord Mayor's [Allen], and Jasper was made drunk, which my Lord was very angry at.

20TH. This morning I rose early and went to my house to put things in a little order against my going, which I conceive will be to-morrow (the weather still very rainy). Took a short melancholy leave of my father and mother, without having them to drink, or say anything of business one to another. And indeed I had a fear upon me I should scarce ever see my mother again, she having a great cold then upon her. Then to Westminster, where by reason of rain and an easterly wind, the water was so high that there was boats rowed in King Street and all our yard was drowned, that one could not go to my house, so as no man has seen the like almost, most houses full of water. Then back by coach to my Lord's, where I met Mr. Sheply, who staid with me waiting for my Lord's coming in till very late. Then he and I, and William Howe went with our swords to bring my Lord home from Sir H. Wright's. He resolved to go to-morrow if the wind ceased.

21ST. To my Lord's, but the wind very high against us, and the weather bad we could not go to-day.

22ND. Up very early and set things in order at my house. But the weather continuing very bad my Lord would not go to-day. I went forth about my own business to buy a pair of riding grey serge stockings and sword and belt and hose, and after that took Wotton and Brigden to the Pope's Head Tavern in Chancery Lane, where Gilb. Holland and Shelston were, and we dined and drank a great deal of wine, and they paid all. Strange how these people do now promise me anything; one a rapier, the other a vessel of wine or a gun, and one offered me his silver hatband to do him a courtesy. I pray God to keep me from being proud or too much lifted up hereby. After that to Westminster, and took leave of Kate Sterpin who was very sorry to part with me.

23RD. Up early, carried my Lord's will in a black box to Mr. William Montagu for him to keep for him. Then to the barber's and put on my cravat there. So to my Lord again, who was almost ready to be gone and had staid for me. Soon as my Lord on board, the guns went off bravely from the ships. And a little while after comes the Vice-Admiral Lawson, and seemed very respectful to my Lord, and so did the rest of the Commanders of the frigates that were thereabouts. I to the cabin allotted for me, which was the best that any had that belonged to my Lord. I got out some things out of my chest for writing and to work presently, Mr. Burr and I both.

24TH. At work hard all day writing letters to the Council, &c. The boy Eliezer flung down a can of beer upon my papers which made me give him a box of the ear, it having all spoiled my papers and cost me a great deal of work. So to bed.

26TH. This day it is two years since it pleased God that I was cut of the stone at Mrs. Turner's in Salisbury Court. And did resolve while I live to keep it a festival, as I did the last year at my house, and for ever to have Mrs. Turner and her company with me. But now it pleases God that I am where I am and so prevented to do it openly; only within my soul I can and do rejoice, and bless God, being at this time, blessed be his holy name, in as good health as ever I was in my life. This morning I rose early, and went about making of an establishment of the whole Fleet, and a list of all the ships, with the number of men and guns.

29TH. We lie still a little below Gravesend. At night Mr. Sheply returned from London, and told us of several elections for the next Parliament. That the King's effigies was new making to be set up in the Exchange again.

30TH. I was saluted in the morning with two letters, from some that I had done a favour to, which brought me in each a piece of gold. This day, while my Lord and we were at dinner, the Nazeby came in sight towards us, and at last came to anchor close by us. After dinner my Lord and many others went on board her, where every thing was out of order, and a new chimney made for my Lord in his bed-chamber, which he was much pleased with. My Lord, in his discourse, discovered a great deal of love to this ship.

APRIL 2ND. Up early, and to get all my things and my boy's packed up. Great concourse of commanders here this morning to take leave of my Lord upon his going into the Nazeby, so that the table was full.

3RD. At night, busy a-writing, and so to bed. My heart exceeding heavy for not hearing of my dear wife, and indeed I do not remember that ever my heart was so apprehensive of her absence as at this very time.

6TH. We under sail as far as the Spitts. In the afternoon, W. Howe and I to our viallins, the first time since we came on board. This afternoon I made even with my Lord to this day, and did give him all the money remaining in my hands. In the evening, it being fine moonshine, I staid late walking upon the quarter-deck with Mr. Cuttance, learning of some sea terms.

7TH. This day, about nine o'clock in the morning, the wind grew high, and we being among the sands lay at anchor; I began to get dizzy and squeamish. Before dinner my Lord sent for me down to eat some oysters, the best my Lord said that ever he ate in his life, though I have ate as good at Bardsey. After dinner, and all the afternoon I walked upon the deck to keep myself from being sick, and at last about five o'clock, went to bed and got a caudle made me, and sleep upon it very well.

8TH (LORD'S DAY). Very calm again, and I pretty well, but my head aked all day. The lieutenant and I lay out of his window with his glass, looking at the women that were on board the vessels nearby, being pretty handsome.

9TH. We having sailed all night, were come in sight of the Nore and South Forelands in the morning, and so sailed all day. In the afternoon we had a very fresh gale, which I brooked better than I thought I should be able to do. This afternoon I first saw France and Calais, with which I was much pleased, though it was at a distance. At night as I was all alone in my cabin, in a melancholy fit playing on my viallin, my Lord and Sir R.

Stayner came into the coach and supped there, and called me out to supper with them.

14TH. Rose and drank a good morning draught there with Mr. Sheply, which occasioned my thinking upon the happy life that I live now, had I nothing to care for but myself.

17TH. So to sleep, every day bringing me a fresh sense of the pleasure of my present life.

23RD. This afternoon I had 40s. given me by Captain Cowes of the Paradox. In the evening the first time that we had any sport among the seamen, and indeed there were extraordinary good sport after my Lord had done playing at ninepins. After that W. Howe and I went to play two trebles in the great cabin below, which my Lord hearing, after supper he called for our instruments, and played a set of Lock's, two trebles, and a base, and that being done, he fell to singing of a song made upon the Rump, with which he played himself well, to the tune of "The Blacksmith." After all that done, then to bed.

26TH. Mr. Sheply, W. Howe and I down with J. Goods into my Lord's stateroom of wine and other drink, where it was very pleasant to observe the massy timbers that the ship is made of. We in the room were wholly under water and yet a deck below that.

27TH. After dinner in the afternoon came on board Sir Thomas Hatton and Sir R. Maleverer going for Flushing; but all the world know that they go where the rest of the many gentlemen go that every day flock to the King at Breda. They supped here, and my Lord treated them as he do the rest that go thither, with a great deal of civility.

MAY 2ND. In the morning at a breakfast of radishes at the Purser's cabin. After that the writing till dinner. At which time comes Dunne from London, with letters that tell us the welcome news of the Parliament's votes yesterday, which will be remembered for the happiest May-day that hath been many a year to England. The King's letter was read in the House, wherein he submits himself and all things to them, as to an Act of Oblivion to all, unless they shall please to except any, as to the confirming of the sales of the King's and Church lands, if they see good. The House upon reading the letter, ordered £50,000 to be forthwith provided to send to His Majesty for his present supply; and a committee chosen to return an answer of thanks to His Majesty for his gracious letter; and that the letter be kept among the records of the Parliament; and in all this not so much as one No. Great joy all yesterday at London, and at night more bonfires than ever, and ringing of bells, and drinking of the King's health upon their knees in the streets, which methinks is a little too much. But every body seems to be very joyfull in the business, insomuch that our sea-commanders now begin to say so too, which a week ago they would not do. And our seamen, as many as had money or credit for drink, did do nothing else this evening.

3RD. This morning my Lord showed me the King's declaration and his letter to the two Generals to be communicated to the fleet. I went up to the quarter-deck with my Lord and the Commanders, and there read both the papers and the vote; which done, and demanding their opinion, the seamen did all of them cry out, "God bless King Charles!" with the greatest joy imaginable. My Lord was much pleased to hear how all the fleet took it in a transport of joy, showed me a private letter of the King's to him, and another from the Duke of York in such familiar style as to their common friend, with all kindness imaginable. My Lord seemed to put great confidence in me, and would take my advice in many things. I perceive his being willing to do all the honour in the world to Monk, and to let him have all the honour of doing the business, though he will many times express his thoughts of him to be but a thick-sculled fool. So that I do believe there is some agreement more than ordinary between the King and my Lord to let Monk carry on the business, for it is he that must do the business, or at least that can hinder it, if he be not flattered and observed. This, my Lord will hint himself sometimes.

4TH. I wrote this morning many letters, and to all the copies of the vote of the council of war I put my name, that if it should come in print my name may be at it. I sent a copy of the vote to Doling, inclosed in this letter:—

"SIR,
    "He that can fancy a fleet (like ours) in her pride, with pendants loose, guns roaring, caps flying, and the loud *'Vive le Roys,'* echoed from one ship's company to another, he, and he only, can apprehend the joy this inclosed vote was received with, or the blessing he thought himself possessed of that bore it, and is
                                            "Your humble servant."

7TH. This morning Captain Cuttance sent me 12 bottles of Margate ale. Three of them I drank presently with some friends in the Coach. My Lord went this morning about the flag-ships in a boat, to see what alterations there must be, as to the arms and flags. He did give me order also to write for silk flags and scarlett waistcloathes. For a rich barge; for a noise of trumpets, and a set of fidlers.

8TH. My Lord and we at nine-pins: I lost 9s. While we were at play Mr. Cook brings me word of my wife. He went to Huntsmore to see her, and brought her and my father Bowyer to London, where he left her at my father's, very well, and speaks very well of her love to me.

9TH. Up very early, writing a letter to the King, as from the two Generals of the fleet, in answer to his letter to them, wherein my Lord do give most humble thanks for his gracious letter and declaration; and promises all duty and obedience to him. As we were sitting down to dinner, in comes Noble with a letter from the House of Lords to my Lord, to desire him to provide ships to transport the Commissioners to the King, which are expected here this week. He brought us certain news that the King was proclaimed yesterday with great pomp, and brought down one of the Proclamations, with great joy to us all; for which God be praised. After dinner to nine pins and lost 5s.

11TH. This morning we began to pull down all the State's arms in the fleet, having first sent to Dover for painters and others to come to set up the King's.

13TH (LORD'S DAY). Trimmed in the morning, after that to the cook's room with Mr. Sheply, the first time that I was there this voyage. Then to the quarter-deck, upon which the tailors and painters were at work, cutting out some pieces of yellow cloth into the fashion of a crown and C. R. and put it upon a fine sheet, and that into the flag instead of the State's arms. In the afternoon a council of war, only to acquaint them that the Harp must be taken out of all their flags, it being very offensive to the King. Mr. Cook, who came after us in the Yarmouth, bringing me a letter from my wife and a Latin letter from my brother John, with both of which I was exceedingly pleased.

14TH. In the morning when I woke and rose, I saw myself out of the scuttle close by the shore, which afterwards I was told to be the Dutch shore; the Hague was clearly to be seen by us. My Lord went up in his nightgown into the cuddy, to see how to dispose thereof for himself and us that belong to him, to give order for our removal to-day. Some nasty Dutchmen came on board to proffer their boats to carry things from us on shore, &c., to get money by us. Before noon some gentlemen came on board from the shore to kiss my Lord's hands. And by and by Mr. North and Dr. Clerke went to kiss the Queen of Bohemia's hands, from my Lord, with twelve attendants from on board to wait on them, among which I sent my boy, who, like myself, is with child to see any strange thing. After noon they came back again after having kissed the Queen of Bohemia's hand, and were sent again by my Lord to do the same to the

Prince of Orange. So I got the Captain to ask leave for me to go, which my Lord did give, and I taking my boy and Judge Advocate with me, went in company with them. The weather bad; we were sadly washed when we came near the shore, it being very hard to land there. The shore is, as all the country between that and the Hague, all sand. The rest of the company got a coach by themselves; Mr. Creed and I went in the fore part of a coach wherein were two very pretty ladies, very fashionable and with black patches, who very merrily sang all the way and that very well, and were very free to kiss the two blades that were with them. I took out my flageolet and piped. The Hague is a most neat place in all respects. The houses so neat in all places and things as is possible. Here we walked up and down a great while, the town being now very full of Englishmen.

15TH. We lay till past three o'clock, then up and down the town, to see it by daylight, where we saw the soldiers of the Prince's guard, all very fine, and the burghers of the town with their arms and muskets as bright as silver. And meeting this morning a school master that spoke good English and French, he went along with us and shewed us the whole town, and indeed I cannot speak enough of the gallantry of the town. Every body of fashion speaks French or Latin, or both. The women many of them very pretty and in good habits, fashionable and black spots. After that to a bookseller's and bought for the love of the binding three books: the French Psalms in four parts, Bacon's Organon, and Farnab. Rhetor.

16TH. Soon as I was up I went down to be trimmed below in the great cabin, but then come in some with visits, among the rest one from Admiral Opdam, who spoke Latin well, but not French nor English, to whom my Lord made me to give his answer and to entertain; he brought my Lord a tierce of wine and a barrel of butter, as a present from the Admiral. This afternoon Mr. Edwd. Pickering told me in what a sad, poor condition for clothes and money the king was, and all his attendants, when he came to him first from my Lord, their clothes not being worth forty shillings the best of them. And how overjoyed the King was when Sir J. Greenville brought him some money; so joyful, that he called the Princess Royal and Duke of York to look upon it as it lay in the portmanteau before it was taken out. My Lord told me, too, that the Duke of York is made High Admiral of England.

17TH. Up early to write down my last two days' observations. Before dinner Mr. Edw. Pickering and I, W. Howe, Pim, and my boy, to Scheveling, where we took coach, and so to the Hague, where walking, intending to find one that might show us the King incognito, I met with Captain Whittington (that had formerly brought a letter to my Lord from the Mayor of London) and he did promise me to do it, but first we went and dined at a French house, but paid 16s. for our part of the club. At dinner in came Dr. Cade, a merry mad parson of the King's. And they two after dinner got the child and me (the others not being able to crowd in) to see the King, who kissed the child very affectionately. Then we kissed his, and the Duke of York's, and the Princess Royal's hands. The King seems to be a sober man; and a very splendid Court he hath in the number of persons of quality that are about him, English very rich in habit. From the King to the Lord Chancellor, who did lie bed-rid of the gout; he spoke very merrily to the child and me. After that, going to see the Queen of Bohemia, I met with Dr. Fuller, whom I sent to a tavern with Mr. Edw. Pickering, while I and the rest went to see the Queen, who used us very respectfully; her hand we all kissed. She seems very debonaire, but plain lady. After that to the Dr.'s, where we drank a while or so.

18TH. Back by water, where a pretty sober Dutch lass sat reading all the way, and I could not fasten any discourse upon her.

20TH. Up early, and with Mr. Pickering and the child by waggon to Scheveling, where it not being yet fit to go off, I went to lie down in a chamber in the house, where in another bed there was a pretty Dutch woman in bed alone, but though I had a month's-mind I had not the boldness to go to her. So there I slept an hour or two. At last she rose, and then I rose and walked up and down the chamber, and saw her dress herself after the Dutch dress, and talked to her as much as I could, and took occasion, from her ring which she wore on her first finger to kiss her hand, but had not the face to offer anything more. So at last I left her there and went to my company. Commissioner Pett at last came to our lodging, and caused the boats to go off; so some in one boat and some in another we all bid adieu to the shore. But through badness of weather we were in great danger, and a great while before we could get to the ship, so that of all the company not one but myself that was not sick. I keeping myself in the open air, though I was soundly wet for it. I having spoke a word or two with my Lord, being not very well settled, partly through last night's drinking and want of sleep, I lay down in my gown upon my bed and slept till the 4 o'clock gun the next morning waked me, which I took for 8 at night, and rising . . . mistook the sun rising for the sun setting on Sunday night.

21ST. So into my naked bed and slept till 9 o'clock, and then John Goods waked me, [by] and by the captain's boy brought me four barrels of Mallows oysters, which Captain Tatnell had sent me from Murlace. The weather foul all this day also. By letters that came hither in my absence, I understand that the Parliament had ordered all persons to be secured, in order to a trial, that did sit as judges in the late King's death, and all the officers too attending the Court. News brought that the two Dukes are coming on board, which, by and by, they did, in a Dutch boat, the Duke of York in yellow trimmings, the Duke of Gloucester in grey and red. My Lord went in a boat to meet them, the captain, myself, and others, standing at the entering port. So soon as they were entered we shot the guns off round the fleet. After that they went to view the ship all over, and were most exceedingly pleased with it. They seem to be both very fine gentlemen. News is sent us that the King is on shore; so my Lord fired all his guns round twice, and all the fleet after him, which in the end fell into disorder, which seemed very handsome. The gun over against my cabin I fired myself to the King, which was the first time that he had been saluted by his own ships since this change; but holding my head too much over the gun, I had almost spoiled my right eye. Nothing in the world but going of guns almost all this day.

23RD. The Doctor and I waked very merry. In the morning came infinity of people on board from the King to go along with him. My Lord, Mr. Crew, and others, go on shore to meet the King as he comes off from shore, where Sir R. Stayner bringing His Majesty into the boat, I hear that His Majesty did with a great deal of affection kiss my Lord upon his first meeting. The King, with the two Dukes and Queen of Bohemia, Princess Royal, and Prince of Orange, came on board, where I in their coming in kissed the King's, Queen's, and Princess's hands, having done the other before. Infinite shooting off of the guns, and that in a disorder on purpose, which was better than if it had been otherwise. All day nothing but Lords and persons of honour on board, that we were exceeding full. Dined in a great deal of state, the Royall company by themselves in the coach, which was a blessed sight to see. After dinner the King and Duke altered the name of some of the ships, viz. the Nazeby into Charles; the Richard, James; the Speaker, Mary; the Dunbar (which was not in company with us), the Henry; Winsly, Happy Return; Wakefield, Richmond; Lambert, the Henrietta; Cheriton, the Speedwell; Bradford, the Success. That done, the Queen, Princess Royal, and Prince of Orange, took leave of the King, and the Duke of York went on board the London, and the Duke of Gloucester, the Swiftsure. Which done, we weighed anchor, and with a fresh gale and most happy weather we set sail for England. All the afternoon the King walked here and there, up and down (quite contrary to what I thought him to have been), very active and stirring. Upon the quarter-deck he fell into discourse of his escape from Worcester, where it made me ready to weep to hear the stories that he told of his difficulties that he had passed through, as his travelling four days and three nights on foot, every step up to his knees in dirt, with nothing but a green coat and a pair of country breeches on, and a pair of country shoes that made him so sore all over his feet, that he could scarce stir. Yet he was forced to run away from a miller and other company, that took them for rogues. His sitting at table at one place, where the master of the house, that had not seen him in eight years, did know him, but kept it private; when at the same table there was one that had been of his own regiment at Worcester, could not know him, but made him drink the King's health, and said that the King was at least four fingers higher than he. At another place he was by some servants of the house made to drink, that they might know him not to be a Roundhead, which they swore he was. In another place at his inn, the master of the house, as the King was standing with his hands upon the back of a chair by the fireside, kneeled down and kissed his hand, privately, saying, that he would not ask who he was, but bid God bless him whither he was going. Then the difficulty of getting a boat to get into France, where he was fain to plot with the master thereof to keep his design from the four men and a boy (which was all his ship's company), and so go to Fécamp in France. At Rouin he looked so poorly, that the people went into the rooms before he went away to see whether he had not stolen something or other. The King supped alone in the coach; after that I got a dish, and we four supped in my cabin, as at noon. So to my cabin again, where the company still was, and were talking more of the King's difficulties; as how he was fain to eat a piece of bread and cheese out of a poor boy's pocket; how, at a Catholique house he was fain to lie in the priest's hole a good while in the house for his privacy. Under sail all night, and most glorious weather.

24TH. Up, and make myself as fine as I could, with the linning stockings on and wide canons that I bought the other day at Hague. Extraordinary press of noble company, and great mirth all the day. Walking upon the decks, where persons of honour all the afternoon, among others, Thomas Killigrew (a merry droll, but a gentleman of great esteem with the King), who told us many merry stories. After this discourse I was called to write a pass for my Lord Mandeville to take up horses to London, which I wrote in the King's name, and carried it to him to sign, which was the first and only one that ever he signed in the ship Charles. To bed, coming in sight of land a little before night.

25TH. By the morning we were come close to the land, and every body made ready to get on shore. The King and the two Dukes did eat their breakfast before they went, and there being set some ship's diet before them, only to show them the manner of the ship's diet, they eat of nothing else but pease and pork, and boiled beef. I spoke with the Duke of York about business, who called me Pepys by name, and upon my desire did promise me his future favour. Great expectation of the King's making some Knights, but there was none. About noon (though the brigantine that Beale made was there ready to carry him) yet he would go in my Lord's barge with the two Dukes. Our Captain steered, and my Lord went along bare with him. I went, and Mr. Mansell, and one of the King's footmen, with a dog that the King loved, (which [dirtied] the boat, which made us laugh, and methink that a King and all that belong to him are but just as others are), in a boat by ourselves, and so got on shore when the King did, who was received by General Monk with all imaginable love and respect at his entrance upon the land of Dover. Infinite the crowd of people and the horsemen, citizens, and noblemen of all sorts. The Mayor of the town came and gave him his white staff, the badge of his place, which the King did give him again. The Mayor also presented him from the town a very rich Bible, which he took and said it was the thing that he loved above all things in the world. A canopy was provided for him to stand under, which he did, and talked awhile with General Monk and others, and so into a stately coach there set for him, and so away through the town towards Canterbury, without making any stay at Dover. The shouting and joy expressed by all is past imagination. My Lord returned late, and at his coming did give me order to cause the marke to be gilded, and a Crown and C. R. to be made at the head of the coach table, where the King to-day with his own hand did mark his height, which accordingly I caused the painter to do, and is now done as is to be seen.

26TH. This night the Captain told me that my Lord had appointed me £30 out of the 1000 ducats which the King had given to the ship, at which my heart was very much joyed. To bed.

27TH (LORD'S DAY). Called up by John Goods to see the Garter and Heralds coat, which lay in the coach, brought by Sir Edward Walker, King at Arms, this morning, for my Lord.

28TH. This morning the Captain did call over the men in the ship (not the boys), and give every one of them a ducat of the King's money that he gave the ship, and the officers according to their quality. I received in the Captain's cabin, for my share, sixty ducats.

31ST. This day my Lord took physic, and came not out of his chamber. All the morning making orders. After dinner a great while below in the great cabin trying with W. Howe some of Mr. Laws' songs, particularly that of "What is a kiss," with which we had a great deal of pleasure.

JUNE 2ND. Being with my Lord in the morning about business in his cabin, I took occasion to give him thanks for his love to me in the share that he had given me of his Majesty's money, and the Duke's. He told me he hoped to do me a more lasting kindness, if all things stand as they are now between him and the King, but, says he, "We must have a little patience and we will rise together; in the mean time I will do you all the good jobs I can." Which was great content for me to hear from my Lord.

4TH. This morning the King's Proclamation against drinking, swearing, and debauchery, was read to our ships' companies in the fleet, and indeed it gives great satisfaction to all.

8TH. Out early, took horses at Deale. I troubled much with the King's gittar, and Fairbrother, the rogue that I intrusted with the carrying of it on foot, whom I thought I had lost. Come to Gravesend. A good handsome wench I kissed, the first that I have seen a great while.

9TH. Up betimes, 25s. the reckoning for very bare. Paid the house and by boats to London, six boats. Mr. Moore, W. Howe, and I, and then the child in the room of W. Howe. Landed at the Temple. To Mr. Crew's. To my father's and put myself into a handsome posture to wait upon my Lord, dined there. To White Hall with my Lord and Mr. Edwd. Montagu. Found the King in the Park. There walked. Gallantly great.

1OTH (LORD'S DAY). At my father's found my wife and to walk with her in Lincoln's Inn walks.

17TH (LORD'S DAY). Lay long abed. To Mr. Mossum's; a good sermon. This day the organs did begin to play at White Hall before the King. After sermon to my Lord. Mr. Edward and I into Gray's Inn walks, and saw many beauties.

18TH. To my Lord's, where much business and some hopes of getting some money thereby. This evening my wife's brother, Balty, came to me to let me know his bad condition and to get a place for him, but I perceive he stands upon a place for a gentleman, that may not stain his family when, God help him, he wants bread.

22ND. To my Lord's, and had the great coach to Brigham's, who went with me to the Half Moon, and gave me a can of good julep, and told me how my Lady Monk deals with him and others for their places, asking him £500, though he was formerly the King's coach-maker, and sworn to it.

23RD. So to my Lord's lodgings, where Tom Guy came to me, and there staid to see the King touch people for the King's evil. But he did not come at all, it rayned so; and the poor people were forced to stand all the morning in the rain in the garden. Afterward he touched them in the Banquetting-house.

26TH. In the afternoon, one Mr. Watts came to me, a merchant, to offer me £500 if I would desist from the Clerk of the Acts place. I pray God direct me in what I do herein.

27TH. With my Lord to the Duke, where he spoke to Mr. Coventry to despatch my business of the Acts, in which place everybody gives me joy, as if I were in it, which God send. So back again, and after a song or two in my chamber in the dark, which do (now that the bed is out) sound very well, I went home and to bed.

JULY 1ST. This morning came home my fine Camlett cloak, with gold buttons, and a silk suit, which cost me much money, and I pray God to make me able to pay for it.

2ND. Infinite of business that my heart and head and all were full. Met with purser Washington, with whom and a lady, a friend of his, I dined at the Bell Tavern in King Street, but the rogue had no more manners than to invite me and to let me pay my club.

4TH. To Westminster Hall, where meeting with Mons. L'Impertinent and W. Bowyer, I took them to the Sun Tavern, and gave them a lobster and some wine, and sat talking like a fool till 4 o'clock.

5TH. This morning my brother Tom brought me my jack-anapes coat with silver buttons. It rained this morning, which makes us fear that the glory of this great day will be lost; the King and Parliament being to be entertained by the City to-day with great pomp. Mr. Hater was with me to-day, and I agreed with him to be my clerk. Being at White Hall, I saw the King, the Dukes, and all their attendants go forth in the rain to the City, and it bedraggled many a fine suit of clothes. I was forced to walk all the morning in White Hall, not knowing how to get out because of the rain.

13TH. Late writing letters; and great doings of music at the next house, which was Whally's; the King and Dukes there with Madame Palmer, a pretty woman that they have a fancy to, to make her husband a cuckold. Here at the old door that did go into his lodgings, my Lord, I, and W. Howe, did stand listening a great while to the music.

14TH. Up early and advised with my wife for the putting of all our things in a readiness to be sent to our new house. Comes in Mr. Pagan Fisher, the poet, and promises me what he had long ago done, a book in praise of the King of France, with my armes, and a dedication to me very handsome.

15TH. In the afternoon to Henry the Seventh's chapel, where I heard a sermon and spent (God forgive me) most of my time in looking upon Mrs. Butler.

28TH. Early in the morning rose, and a boy brought me a letter from Poet Fisher, who tells me that he is upon a panegyrique of the King, and desired to borrow a piece of me; and I sent him half a piece.

31ST. To White Hall, where my Lord and the principal officers met, and had a great discourse about raising of money for the Navy, which is in very sad condition, and money must be raised for it.

AUGUST 4TH. After that I went and bespoke some linen of Betty Lane in the Hall, and after that to the Trumpet, where I sat and talked with her, &c.

6TH. This morning at the office, and, that being done, home to dinner all alone, my wife being ill in pain a-bed, which I was troubled at, and not a little impatient. This night Mr. Man offered me £1,000 for my office of Clerk of the Acts, which made my mouth water; but yet I dare not take it till I speak with my Lord to have his consent.

9TH. Having my head full of drink from having drunk so much Rhenish wine in the morning, and more in the afternoon at Mrs. Blackburne's, came thence home and so to bed, not well, and very ill all night.

11TH. I rose to-day without any pain, which makes me think that my pain yesterday was nothing but from my drinking too much the day before.

12TH (LORD's DAY). To my Lord, and with him to White Hall Chappell, where Mr. Calamy preached, and made a good sermon upon these words: "To whom much is given, of him much is required." He was very officious with his three reverences to the King, as others do. After that I went to walk, and meeting Mrs. Lane of Westminster Hall, I took her to my Lord's, and did give her a bottle of wine in the garden, where Mr. Fairbrother, of Cambridge, did come and found us, and drank with us. After that I took her to my house, where I was exceeding free in dallying with her, and she not unfree to take it.

15TH. To the office, and after dinner by water to White Hall, where I found the King gone this morning by 5 of the clock to see a Dutch pleasure-boat below bridge, where he dines, and my Lord with him. The King do tire all his people that are about him with early rising since he came.

16TH. This morning my Lord (all things being ready) carried me by coach to Mr. Crew's, (in the way talking how good he did hope my place would be to me, and in general speaking that it was not the salary of any place that did make a man rich, but the opportunity of getting money while he is in the place,) where he took leave, and went into the coach, and so for Hinchinbroke.

18TH. This morning I took my wife towards Westminster by water, and landed her at Whitefriars, with £5 to buy her a petticoat, and I to the Privy Seal. By and by comes my wife to tell me that my father has persuaded her to buy a most fine cloth of 26s. a yard, and a rich lace, that the petticoat will come to £5, at which I was somewhat troubled, but she doing it very innocently, I could not be angry.... Dined at the Leg in King Street, where Captain Ferrers, my Lord's Cornet, comes to us, who after dinner took me and Creed to the Cockpitt play, the first that I have had time to see since my coming from sea, "The Loyall Subject," where one Kinaston, a boy, acted the Duke's sister, but made the loveliest lady that ever I saw in my life, only her voice not very good. After the play done, we three went to drink, and by Captain Ferrers' means, Kinaston and another that acted Archas, the General, came and drank with us. Hence home by coach, and after being trimmed, leaving my wife to look after her little bitch, which was just now a-whelping, I to bed.

19TH (LORD'S DAY). In the morning my wife tells me that the bitch has whelped four young ones and is very well after it, my wife having had a great fear that she would die thereof, the dog that got them being very big. After dinner my wife went and fetched the little puppies to us, which are very pretty ones. After they were gone, I went up to put my papers in order, and finding my wife's clothes lie carelessly laid up, I was angry with her, which I was troubled for. After that my wife and I went and walked in the garden, and so home to bed.

28TH. At home looking over my papers and books and house as to the fitting of it to my mind till two in the afternoon. Some time I spent this morning beginning to teach my wife some scale in music, and found her apt beyond imagination. To bed, a little troubled that I fear my boy Will is a thief and has stole some money of mine, particularly a letter that Mr. Jenkins did leave the last week with me with half a crown in it to send to his son.

29TH (OFFICE DAY). Before I went to the office my wife and I examined my boy Will about his stealing of things, but he denied all with the greatest subtlety and confidence in the world. Home to dinner, and there I found my wife had discovered my boy Will's theft and a great deal more than we imagined, at which I was vexed and intend to put him away. Home at night, and find that my wife had found out more of the boy's stealing 6s. out of W. Hewer's closet, and hid it in the house of office, at which my heart was troubled. To bed, and caused the boy's clothes to be brought up to my chamber. But after we were all a-bed, the wench (which lies in our chamber) called us to listen of a sudden, which put my wife into such a fright that she shook every joint of her, and a long time that I could not get her out of it. The noise was the boy, we did believe, got in a desperate mood out of his bed to do himself or William [Hewer] some mischief. But the wench went down and got a candle lighted, and finding the boy in bed, and locking the doors fast, with a candle burning all night, we slept well, but with a great deal of fear.

30TH. We found all well in the morning below stairs, but the boy in a sad plight of seeming sorrow; but he is the most cunning rogue that ever I met with of his age. This the first day that ever I saw my wife wear black patches since we were married.

SEPTEMBER 4TH. From thence to Axe Yard to my house, where standing at the door Mrs. Diana comes by, whom I took into my house upstairs, and there did dally with her a great while, and found that in Latin *"Nulla puella negat."*

5TH. In the evening my wife being a little impatient I went along with her to buy her a necklace of pearl, which will cost £4 10s., which I am willing to comply with her in for her encouragement, and because I have lately got money, having now about £200 in cash beforehand in the world. Home, and having in our way bought a rabbit and two little lobsters, my wife and I did sup late, and so to bed.

22ND. To Westminster to my Lord's. I staid here all day in my Lord's chamber and upon the leads gazing upon Diana, who looked out of a window upon me. At last I went out to Mr. Harper's, and she standing over the way at the gate, I went over to her and appointed to meet to-morrow in the afternoon at my Lord's.

23RD (LORD'S DAY). After sermon with Mr. Pierce to Whitehall, and from thence to my Lord, but Diana did not come according to our agreement.

25TH. And afterwards I did send for a cup of tea (a China drink) of which I never had drank before, and went away.

28TH. All the afternoon among my workmen till 10 or 11 at night, and did give them drink and very merry with them, it being my luck to meet with a sort of drolling workmen on all occasions. To bed.

OCTOBER 7TH (LORD'S DAY). To my Lord's and dined with him; he all dinner time talking French to me, and telling me the story how the Duke of York hath got my Lord Chancellor's daughter with child, and that she do lay it to him, and that for certain he did promise her marriage, and had signed it with his blood, but that he by stealth had got the paper out of her cabinet. And that the King would have him to marry her, but that he will not.

13TH. To my Lord's in the morning, where I met with Captain Cuttance, but my Lord not being up I went out to Charing Cross, to see Major-general Harrison hanged, drawn, and quartered; which was done there, he looking as cheerful as any man could do in that condition. He was presently cut down, and his head and heart shown to the people, at which there was great shouts of joy. It is said, that he said that he was sure to come shortly at the right hand of Christ to judge them that now had judged him; and that his wife do expect his coming again. Thus it was my chance to see the King beheaded at White Hall, and to see the first blood shed in revenge for the blood of the King at Charing Cross. From thence to my Lord's, and took Captain Cuttance and Mr. Sheply to the Sun Tavern, and did give them some oysters. After that I went by water home, where I was angry with my wife for her things lying about, and in my passion kicked the little fine basket which I bought her in Holland, and broke it, which troubled me after I had done it. Within all the afternoon setting up shelves in my study. At night to bed.

14TH (LORD'S DAY). To White Hall Chappell, where one Dr. Crofts made an indifferent sermon, and after it an anthem, ill sung, which made the King laugh. Here I first did see the Princess Royal since she came into England. Here I also observed, how the Duke of York and Mrs. Palmer did talk to one another very wantonly through the hangings that parts the King's closet and the closet where the ladies sit.

15TH. This morning Mr. Carew was hanged and quartered at Charing Cross; but his quarters, by a great favour, are not to be hanged up.

18TH. This morning, it being expected that Colonel Hacker and Axtell should die, I went to Newgate, but found they were reprieved till to-morrow.

19TH. Office in the morning. This morning my dining-room was finished with green serge hanging and gilt leather, which is very handsome. This morning Hacker and Axtell were hanged and quartered, as the rest are.

20TH. This afternoon, going through London, and calling at Crowe's the upholsterer's, in Saint Bartholomew's, I saw the limbs of some of our new traitors set upon Aldersgate, which was a sad sight to see; and a bloody week this and the last have been, there being ten hanged, drawn, and quartered.

21ST (LORD'S DAY). To the Crown in the Palace Yard, I and George Vines by the way calling at their house, where he carried me up to the top of his turret, where there is Cooke's head set up for a traytor, and Harrison's set up on the other side of Westminster Hall. Here I could see them plainly, as also a very fair prospect about London. This day or two my wife has been troubled with her boils in the old place, which do much trouble her. To-day at noon (God forgive me) I strung my lute, which I had not touched a great while before.

26TH. Office. My father and Dr. Thomas Pepys dined at my house, the last of whom I did almost fox with Margate ale. My father is mightily pleased with my ordering of my house. I did give him money to pay several bills. After that I to Westminster to White Hall, where I saw the Duke de Soissons go from his audience with a very great deal of state: his own coach all red velvet covered with gold lace, and drawn by six barbes, and attended by twenty pages very rich in clothes. To Westminster Hall, and bought, among other books, one of the life of our Queen, which I read at home to my wife; but it was so sillily writ, that we did nothing but laugh at it; among other things it is dedicated to that paragon of virtue and beauty, the Duchess of Albemarle. Great talk as if the Duke of York do now own the marriage between him and the Chancellor's daughter.

NOVEMBER 4TH (LORD'S DAY). My wife seemed very pretty to-day, it being the first time I had given her leave to wear a black patch.

5TH (OFFICE DAY). Home, and fell a-reading of the tryalls of the late men that were hanged for the King's death, and found good satisfaction in reading thereof. At night to bed, and my wife and I did fall out about the dog's being put down in the cellar, which I had a mind to have done because of his fouling the house, and I would have my will, and so we went to bed and lay all night in a quarrel. This night I was troubled all night with a dream that my wife was dead, which made me that I slept ill all night.

11TH (LORD'S DAY). Went to my father's where I found my wife, and there we supped, and Dr. Thomas Pepys, who my wife told me after I was come home, that he had told my brother Thomas that he loved my wife so well that if she had a child he would never marry, but leave all that he had to my child, and after supper we walked home, my little boy carrying a link, and Will leading my wife. So home, and to prayers and to bed.

12TH. My father and I took occasion to go forth, and went and drank at Mr. Standing's, and there discoursed seriously about my sister's coming to live with me, which I have much mind for her good to have, and yet I am much afeard of her ill-nature. Coming home again, he and I, and my wife, my mother and Pall, went all together into the little room, and there I told her plainly what my mind was, to have her come not as a sister in any respect, but as a servant, which she promised me that she would, and with many thanks did weep for joy, which did give me and my wife some content and satisfaction.

19TH (OFFICE DAY). After we had done a little at the office this morning, I went with the Treasurer in his coach to White Hall, and in our way, in discourse, do find him a very good-natured man; and, talking of those men who now stand condemned for murdering the King, he says that he believes that, if the law would give leave, the King is a man of so great compassion that he would wholly acquit them. So to my musique and sat up late at it, and so to bed, leaving my wife to sit up till 2 o'clock that she may call the wench up to wash.

20TH. About two o'clock my wife wakes me, and comes to bed, and so both to sleep and the wench to wash. I rose and with Will to my Lord's by land, it being a very hard frost, the first we have had this year.

22ND. Mr. Fox came in presently and did receive us with a great deal of respect; and then did take my wife and I to the Queen's presence-chamber, where he got my wife placed behind the Queen's chair, and I got into the crowd, and by and by the Queen and the two Princesses came to dinner. The Queen a very little plain old woman, and nothing more in her presence in any respect nor garb than any ordinary woman. The Princess of Orange I had often seen before. The Princess Henrietta is very pretty, but much below my expectation; and her dressing of herself with her hair frized short up to her ears, did make her seem so much the less to me. But my wife standing near her with two or three black patches on, and well dressed, did seem to me much handsomer than she.

24TH. To my Lord's, where after I had done talking with him Mr. Townsend, Rumball, Blackburn, Creed and Shepley and I to the Rhenish winehouse, and there I did give them two quarts of Wormwood wine, and so we broke up.

26TH (OFFICE DAY). The Comptroller and I to the Mitre to a glass of wine, when we fell into a discourse of poetry, and he did repeat some verses of his own making which were very good.

27TH. To Whitehall, where I found my Lord gone abroad to the wardrobe, whither he do now go every other morning, and do seem to resolve to understand and look after the business himself. From thence to Westminster Hall, and in King Street there being a great stop of coaches, there was falling out between a drayman and my Lord Chesterfield's coachman, and one of his footmen killed. At the Hall I met with Mr. Creed, and he and I to Hell to drink our morning draught, and so to my Lord's again, where I found my wife, and she and I dined with him and my Lady, and great company of my Lord's friends, and my Lord did show us great respect.

DECEMBER 1ST. This morning, observing some things to be laid up not as they should be by the girl, I took a broom and basted her till she cried extremely, which made me vexed, but before I went out I left her appeased.

2ND (LORD'S DAY). My head not very well, and my body out of order by last night's drinking, which is my great folly.

3RD. This morning I took a resolution to rise early in the morning, and so I rose by candle, which I have not done all this winter, and spent my morning in fiddling till time to go to the office.

4TH. This day the Parliament voted that the bodies of Oliver, Ireton, Bradshaw, &c., should be taken up out of their graves in the Abbey, and drawn to the gallows, and there hanged and buried under it: which (methinks) do trouble me that a man of so great courage as he was, should have that dishonour, though otherwise he might deserve it enough.

5TH. I dined at home, and after dinner I went to the new Theatre and there I saw "The Merry Wives of Windsor" acted, the humours of the country gentleman and the French doctor very well done, but the rest but very poorly, and Sir J. Falstaffe as bad as any.

6TH. I carried my wife to White Friars and landed her there, and myself to Whitehall to the Privy Seal, where abundance of pardons to seal, but I was much troubled for it because that there are no fees now coming for them to me.

7TH. Before dinner I examined Laud in his Latin and found him a very pretty boy and gone a great way in Latin. So to the Privy Seal, where I signed a deadly number of pardons, which do trouble me to get nothing by.

9TH (LORD'S DAY). Dined with my Lady and staid all the afternoon with her, and had infinite of talk of all kind of things, especially of beauty of men and women, with which she seems to be much pleased to talk of.

10TH. Up exceedingly early to go to the Comptroller, but he not being up and it being a very fine, bright, moonshine morning I went and walked all alone twenty turns in Cornhill, from Gracious Street corner to the Stockes and back again, from 6 o'clock till past 7, so long that I was weary, and going to the Comptroller's thinking to find him ready, I found him gone, at which I was troubled, and being weary went home.

11TH. My wife and I up very early this day, and though the weather was very bad and the wind high, yet my Lady Batten and her maid and we two did go by our barge to Woolwich (my Lady being very fearfull) where we found both Sir Williams and much other company, expecting the weather to be better, that they might go about weighing up the Assurance, which lies there (poor ship, that I have been twice merry in, in Captn. Holland's time,) under water, only the upper deck may be seen and the masts. Captain Stoakes is very melancholy, and being in search for some clothes and money of his, which he says he hath lost out of his cabin. I did the first office of a Justice of Peace to examine a seaman thereupon, but could find no reason to commit him.

12TH. Up with J. Spicer to his office and took £100, and by coach with it as far as my father's, where I called to see them, and my father did offer me six pieces of gold, in lieu of six pounds that he borrowed of me the other day, but it went against me to take it of him and therefore did not, though I was afterwards a little troubled that I did not. Thence home, and took out this £100 and sealed it up with the other last night, it being the first £200 that ever I saw together of my own in my life. After that home and to bed, reading myself asleep, while the wench sat mending my breeches by my bedside.

14TH. Also all this day looking upon my workmen. Only met with the Comptroller at the office a little both forenoon and afternoon, and at night step a little with him to the Coffee House where we light upon very good company and had very good discourse concerning insects and their having a generative faculty as well as other creatures.

16TH. With Tom Doling and Boston and D. Vines (whom we met by the way) to Price's, and there we drank, and in discourse I learnt a pretty trick to try whether a woman be a maid or no, by a string going round her head to meet at the end of her nose, which if she be not will come a great way beyond.

27TH. About the middle of the night I was very ill—I think with eating and drinking too much—and so I was forced to call the maid, who pleased my wife and I in her running up and down so innocently in her smock, and vomited in the bason, and so to sleep, and in the morning was pretty well, only got cold, and so had pain . . . as I used to have.

1661

At the end of the last and the beginning of this year, I do live in one of the houses belonging to the Navy Office, as one of the principal officers, and have done now about half a year. After much trouble with workmen I am now almost settled; my family being, myself, my wife, Jane, Will, Hewer, and Wayneman, my girle's brother. Myself in constant good health, and in a most handsome and thriving condition. Blessed be Almighty God for it. I am now taking of my sister to come and live with me. As to things of State.—The King settled, and loved of all. The Duke of York matched to my Lord Chancellor's daughter, which do not please many. The Queen upon her return to France with the Princess Henrietta. The Princess of Orange lately dead, and we into new mourning for her. We have been lately frighted with a great plot, and many taken up on it, and the fright not quite over. The Parliament, which had done all this great good to the King, beginning to grow factious, the King did dissolve it December 29th last, and another likely to be chosen speedily. I take myself now to be worth £300 clear in money, and all my goods and all manner of debts paid, which are none at all.

JANUARY 2ND. I by water to my office, and there all the morning, and so home to dinner, where I found Pall (my sister) was come; but I do not let her sit down at table with me, which I do at first that she may not expect it hereafter from me.

3RD. To Will's, where Spicer and I eat our dinner of a roasted leg of pork which Will did give us, and after that to the Theatre, where was acted "Beggars' Bush," it being very well done; and here the first time that ever I saw women come upon the stage.

7TH. This morning, news was brought to me to my bedside, that there had been a great stir in the City this night by the Fanatiques, who had been up and killed six or seven men, but all are fled. My Lord Mayor and the whole City had been in arms, above 40,000.

8TH. My wife and I lay very long in bed to-day talking and pleasing one another in discourse.

10TH. So to Mrs. Hunt, where I found a Frenchman, a lodger of her's, at dinner, and just as I came in was kissing my wife, which I did not like, though there could not be any hurt in it.

11TH. Dined at home, discontented that my wife do not go neater now she has two maids.

12TH. With Colonel Slingsby and a friend of his, Major Waters (a deaf and most amorous melancholy gentleman, who is under a despayr in love, as the Colonel told me, which makes him bad company, though a most goodnatured man), by water to Redriffe, and so on foot to Deptford.

19TH. To the Comptroller's, and with him by coach to White Hall; in our way meeting Venner and Pritchard upon a sledge, who with two more Fifth Monarchy men were hanged to-day, and the two first drawn and quartered.

20TH (LORD'S DAY). So home to supper and then to bed, having eat no dinner to-day. It is strange what weather we have had all this winter; no cold at all; but the ways are dusty, and the flyes fly up and down, and the rosebushes are full of leaves, such a time of the year as was never known in this world before here. This day many more of the Fifth Monarchy men were hanged.

26TH. Within all the morning. About noon comes one that had formerly known me and I him, but I know not his name, to borrow £5 of me, but I had the wit to deny him.

28TH. At the office all the morning; dine at home, and after dinner to Fleet Street, with my sword to Mr. Brigden (lately made Captain of the Auxiliaries) to be refreshed, and with him to an ale-house, where I met Mr. Davenport, and after some talk of Cromwell, Ireton and Bradshaw's bodies being taken out of their graves to-day, I went to Mr. Crew's and thence to the Theatre, where I saw again "The Lost Lady," which do now please me better than before; and here I sitting behind in a dark place, a lady spit backward upon me by mistake, not seeing me, but after seeing her to be a very pretty lady, I was not troubled at it at all.

30TH (FAST DAY). The first time that this day hath been yet observed: and Mr. Mills made a most excellent sermon, upon "Lord forgive us our former iniquities;" speaking excellently of the justice of God in punishing men for the sins of their ancestors. Then to my Lady Batten's; where my wife and she are lately come back again from being abroad, and seeing of Cromwell, Ireton, and Bradshaw hanged and buried at Tyburn.

FEBRUARY 3RD (LORD'S DAY). This day I first begun to go forth in my coat and sword, as the manner now among gentlemen is. So to White Hall; where I staid to hear the trumpets and kettledrums, and then the other drums, which are much cried up, though I think it dull, vulgar musique.

5TH. Washing-day. My wife and I by water to Westminster. Into the Hall and there saw my Lord Treasurer (who was sworn to-day at the Exchequer, with a great company of Lords and persons of honour to attend him) go up to the Treasury Offices, and take possession thereof; and also saw the heads of Cromwell, Bradshaw, and Ireton, set up upon the further end of the Hall.

10TH (LORD's DAY). Took physique all day, and, God forgive me, did spend it in reading of some little French romances. At night my wife and I did please ourselves talking of our going into France, which I hope to effect this summer.

14TH (VALENTINE's DAY). Up early and to Sir W. Batten's, but would not go in till I asked whether they that opened the door was a man or a woman, and Mingo, who was there, answered a woman, which, with his tone, made me laugh; so up I went and took Mrs. Martha for my Valentine (which I do only for complacency), and Sir W. Batten he go in the same manner to my wife, and so we were very merry.

17TH (LORD's DAY). A most tedious, unreasonable, and impertinent sermon, by an Irish Doctor. His text was "Scatter them, O Lord, that delight in war." Sir Wm. Batten and I very much angry with the parson.

18TH. In the afternoon my wife and I and Mrs. Martha Batten, my Valentine, to the Exchange, and there upon a payre of embroydered and six payre of plain white gloves I laid out 40s. upon her. Then we went to a mercer's at the end of Lombard Street, and there she bought a suit of Lutestring for herself, and so home.

21ST. To Westminster by coach with Sir W. Pen, and in our way saw the city begin to build scaffolds against the Coronacion.

22ND. Then my wife to Sir W. Batten's, and there sat awhile; he having yesterday sent my wife half-a-dozen pairs of gloves, and a pair of silk stockings and garters, for her Valentine's gift. Then home and to bed.

23RD. This my birthday, 28 years. By water to Whitefriars to the Play house, and there saw "The Changeling," the first time it hath been acted these twenty years, and it takes exceedingly. Besides, I see the gallants do begin to be tyred with the vanity and pride of the theatre actors who are indeed grown very proud and rich. Then by link home, and there to my book awhile and to bed. This is now 28 years that I am born. And blessed be God, in a state of full content, and great hopes to be a happy man in all respects, both to myself and friends.

28TH. After dinner we went to Captain Bodilaw's, and there made sale of many old stores by the candle, and a good sport it was to see how from a small matter bid at first they would come to double and treble the price of things.

MARCH 3RD (LORD'S DAY). So to my Lord's, who comes in late and tells us how news is come to-day of Mazarin's being dead, which is very great news and of great consequence. I lay to-night with Mr. Shepley here, because of my Lord's going to-morrow.

4TH. My Lord went this morning on his journey to Hinchingbroke, Mr. Parker with him. Before his going he did give me some jewells to keep for him, viz., that that the King of Sweden did give him, with the King's own picture in it, most excellently done; and a brave George, all of diamonds, and this with the greatest expressions of love and confidence that I could imagine or hope for, which is a very great joy to me.

11TH. At night home and found my wife come home, and among other things she hath got her teeth new done by La Roche, and are indeed now pretty handsome, and I was much pleased with it. So to bed.

13TH. Early up in the morning to read "The Seaman's Grammar and Dictionary" I lately have got, which do please me exceeding well.

14TH. Then to my Lord's, and so with Mr. Creed to an ale-house, where he told me a long story of his amours at Portsmouth to one of Mrs. Boat's daughters, which was very pleasant. Dined with my Lord and Lady, and so with Mr. Creed to the Theatre, and there saw "King and no King," well acted. Thence with him to the Cock alehouse at Temple Bar, where he did ask my advice about his amours, and I did give him it, which was to enquire into the condition of his competitor, who is a son of Mr. Gauden's, and that I promise to do for him, and he to make [what] use he can of it to his advantage. Home and to bed.

18TH. To bed with my head and mind full of business, which do a little put me out of order, and I do find myself to become more and more thoughtful about getting of money than ever heretofore.

25TH (LADY DAY). So homewards and took up a boy that had a lanthorn, that was picking up of rags, and got him to light me home, and had great discourse with him how he could get sometimes three or four bushells of rags in a day, and got 3d. a bushell for them, and many other discourses, what and how many ways there are for poor children to get their livings honestly.

26TH. Up early to do business in my study. This is my great day that three years ago I was cut of the stone, and, blessed be God, I do yet find myself very free from pain again.

31ST (SUNDAY). At church, where a stranger preached like a fool.

APRIL 6TH. With Mr. Creed and Moore to the Leg in the Palace to dinner which I gave them, and after dinner I saw the girl of the house, being very pretty, go into a chamber, and I went in after her and kissed her.

7TH. I went to Sir W. Batten's and resolved of a journey to-morrow to Chatham, and so home and to bed.

11TH. At 2 o'clock, with very great mirth, we went to our lodging and to bed, and lay till 7, and then called up by Sir W. Batten, so I arose and we did some business, and then came Captn. Allen, and he and I withdrew and sang a song or two, and among others took pleasure in "Goe and bee hanged, that's good-bye." The young ladies come too, and so I did again please myself with Mrs. Rebecca, and about 9 o'clock, after we had breakfasted, we set forth for London, and indeed I was a little troubled to part with Mrs. Rebecca, for which God forgive me. Thus we went away through Rochester. We baited at Dartford, and thence to London, but of all the journeys that ever I made this was the merriest, and I was in a strange mood for mirth. Among other things, I got my Lady to let her maid, Mrs. Anne, to ride all the way on horseback, and she rides exceedingly well; and so I called her my clerk, that she went to wait upon me. I met two little schoolboys going with pitchers of ale to their school-master to break up against Easter, and I did drink of some of one of them and give him two pence. By and by we come to two lit-tle girls keeping cows, and I saw one of them very pretty, so I had a mind to make her ask my blessing, and telling her that I was her godfather, she asked me innocently whether I was not Ned Wooding, and I said that I was, so she kneeled down and very simply called, "Pray, godfather, pray to God to bless me," which made us very merry, and I gave her two-pence. In several places, I asked women whether they would sell me their chil-dren, but they denied me all, but said they would give me one to keep for them, if I would. Mrs. Anne and I rode under the man that hangs upon Shooter's Hill, and a filthy sight it was to see how his flesh is shrunk to his bones. So home and I found all well.

13TH. So to Whitehall again and met with my Lord above with the Duke; and after a little talk with him, I went to the

Banquet-house, and there saw the King heal, the first time that ever I saw him do it; which he did with great gravity, and it seemed to me to be an ugly office and a simple one.

20TH. So back to the Cockpit, and there, by the favour of one Mr. Bowman, he and I got in, and there saw the King and Duke of York and his Duchess (which is a plain woman, and like her mother, my Lady Chancellor). And so saw "The Humersome Lieutenant" acted before the King, but not very well done. But my pleasure was great to see the manner of it, and so many great beauties, but above all Mrs. Palmer, with whom the King do discover a great deal of familiarity.

22ND. Up early and made myself as fine as I could, and put on my velvet coat, the first day that I put it on, though made half a year ago. And being ready, Sir W. Batten, my Lady, and his two daughters and his son and wife, and Sir W. Pen and his son and I, went to Mr. Young's, the flag-maker, in Corne-hill; and there we had a good room to ourselves, with wine and good cake, and saw the show very well. In which it is impossible to relate the glory of this day, expressed in the clothes of them that rid, and their horses and horses-clothes, among others, my Lord Sandwich's. Embroidery and diamonds were ordinary among them. The Knights of the Bath was a brave sight of itself; and their Esquires, among which Mr. Armiger was an Esquire to one of the Knights. Remarquable were the two men that represent the two Dukes of Normandy and Aquitane. The Bishops come next after Barons, which is the higher place; which makes me think that the next Parliament they will be called to the House of Lords. My Lord Monk rode bare after the King, and led in his hand a spare horse, as being Master of the Horse. The King, in a most rich embroidered suit and cloak, looked most noble. Waldlow, the vintner, at the Devil, in Fleet-street, did lead a fine company of soldiers, all young comely men, in white doublets. There followed the Vice-Chamberlain, Sir G. Carteret, a company of men all like Turks; but I know not yet what they are for. The streets all gravelled, and the houses hung with carpets before them, made a brave show, and the ladies out of the windows, one of which over against us I took much notice of, and spoke of her, which made good sport among us. So glorious was the show with gold and silver, that we were not able to look at it, our eyes at last being so much overcome with it. Both the King and the Duke of York took notice of us, as he saw us at the window. The show being ended, Mr. Young did give us a dinner, at which we were very merry, and pleased above imagination at what we have seen.

Coronačon Day.

23RD. About 4 I rose and got to the Abbey, where I followed Sir J. Denham, the Surveyor, with some company that he was leading in. And with much ado, by the favour of Mr. Cooper, his man, did get up into a great scaffold across the North end of the Abbey, where with a great deal of patience I sat from past 4 till 11 before the King came in. And a great pleasure it was to see the Abbey raised in the middle, all covered with red, and a throne (that is a chair) and footstool on the top of it; and all the officers of all kinds, so much as the very fidlers, in red vests. At last comes in the Dean and Prebends of Westminster, with the Bishops (many of them in cloth of gold copes), and after them the Nobility, all in their Parliament robes, which was a most magnificent sight. Then the Duke, and the King with a scepter (carried by my Lord Sandwich) and sword and mond before him, and the crown too. The King in his robes, bare-headed, which was very fine. And after all had placed themselves, there was a sermon and the service; and then in the Quire at the high altar, the King passed through all the ceremonies of the Coronačon, which to my great grief I and most in the Abbey could not see. The crown being put upon his head, a great shout begun, and he came forth to the throne, and there passed more ceremonies: as taking the oath, and having things read to him by the Bishop; and his lords (who put on their caps as soon as the King put on his crown) and bishops come, and kneeled before him. And three times the King at Arms went to the three open places on the scaffold, and proclaimed, that if any one could show any reason why Charles Stewart should not be King of England, that now he should come and speak. And a Generall Pardon also was read by the Lord Chancellor, and meddalls flung up and down by my Lord Cornwallis, of silver, but I could not come by any. And the King came in with his crown on, and his sceptre in his hand, under a canopy borne up by six silver staves, carried by Barons of the Cinque Ports, and little bells at every end. After a long time, he got up to the farther end, and all set themselves down at their several tables; and that was also a brave sight: and the King's first course carried up by the Knights of the Bath. And many fine ceremonies there was of the Heralds leading up people before him, and bowing; and my Lord of Albemarle's going to the kitchen and eat a bit of the first dish that was to go to the King's table. But, above all, was these three Lords, Northumberland, and Suffolk, and the Duke of Ormond, coming before the courses on horseback, and staying so all dinner-time, and at last to bring up [Dymock] the King's Champion, all in armour on horseback, with his spear and targett carried before him. And a Herald proclaims "That if any dare deny Charles Stewart to be lawful King of England, here was a Champion that would fight with him;" and with these words, the Champion flings down his gauntlet, and all this he do three times in his going up towards the King's table. At last when he is come, the King drinks to him, and then sends him the cup which is of gold, and he drinks it off, and then rides back again with the cup in his hand. I went from table to table to see the Bishops and all others at their dinner, and was infinitely pleased with it. At Mr. Bowyer's; a great deal of company, some I knew, others I did not. Here we staid upon the leads and below till it was late, expecting to see the fire-works, but they were not performed to-night: only the City had a light like a glory round about it with bonfires. And after a little stay more I took my wife and Mrs. Frankleyn (who I proffered the civility of lying with my wife at Mrs. Hunt's to-night) to Axe-yard, in which at the further end there were three great bonfires, and a great many great gallants, men and women; and they laid hold of us, and would have us drink the King's health upon our knees, kneeling upon a faggot, which we all did, they drinking to us one after another. Which we thought a strange frolique; but these gallants continued thus a great while, and I wondered to see how the ladies did tipple. Thus did the day end with joy everywhere. Now, after all this, I can say that, besides the pleasure of the sight of these glorious things, I may now shut my eyes against any other objects, nor for the future trouble myself to see things of state and show, as being sure never to see the like again in this world.

24TH. Waked in the morning with my head in a sad taking through the last night's drink, which I am very sorry for; so rose and went out with Mr. Creed to drink our morning draft, which he did give me in chocolate to settle my stomach.

MAY 11TH. I went to Graye's Inne, and there to a barber's where I was trimmed, and had my haire cut, in which I am lately become a little curious, finding that the length of it do become me very much.

JUNE 4TH. To my Lord's Crew's to dinner with him, and had very good discourse about having of young noblemen and gentlemen to think of going to sea, as being as honourable service as the land war. And among other things he told us how, in Queen Elizabeth's time, one young nobleman would wait with a trencher at the back of another till he came to age himself. And witnessed in my young Lord of Kent, that then was, who waited upon my Lord Bedford at table, when a letter came to my Lord Bedford that the Earldom of Kent was fallen to his servant, the young Lord; and so he rose from table, and made him sit down in his place, and took a lower for himself, for so he was by place to sit.

23RD (LORD'S DAY). After dinner to church all of us and had a very good sermon of a stranger, and so I and the young company to walk first to Graye's Inn Walks, where great store of gallants, but above all the ladies that I there saw, or ever did see, Mrs. Frances Butler (Monsieur L'Impertinent's sister) is the greatest beauty.

28TH. At home all the morning practising to sing, which is now my great trade, and at noon to my Lady and dined with her.

JULY 26TH. Back to the office all the afternoon, and that done home for all night. Having the beginning of this week made a vow to myself to drink no wine this week (finding it too unfit for me to look after business), and this day breaking of it against my will, I am much troubled for it, but I hope God will forgive me.

AUGUST 10TH. This morning came the maid that my wife hath lately hired for a chamber maid. She is very ugly, so that I cannot care for her, but otherwise she seems very good.

19TH. I am forced to go to Worcester House, where several Lords are met in Council this afternoon. And while I am waiting there, in comes the King in a plain common riding-suit and velvet cap, in which he seemed a very ordinary man to one that had not known him.

24TH. To the Opera, and there saw "Hamlet, Prince of Denmark," done with scenes very well, but above all, Betterton did the prince's part beyond imagination.

25TH (LORD'S DAY). By and by comes in my father (he intends to go into the country to-morrow), and he and I among other discourse at last called Pall up to us, and there in great anger told her before my father that I would keep her no longer, and my father he said he would have nothing to do with her. At last, after we had brought down her high spirit, I got my father to yield that she should go into the country with my mother and him, and stay there awhile to see how she will demean herself.

SEPTEMBER 7TH. At the office all the morning. So I having appointed the young ladies at the Wardrobe to go with them to a play to-day, my wife and I took them to the Theatre, where we seated ourselves close by the King, and Duke of York, and Madame Palmer, which was great content; and, indeed, I can never enough admire her beauty. And here was "Bartholomew Fayre," with the puppet-show, acted to-day, which had not been these forty years (it being so satyricall against Puritanism, they durst not till now, which is strange they should already dare to do it, and the King do countenance it).

15TH (LORD'S DAY). To my aunt Kite's in the morning to help my uncle Fenner to put things in order against anon for the buriall, and at noon home again; and after dinner to church, my wife and I, and after sermon with my wife to the buriall of my aunt Kite, where besides us and my uncle Fenner's family, there was none of any quality but poor rascally people. So we went to church with the corps, and there had service read at the grave, and back again with Pegg Kite, who will be, I doubt, a troublesome carrion to us executors; but if she will not be ruled, I shall fling up my executorship.

30TH. This morning up by moon-shine, at 5 o'clock, to White Hall, to meet Mr. Moore at the Privy Seal, but he not being come as appointed, I went into King Street to the Red Lyon to drink my morning draft, and there I heard of a fray between the two Embassadors of Spain and France; and that, this day, being the day of the entrance of an Embassador from Sweden, they intended to fight for the precedence. Then to the Wardrobe, and dined there, and then abroad and in Cheapside hear that the Spanish hath got the best of it, and killed three of the French coach-horses and several men, and is gone through the City next to our King's coach; at which, it is strange to see how all the City did rejoice. And indeed we do naturally all love the Spanish, and hate the French. But I, as I am in all things curious, presently got to the water-side, and there took oars to Westminster Palace, thinking to have seen them come in thither with all the coaches, but they being come and returned, I ran after them with my boy after me through all the dirt and the streets full of people; till at last, at the Mewes, I saw the Spanish coach go, with fifty drawn swords at least to guard it, and our soldiers shouting for joy. And so I followed the coach, and then met it at York House, where the embassador lies; and there it went in with great state. So then I went to the French house, where I observe still, that there is no men in the world of a more insolent spirit where they do well, nor before they begin a matter, and more abject if they do miscarry, than these people are; for they all look like dead men, and not a word among them, but shake their heads.

OCTOBER 1ST. This morning my wife and I lay long in bed, and among other things fell into talk of musique, and desired that I would let her learn to sing, which I did consider, and promised her she should. So before I rose, word was brought me that my singing master, Mr. Goodgroome, was come to teach me; and so she rose and this morning began to learn also.

28TH. At the office all the morning, and dined at home, and so to Paul's Churchyard to Hunt's, and there found my Theorbo done, which pleases me very well, and costs me 26s. to the altering. But now he tells me it is as good a lute as any is in England, and is worth well £10. Hither I sent for Captain Ferrers to me, who comes with a friend of his, and they and I to the Theatre, and there saw "Argalus and Parthenia," where a woman acted Parthenita, and came afterwards on the stage in men's clothes, and had the best legs that ever I saw, and I was very well pleased with it. Thence to the Ringo alehouse.

NOVEMBER 6TH. Going forth this morning I met Mr. Davenport and a friend of his, one Mr. Furbisher, to drink their morning draft with me, and I did give it them in good wine, and anchovies, and pickled oysters, and took them to the Sun in Fish Street, there did give them a barrel of good ones, and a great deal of wine.

9TH. After dinner I to the Wardrobe, and there staid talking with my Lady all the afternoon till late at night. Among other things my Lady did mightily urge me to lay out money upon my wife, which I perceived was a little more earnest than ordinary, and so I seemed to be pleased with it, and do resolve to bestow a lace upon her, and what with this and other talk, we were exceeding merry. So home at night.

10TH (LORD's DAY). At our own church in the morning, where Mr. Mills preached. Thence alone to the Wardrobe to dinner with my Lady, where my Lady continues upon yesterday's discourse still for me to lay out money upon my wife, which I think it is best for me to do for her honour and my own.

13TH. By appointment, we all went this morning to wait upon the Duke of York, which we did in his chamber, as he was dressing himself in his riding suit to go this day by sea to the Downs. After we had given him our letter relating the bad condition of the Navy for want of money, he referred it to his coming back and so parted, and I to Whitehall and to see la belle Pierce, and so on foot to my Lord Crew's. From thence to the Theatre, and there saw "Father's own Son" again, and so it raining very hard I went home by coach, with my mind very heavy for this my expensefull life, which will undo me, I fear, after all my hopes, if I do not take up, for now I am coming to lay out a great deal of money in clothes for my wife, I must forbear other expenses. To bed, and this night began to lie in the little green chamber, where the maids lie, but we could not a great while get Nell to lie there, because I lie there and my wife, but at last, when she saw she must lie there or sit up, she, with much ado, came to bed.

17TH (LORD's DAY). So to church again, and heard a simple fellow upon the praise of Church musique, and exclaiming against men's wearing their hats on in the church, but I slept part of the sermon, till latter prayer and blessing and all was done without waking which I never did in my life.

20TH. To Westminster Hall by water in the morning, where I saw the King going in his barge to the Parliament House; this being the first day of their meeting again. And the Bishops, I hear, do take their places in the Lords' House this day.

29TH. After dinner to White Hall to the Duke, who met us in his closet; and there he did discourse to us the business of Holmes, and did desire of us to know what hath been the common practice about making of forrayne ships to strike sail to us, which they did all do as much as they could; but I could say nothing to it, which I was sorry for. So indeed I was forced to study a lie, and so after we were gone from the Duke, I told Mr. Coventry that I had heard Mr. Selden often say, that he could prove that in Henry the 7th's time, he did give commission to his captains to make the King of Denmark's ships to strike to him in the Baltique. So home, calling at Paul's Churchyard for a *"Mare Clausum,"* having it in my mind to write a little matter, what I can gather, about the business of striking sayle, and present it to the Duke, which I now think will be a good way to make myself known. So home and to bed.

DECEMBER 1ST (LORD'S DAY). There hath lately been great clapping up of some old statesmen, such as Ireton, Moyer, and others, and they say, upon a great plot, but I believe no such thing; but it is but justice that they should be served as they served the poor Cavaliers; and I believe it will oftentimes be so as long as I live, whether there be cause or no.

3RD. To the Paynter's and sat and had more of my picture done; but it do not please me, for I fear it will not be like me. To my Lady, where my Lady Wright was at dinner with her, and all our talk about the great happiness that my Lady Wright says there is in being in the fashion and in variety of fashions, in scorn of others that are not so, as citizens' wives and country gentlewomen, which though it did displease me enough, yet I said nothing to it.

1662

JANUARY 1ST. Waking this morning out of my sleep on a sudden, I did with my elbow hit my wife a great blow over her face and nose, which waked her with pain, at which I was sorry, and to sleep again.

16TH. Towards Cheapside and in Paul's Churchyard saw the funeral of my Lord Cornwallis, late Steward of the King's House, a bold profane talking man, go by, and thence I to the Paynter's, and there paid him £6 for the two pictures, and 36s. for the two frames.

26TH (LORD'S DAY). To church in the morning. But thanks be to God, since my leaving drinking of wine, I do find myself much better and do mind my business better, and do spend less money, and less time lost in idle company.

27TH. This morning, going to take water upon Towerhill, we met with three sleddes standing there to carry my Lord Monson and Sir H. Mildmay and another to the gallows and back again, with ropes about their necks; which is to be repeated every year, this being the day of their sentencing the King.

FEBRUARY 4TH. To Westminster Hall, where it was full term. Here all the morning, and at noon to my Lord Crew's, where one Mr. Templer (an ingenious man and a person of honour he seems to be) dined; and, discoursing of the nature of serpents, he told us some that in the waste places of Lancashire do grow to a great bigness, and that do feed upon larks, which they take thus:—They observe when the lark is soared to the highest, and do crawl till they come to be just underneath them; and there they place themselves with their mouths uppermost, and there, as is conceived, they do eject poyson up to the bird; for the bird do suddenly come down again in its course of a circle, and falls directly into the mouth of the serpent; which is very strange. He is a great traveller; and, speaking of the tarantula, he says that all the harvest long (about which times they are most busy) there are fidlers go up and down the fields every where, in expectation of being hired by those that are stung.

10TH. Musique practice a good while, then to Paul's Churchyard, and here I met with Dr. Fuller's "England's Worthys," the first time that I ever saw it; and so I sat down reading in it, till it was two o'clock before I thought of the time going, and so I rose and went home to dinner, being much troubled that (though he had some discourse with me about my family and arms) he says nothing at all, nor mentions us either in Cambridgeshire or Norfolk. But I believe, indeed, our family were never considerable.

23RD (LORD'S DAY). This day by God's mercy I am 29 years of age, and in very good health, and like to live and get an estate and if I have a heart to be contented, I think I may reckon myself as happy a man as any is in the world, for which God be praised. So to prayers and to bed.

24TH. Long with Mr. Berkenshaw in the morning at my musique practice, finishing my song of "Gaze not on Swans," in two parts, which pleases me well, and I did give him £5 for this month or five weeks that he hath taught me, which is a great deal of money and troubled me to part with it. So home and to supper, and then called Will up, and chid him before my wife for refusing to go to church with the maids yesterday, and telling his mistress that he would not be made a slave of, which vexes me. So to bed.

28TH. The boy failing to call us up as I commanded, I was angry, and resolved to whip him for that and many other faults, to-day. Home, and to be as good my word, I bade Will get me a rod, and he and I called the boy up to one of the upper rooms of the Comptroller's house towards the garden, and there I reckoned all his faults, and whipped him soundly, but the rods were so small that I fear they did not much hurt to him, but only to my arm, which I am already, within a quarter of an hour, not able to stir almost. After supper to bed.

MARCH 1ST. Thence my wife and I by coach, first to see my little picture that is a drawing, and thence to the Opera, and there saw "Romeo and Juliet," the first time it was ever acted; but it is a play of itself the worst that ever I heard in my life, and the worst acted that ever I saw these people do, and I am resolved to go no more to see the first time of acting, for they were all of them out more or less.

2ND (LORD'S DAY). With my mind much eased talking long in bed with my wife about our frugall life for the time to come, proposing to her what I could and would do if I were worth £2,000, that is, be a knight, and keep my coach, which pleased her, and so I do hope we shall hereafter live to save something, for I am resolved to keep myself by rules from expenses.

5TH. In the morning to the Painter's about my little picture. Thence to Tom's about business, and so to the pewterer's, to buy a poore's-box to put my forfeit in, upon breach of my late vows. So to the Wardrobe and dined, and thence home and to my office, and there sat looking over my papers of my voyage, when we fetched over the King, and tore so many of these that were worth nothing, as filled my closet as high as my knees. I staid doing this till 10 at night, and so home and to bed.

24TH. By and by comes La Belle Pierce to see my wife, and to bring her a pair of peruques of hair, as the fashion now is for ladies to wear; which are pretty, and are of my wife's own hair, or else I should not endure them.

26TH. Up early. This being, by God's great blessing, the fourth solemn day of my cutting for the stone this day four years, and am by God's mercy in very good health, and like to do well, the Lord's name be praised for it. At noon come my good guests, Madame Turner, The., and Cozen Norton, and a gentleman, one Mr. Lewin of the King's Life Guard; by the same token he told us of one of his fellows killed this morning in a duel. I had a pretty dinner for them, viz., a brace of stewed carps, six roasted chickens, and a jowl of salmon, hot, for the first course a tanzy and two neats' tongues, and cheese the second and were very merry all the afternoon, talking and singing and piping upon the flageolette. In the evening they went with great pleasure away, and I with great content and my wife walked half an hour in the garden, and so home to supper and to bed.

27TH. Early Sir G. Carteret, both Sir Williams and I by coach to Deptford, it being very windy and rainy weather, taking a codd and some prawnes in Fish Street with us. We settled to pay the Guernsey, a small ship, but come to a great deal of money, it having been unpaid ever since before the King came in, by which means not only the King pays wages while the ship has lain still, but the poor men have most of them been forced to borrow all the money due for their wages before they receive it, and that at a dear rate, God knows, so that many of them had very little to receive at the table, which grieved me to see it. To dinner, very merry.

APRIL 6TH (LORD'S DAY). By water to White Hall. Thence to the Chappell, and there, though crowded, heard a very honest sermon before the King by a Canon of Christ Church, upon these words, "Having a form of goodliness, but denying," &c. Among other things, did much insist upon the sin of adultery: which methought might touch the King, and the more because he forced it into his sermon, methinks, besides his text. So up and saw the King at dinner.

11TH. Up early to my lute and a song, then about six o'clock with Sir W. Pen by water to Deptford; and among the ships now going to Portugall with men and horse, to see them dispatched. So to Greenwich; and had a fine pleasant walk to Woolwich, having in our company Captn. Minnes, with whom I was much pleased to hear him talk in fine language, but pretty well for all that. Among other things, he and the other Captains that were with us tell me that negroes drowned look white and lose their blackness, which I never heard before.

MAY 4TH (LORD'S DAY). Lay long talking with my wife, then Mr. Holliard came to me and let me blood, about sixteen ounces, I being exceedingly full of blood and very good. I begun to be sick; but lying on my back I was presently well again, and did give him 5s. for his pains.

1OTH. At noon to the Wardrobe; there dined. My Lady told me how my Lady Castlemaine do speak of going to lie in at Hampton Court; which she and all our ladies are much troubled at, because of the King's being forced to show her countenance in the sight of the Queen when she comes.

14TH. All the morning at Westminster and elsewhere about business, and dined at the Wardrobe; and after dinner, sat talking an hour or two alone with my Lady. She is afeared that my Lady Castlemaine will keep still with the King, and I am afeared she will not, for I love her well.

15TH. At night, all the bells of the town rung, and bonfires made for the joy of the Queen's arrival, who came and landed at Portsmouth last night. But I do not see much thorough joy, but only an indifferent one, in the hearts of people, who are much discontented at the pride and luxury of the Court, and running in debt.

18TH (WHITSUNDAY). By water to White Hall, and there to chappell in my pew belonging to me as Clerk of the Privy Seal; and there I heard a most excellent sermon of Dr. Hackett, Bishop of Lichfield and Coventry, upon these words: "He that drinketh this water shall never thirst." We had an excellent anthem, sung by Captain Cooke and another, and brave musique. And then the King came down and offered, and took the sacrament upon his knees; a sight very well worth seeing. At home I found my wife discontented at my being abroad, but I pleased her. She was in her new suit of black sarcenet and yellow petticoat very pretty. So to bed.

19TH. Long in bed, sometimes scolding with my wife, and then pleased again, and at last up, and put on my riding cloth suit, and a camelott coat new, which pleases me well enough.

20TH. My wife and I by coach to the Opera, and there saw the 2nd part of "The Siege of Rhodes," but it is not so well done as when Roxalana was there, who, it is said, is now owned by my Lord of Oxford. Thence to Tower-wharf, and there took boat and we all walked to Halfeway House, and there eat and drank, and were pleasant, and so finally home again in the evening, and so good night, this being a very pleasant life that we now lead, and have long done, the Lord be blessed, and make us thankful. But, though I am much against too much spending, yet I do think it best to enjoy some degree of pleasure now that we have health, money, and opportunity, rather than to leave pleasures to old age or poverty, when we cannot have them so properly.

21ST. My wife and I by water to Westminster, and after she had seen her father (of whom lately I have heard nothing at all what he does or her mother), she comes to me to my Lord's lodgings, where she and I staid walking in White Hall garden.

And in the Privy-garden saw the finest smocks and linnen petticoats of my Lady Castlemaine's, laced with rich lace at the
bottom, that ever I saw; and did me good to look upon them. So
to Wilkinson's, she and I and Sarah to dinner, where I had a
good quarter of lamb and a salat. Here Sarah told me how the
King dined at my Lady Castlemaine's, and supped, every day
and night the last week; and that the night that the bonfires
were made for joy of the Queen's arrivall, the King was there;
but there was no fire at her door, though at all the rest of the
doors almost in the street; which was much observed: and that
the King and she did send for a pair of scales and weighed one
another; and she, being with child, was said to be heaviest. But
she is now a most disconsolate creature, and comes not out of
doors, since the King's going. But we went to the Theatre to
"The French Dancing Master," and there with much pleasure
gazed upon her (Lady Castlemaine); but it troubles us to see
her look dejectedly and slighted by people already. The play
pleases us very well; but Lacy's part, the Dancing Master, the
best in the world.

23RD. News was brought me that my Lord Sandwich is
come and gone up to my Lady, which put me into great sus-
pense of joy, so I went up waiting my Lord's coming out of my
Lady's chamber, which by and by he did, and looks very well,
and my soul is glad to see him. He very merry, and hath left the
King and Queen at Portsmouth, and is come up to stay here till
next Wednesday, and then to meet the King and Queen at
Hampton Court. So to dinner, Mr. Browne, Clerk of the House
of Lords, and his wife and brother there also and my Lord
mighty merry; among other things, saying that the Queen is a
very agreeable lady, and paints still. My wife and I to the puppet play in Covent Garden, which I saw the other day, and indeed it is very pleasant. Here among the fidlers I first saw a
dulcimere played on with sticks knocking of the strings, and is
very pretty.

25TH (LORD'S DAY). To trimming myself, which I have this
week done every morning, with a pumice stone, which I learnt

of Mr. Marsh, when I was last at Portsmouth and I find it very easy, speedy, and cleanly, and shall continue the practice of it. Then to the Wardrobe, where I found my Lord takes physic, so I did not see him, but with Capn. Ferrers in Mr. George Montagu's coach to Charing Cross; and there at the Triumph tavern he showed me some Portugall ladys, which are come to town before the Queen. They are not handsome, and their farthingales a strange dress. Many ladies and persons of quality come to see them. I find nothing in them that is pleasing; and I see they have learnt to kiss and look freely up and down already, and I do believe will soon forget the recluse practice of their own country. They complain much for lack of good water to drink.

26TH. Up by four o'clock in the morning, and fell to the preparing of some accounts for my Lord of Sandwich. Thence home, and to the Trinity House; where the Brethren about three o'clock came hither, and so to dinner. I seated myself close by Mr. Prin, who, in discourse with me, fell upon what records he hath of the lust and wicked lives of the nuns heretofore in England, and showed me out of his pocket one wherein thirty nuns for their lust were ejected of their house, being not fit to live there, and by the Pope's command to be put, however, into other nunnerys.

31ST. So home, and had Sarah to comb my head clean, which I found so foul with powdering and other troubles, that I am resolved to try how I can keep my head dry without powder; and I did also in a suddaine fit cut off all my beard, which I had been a great while bringing up, only that I may with my pumice-stone do my whole face, as I now do my chin, and to save time, which I find a very easy way and gentile. So she also washed my feet in a bath of herbs, and so to bed. I have by a late oath obliged myself from wine and plays, of which I find good effect.

JUNE 8TH (LORD'S DAY). Home, and observe my man Will to walk with his cloak flung over his shoulder, like a Ruffian, which, whether it was that he might not be seen to walk along with the footboy, I know not, but I was vexed at it; and coming home, and after prayers, I did ask him where he learned that immodest garb, and he answered me that it was not immodest, or some such slight answer, at which I did give him two boxes on the ears, which I never did before, and so was after a little troubled at it.

9TH. Dined at home, and after dinner to Greatorex's, and with him and another stranger to the Tavern, but I drank no wine.

12TH. To dinner, by Mr. Gauden's invitation, to the Dolphin, where a good dinner; but what is to myself a great wonder, that with ease I past the whole dinner without drinking a drop of wine.

13TH. Up by 4 o'clock in the morning, and read Cicero's Second Oration against Catiline, which pleased me exceedingly; and more I discern therein than ever I thought was to be found in him; but I perceive it was my ignorance, and that he is as good a writer as ever I read in my life.

14TH. Up by four o'clock in the morning and up on business at my office. Then we sat down to business, and about 11 o'clock, having a room got ready for us, we all went out to the Tower-hill; and there, over against the scaffold, made on purpose this day, saw Sir Henry Vane brought. A very great press of people. He made a long speech, many times interrupted by the Sheriff and others there; and they would have taken his paper out of his hand but he would not let it go. But they caused all the books of those that writ after him to be given the Sheriff; and the trumpets were brought under the scaffold that he might not be heard. Then he prayed, and so fitted himself, and received the blow; but the scaffold was so crowded that we could not see it done. He had a blister, or issue, upon his neck, which he desired them not hurt: he changed not his colour or speech to the last, but died justifying himself and the cause he had stood for; and spoke very confidently of his being presently at the right hand of Christ; and in all things appeared the most resolved man that ever died in that manner, and showed more heat than cowardize, but yet with all humility and gravity. One asked him why he did not pray for the King. He answered, "Nay," says he, "you shall see I can pray for the King: I pray God bless him!" The King had given his body to his friends; and, therefore, he told them that he hoped they would be civil to his body when dead; and desired they would let him die like a gentleman and a Christian, and not crowded and pressed as he was.

18TH. Up early; and after reading a little in Cicero, I made me ready and to my office, where all the morning very busy. That done I walked to Lilly's, the painter's, where I saw among other rare things, the Duchess of York, her whole body, sitting in state in a chair, in white sattin, and another of the King, that is not finished; most rare things. So home, and after some merry discourse in the kitchen with my wife and maids as I now-a-days often do, I being well pleased with both my maids, to bed.

19TH. Up at five o'clock, and while my man Will was getting himself ready to come up to me I took and played upon my lute a little. So home and at the office preparing papers and things, and indeed my head has not been so full of business a great while, and with so much pleasure, for I begin to see the pleasure it gives. God give me health. So to bed.

21ST. Hearing from my wife and the maids complaints made of the boy, I called him up, and with my whip did whip him till I was not able to stir, and yet I could not make him confess any of the lies that they tax him with. At last, not willing to let him go away a conqueror, I took him in task again, and pulled off his frock to his shirt, and whipped him till he did confess that he did drink the whey, which he had denied, and pulled a pink, and above all did lay the candlestick upon the ground in his chamber, which he had denied this quarter of a year. I confess it is one of the greatest wonders that ever I met with that such a little boy as he could possibly be able to suffer half so much as he did to maintain a lie. I think I must be forced to put him away. So to bed, with my arm very weary.

22ND (LORD'S DAY). This day I first put on my slasht doublet, which I like very well.

23RD. Meeting with Frank Moore, my Lord Lambeth's man formerly, we, and two or three friends of his did go to a tavern, and there they drank, but I nothing but small beer. In the next room one was playing very finely of the dulcimer, which well played I like well.

28TH. This day a genteel woman came to me, claiming kindred of me, as she had once done before, and borrowed 10s. of me, promising to repay it at night, but I hear nothing of her. I shall trust her no more. Great talk there is of a fear of a war with the Dutch; and we have order to pitch upon twenty ships to be forthwith set out; but I hope it is but a scarecrow to the world, to let them see that we can be ready for them; though, God knows! the King is not able to set out five ships at this present without great difficulty, we neither having money, credit, nor stores. My mind is now in a wonderful condition of quiet and content, more than ever in all my life, since my minding the business of my office, which I have done most constantly; and I find it to be the very effect of my late oaths against wine and plays, which, if God please, I will keep constant in, for now my business is a delight to me, and brings me great credit, and my purse encreases too.

30TH. Up betimes, and to my office, where I found Griffin's girl making it clean, but, God forgive me! what a mind I had to her, but did not meddle with her. She being gone, I fell upon boring holes for me to see from my closet into the great office, without going forth, wherein I please myself much.

OBSERVATIONS

This I take to be as bad a juncture as ever I observed. The King and his new Queen minding their pleasures at Hampton Court. All people discontented; some that the King do not gratify them enough; and the others, Fanatiques of all sorts, that the

King do take away their liberty of conscience; and the height of the Bishops, who I fear will ruin all again. They do much cry up the manner of Sir H. Vane's death, and he deserves it. They clamour against the chimney-money, and say they will not pay it without force.

JULY 4TH. By and by comes Mr. Cooper, mate of the Royall Charles, of whom I intend to learn mathematiques, and do begin with him to-day, he being a very able man, and no great matter, I suppose, will content him. After an hour's being with him at arithmetique (my first attempt being to learn the multiplicacion-table); then we parted till to-morrow.

9TH. Up by four o'clock, and at my multiplicacion-table hard, which is all the trouble I meet withal in my arithmetique.

11TH. Up by four o'clock, and hard at my multiplicacion-table, which I am now almost master of.

16TH. This day I was told that my Lady Castlemaine (being quite fallen out with her husband) did yesterday go away from him, with all her plate, jewels, and other best things; and is gone to Richmond to a brother of her's; which, I am apt to think, was a design to get out of town, that the King might come at her the better. But strange it is how for her beauty I am willing to construe all this to the best and to pity her wherein it is to her hurt, though I know well enough she is a whore.

19TH. In the afternoon I went upon the river to look after some tarr I am sending down and some coles, and so home again; it raining hard upon the water, I put ashore and sheltered myself, while the King came by in his barge, going down towards the Downs to meet the Queen: the Duke being gone yesterday. But methought it lessened my esteem of a king, that he should not be able to command the rain.

30TH. Thence with Captain Fletcher, of the Gage, in his ship's boat with 8 oars (but every ordinary oars outrowed us) to

Woolwich, expecting to find Sir W. Batten there upon his survey, but he is not come, and so we got a dish of steaks at the White Hart, while his clarkes and others were feasting of it in the best room of the house, and after dinner playing at shuffleboard, and when at last they heard I was there, they went about their survey. But God help the King! what surveys shall be taken after this manner! I after dinner about my business to the Rope-yard, and there staid till night, repeating several trialls of the strength, wayte, waste, and other things of hemp, by which I have furnished myself enough to finish my intended business of stating the goodness of all sorts of hemp.

August 1st. So at the office all the afternoon till evening to my chamber, where, God forgive me, I was sorry to hear that Sir W. Pen's maid Betty was gone away yesterday, for I was in hopes to have had a bout with her before she had gone, she being very pretty. I had also a mind to my own wench, but I dare not for fear she should prove honest and refuse and then tell my wife.

6th. Thence home, and at my office all the morning, and dined at home, and can hardly keep myself from having a mind to my wench, but I hope I shall not fall to such a shame to myself.

8th. Up by four o'clock in the morning, and at five by water to Woolwich, there to see the manner of tarring, and all the morning looking to see the several proceedings in making of cordage, and other things relative to that sort of works, much to my satisfaction. To Deptford, and there surprised the Yard, and called them to a muster, and discovered many abuses, which we shall be able to understand hereafter and amend.

13th. Up early, and to my office, where people come to me about business, and by and by we met on purpose to enquire into the business of the flagmakers, where I am the person that do chiefly manage the business against them on the King's part; and I do find it the greatest cheat that I have yet found.

15TH. At noon to the Change, and there hear of some Quakers that are seized on, that would have blown up the prison in Southwark where they are put.

17TH (LORD'S DAY). Walked to St. Dunstan's, where, it not being seven o'clock yet, the doors were not open; and so I went and walked an hour in the Temple-garden, reading my vows, which it is a great content to me to see how I am a changed man in all respects for the better, since I took them, which the God of Heaven continue to me, and make me thankful for. Besides the sermon, I was very well pleased with the sight of a fine lady that I have often seen walk in Graye's Inn Walks, and it was my chance to meet her again at the door going out, and very pretty and sprightly she is, and I believe the same that my wife and I some years since did meet at Temple Bar gate and have sometimes spoke of.

18TH. Up very early, and up upon my house to see how work goes on, which do please me very well. So about seven o'clock took horse and rode to Bowe, and three staid at the King's Head, and eat a breakfast of eggs till Mr. Deane of Woolwich came to me, and he and I rid into Waltham Forest, and there we saw many trees of the King's a-hewing; and he showed me the whole mystery of off square, wherein the King is abused in the timber that he buys, which I shall with much pleasure be able to correct. After we had been a good while in the wood, we rode to Illford, and there, while dinner was getting ready, he and I practised measuring of the tables and other things till I did understand measuring of timber and board very well.

2OTH. Up early, and to my office, and thence to my Lord Sandwich. By and by comes in Mr. Coventry to us, whom my Lord tells that he is also put into the commission, and that I am there, of which he said he was glad; and did tell my Lord that I was indeed the life of this office, and much more to my commendation beyond measure. So that on all hands, by God's blessing, I find myself a very rising man. We had a venison pasty, and other good plain and handsome dishes; the mistress of the house a pretty, well-carriaged woman, and a fine hand she hath; and her maid a pretty brown lass. But I do find my nature ready to run back to my old course of drinking wine and staying from my business, and yet, thank God, I was not fully contented with it, but did stay at little ease, and after dinner hastened home by water, and so to my office till late at night.

23RD. And so all along Thames-street, but could not get a boat: I offered eight shillings for a boat to attend me this afternoon, and they would not, it being the day of the Queen's coming to town from Hampton Court. Anon come the King and Queen in a barge under a canopy with 10,000 barges and boats, I think, for we could see no water for them, nor discern the King nor Queen. And so they landed at White Hall Bridge, and the great guns on the other side went off. But that which pleased me best was, that my Lady Castlemaine stood over against us upon a piece of White Hall, where I glutted myself with looking on her. One thing more; there happened a scaffold below to fall, and we feared some hurt, but there was none, but she of all the great ladies only run down among the common rabble to see what hurt was done, and did take care of a child that received some little hurt, which methought was so noble. Anon there came one there booted and spurred that she talked long with. And by and by, she being in her hair, she put on his hat, which was but an ordinary one, to keep the wind off. But methinks it became her mightily, as every thing else do. The show being over, I went away, not weary with looking on her.

27TH. This afternoon Mrs. Hunt came to see me, and I did give her a Muske Millon. To-day my hogshead of sherry I have sold to Sir W. Batten, and am glad of my money instead of wine.

31ST (LORD'S DAY). So to my office, and there made my monthly [accounts], and find myself worth in money about £686 19s. 2 ½d., for which God be praised; and indeed greatly I hope to thank Almighty God, who do most manifestly bless me in my endeavours to do the duties of my office, I now saving money, and my expenses being little.

SEPTEMBER 1ST. And so Mr. Paget being there, Will Howe and I and he played over some things of Locke's that we used to play at sea, that pleased us three well, it being the first music I have heard a great while, so much has my business of late taken me off from all my former delights.

3RD. Up betimes, but now the days begin to shorten, and so whereas I used to rise by four o'clock it is not broad daylight now till after five o'clock, so that it is after five before I do rise.

5TH. To Mr. Bland's, the merchant, by invitation, I alone of all our company of this office; where I found all the officers of the Customs, very grave fine gentlemen, and I am very glad to know them. And among other pretty discourse, some was of Sir Jerom Bowes, Embassador from Queene Elizabeth to the Emperor of Russia; who because some of the noblemen there would go up the stairs to the Emperor before him, he would not go up till the Emperor had ordered those two men to be dragged down-stairs, with their heads knocking upon every stair till they were killed. And when he was come, up they demanded his sword of him before he entered the room. He told them, if they would have his sword, they should have his boots too. And so caused his boots to be pulled off, and his night-gown and night-cap and slippers to be sent for; and made the Emperor stay till he could go in his night-dress, since he might not go as a soldier. And lastly, when the Emperor in contempt, to show his command of his subjects, did command one to leap from the window down and broke his neck in the sight of our Embassador, he replied that his mistress did set more by, and did make better use of the necks of her subjects; but said that, to show what her subjects would do for her, he would, and did, fling down his gauntlet before the Emperor; and challenged all the nobility there to take it up, in defence of the Emperor against his Queen: for which, at this very day, the name of Sir Jerom Bowes is famous and honoured there.

7TH (LORD'S DAY). Meeting Mr. Pierce, the chyrurgeon, he took me into Somersett House; and there carried me into the Queen-Mother's presence-chamber, where she was with our own Queen sitting on her left hand (whom I did never see before); and though she be not very charming, yet she hath a good, modest, and innocent look which is pleasing. Here I also saw Madam Castlemaine, and, which pleased me most, Mr. Crofts, the King's bastard, a most pretty spark of about 15 years old, who, I perceive, do hang much upon my Lady Castlemaine, and is always with her; and I hear, the Queens, both of them are mighty kind to him. By and by in comes the King, and anon the Duke and his Duchess; so that, they being all together, was such a sight as I never could almost have happened to see with so much ease and leisure. They staid till it was dark, and then went away; the King and his Queen, and my Lady Castlemaine and young Crofts, in one coach and the rest in other coaches. Here were great store of great ladies, but very few handsome. The King and Queen were very merry; and he would have made the Queen-Mother believe that his Queen was with child, and said that she said so. And the young Queen answered, "You lye;" which was the first English word that I ever heard her say: which made the King good sport; and he would have taught her to say in English, "Confess and be hanged."

14TH (LORD'S DAY). Called in at the Legg and drank a cup of ale and a toast, which I have not done many a month before, but it served me for my two glasses of wine to-day.

19TH. Up betimes and to my office, and at 9 o'clock, none of the rest going, I went alone to Deptford, and there went on where they left last night to pay Woolwich yard, and so at noon dined well, being chief at the table, and do not see but every body begins to give me as much respect and honour as any of the rest. After dinner to Pay again, and so till 9 at night, my great trouble being that I was forced to begin an ill practice of bringing down the wages of servants, for which people did curse me, which I do not love. At night, after I had eaten a cold pullet, I walked by brave moonshine, with three or four armed men to guard me, to Redriffe, it being a joy to my heart to think of the condition that I am now in, that people should of themselves provide this for me, unspoke to. I hear this walk is dangerous to walk alone by night, and much robbery committed here. So from thence by water home, and so to my lodgings to bed.

21st (LORD'S DAY). The Queen coming by in her coach, going to her chappell at St. James's (the first time it hath been ready for her), I crowded after her, and I got up to the room where her closet is; and there stood and saw the fine altar, ornaments, and the fryers in their habits, and the priests come in with their fine copes and many other very fine things. I heard their musique too; which may be good, but it did not appear so to me, neither as to their manner of singing, nor was it good concord to my ears, whatever the matter was. The Queene very devout: but what pleased me best was to see my dear Lady Castlemaine, who, tho' a Protestant, did wait upon the Queen to chappell. By and by, after mass was done, a fryer with his cowl did rise up and preach a sermon in Portuguese; which I not understanding, did go away, and to the King's chappell.

29th (MICHAELMAS DAY). This day my oaths for drinking of wine and going to plays are out, and so I do resolve to take a liberty to-day, and then to fall to them again. To the King's Theatre, where we saw "Midsummer's Night's Dream," which I had never seen before, nor shall ever again, for it is the most insipid ridiculous play that ever I saw in my life. I saw, I confess, some good dancing and some handsome women, which was all my pleasure.

30th. I arose, and about my business, and then to my house to look over my workmen but good God! how I do find myself by yesterday's liberty hard to be brought to follow business again, but however, I must do it, considering the great sweet and pleasure and content of mind that I have had since I did leave drink and plays, and other pleasures, and followed my business.

OCTOBER 8TH. Up and by water to my Lord Sandwich's, and was with him a good while in his chamber, and among other things to my extraordinary joy, he did tell me how much I was beholding to the Duke of York, who did yesterday of his own accord tell him that he did thank him for one person brought into the Navy, naming myself, and much more to my commendation, which is the greatest comfort and encouragement that ever I had in my life, and do owe it all to Mr. Coventry's goodness and ingenuity. I was glad above measure of this.

13TH. With my father took a melancholy walk to Portholme, seeing the countrymaids milking their cows there, they being there now at grass, and to see with what mirth they come all home together in pomp with their milk, and sometimes they have musique go before them.

17TH. With Mr. Creed to Westminster Hall, and by and by thither comes Captn. Ferrers, upon my sending for him, and we three to Creed's chamber, and there sat a good while and drank chocolate. Here I am told how things go at Court; that the young men get uppermost, and the old serious lords are out of favour.

19TH (LORD'S DAY). Got me ready in the morning and put on my first new lace-band; and so neat it is, that I am resolved my great expense shall be lace-bands, and it will set off anything else the more. I am sorry to hear that the news of the selling of Dunkirk is taken so generally ill, as I find it is among the merchants; and other things, as removal of officers at Court, good for worse; and all things else made much worse in their report among people than they are. And this night, I know not upon what ground, the gates of the City ordered to be kept shut, and double guards every where.

20TH. With Commissioner Pett to Mr. Lilly's, the great painter, who came forth to us; but believing that I come to bespeak a picture, he prevented us by telling us, that he should not be at leisure these three weeks; which methinks is a rare thing. And then to see in what pomp his table was laid for himself to go to dinner; and here, among other pictures, saw the so much desired by me picture of my Lady Castlemaine, which is a most blessed picture; and that I must have a copy of.

24TH. After with great pleasure lying a great while talking and sporting in bed with my wife (for we have been for some years now, and at present more and more, a very happy couple, blessed be God), I got up and to my office. So home and dined there with my wife upon a most excellent dish of tripes of my own directing, covered with mustard, as I have heretofore seen them done at my Lord Crew's, of which I made a very great meal.

26TH (LORD'S DAY). All this day soldiers going up and down the town, there being an alarm and many Quakers and others clapped up; but I believe without any reason: only they say in Dorsetshire there hath been some rising discovered.

30TH. Could sleep but little to-night for thoughts of my business. So up by candlelight and by water to Whitehall, and so to my Lord Sandwich, who was up in his chamber and all alone, did acquaint me with his business which was, that our old acquaintance Mr. Wade (in Axe Yard) hath discovered to him £7,000 hid in the Tower, of which he was to have two for discovery my Lord himself two, and the King the other three, when it was found; and that the King's warrant runs for me on my Lord's part, and one Mr. Lee for Sir Harry Bennet, to demand leave of the Lieutenant of the Tower for to make search. After dinner, Sir H. Bennet did call aside the Lord Mayor and me, and did break the business to him, who did not, nor durst appear the least averse to it, but did promise all assistance forthwith to set upon it. So Mr. Lee and I to our office, and there walked till Mr. Wade and one Evett his guide did come, and W. Griffin, and a porter with his picke-axes, &c.; and so they walked along with us to the Tower, and Sir H. Bennet and my Lord Mayor did give us full power to fall to work. So our guide demands a candle, and down into the cellars he goes, inquiring whether they were the same that Baxter always had. We went into several little cellars, and then went out a-doors to view, and to the Cole Harbour; but none did answer so well to the marks which was given him to find it by, as one arched vault. Where, after a great deal of council whether to set upon it now, or delay for better and more full advice, we set to it, to digging we went to almost eight o'clock at night, but could find nothing. But, however, our guides did not at all seem discouraged; for that they being confident that the money is there they look for but having never been in the cellars, they could not be positive to the place, and therefore will inform themselves more fully now they have been there, of the party that do advise them. So locking the door after us, we left work to-night, and up to the Deputy Governor; and he do undertake to keep the key of the cellars, that none shall go down without his privity. But, Lord! to see what a young simple fantastique coxcombe is made Deputy Governor, would make one mad; and how he called out for his night-gown of silk, only to make a show to us.

NOVEMBER 1ST. Thence to my office, sent for to meet Mr. Leigh again, from Sir H. Bennet. And he and I, with Wade and his intelligencer and labourers, to the Tower cellars, to make one tryall more; where we staid two or three hours digging, and dug a great deal all under the arches, as it was now most confidently directed, and so seriously, and upon pretended good grounds, that I myself did truly expect to speed but we missed of all: and so we went away the second time like fools. And to our office, whither, a coach being come, Mr. Leigh goes home to Whitehall; and I by appointment to the Dolphin Tavern, to meet Wade and the other, Captn. Evett, who now do tell me plainly, that he that do put him upon this is one that had it from Barkestead's own mouth, and was advised with by him, just before the King's coming in, how to get it out, and had all the signs told him how and where it lay, and had always been the great confident of Barkestead even to the trusting him with his life and all he had. So that he did much convince me that there is good ground for what we go about. But I fear it may be that he did find some conveyance of it away, without the help of this man, before he died. But he is resolved to go to the party once more, and then to determine what we shall do further.

2ND (LORD'S DAY). Lay long with pleasure talking with my wife, in whom I never had greater content, blessed be God! than now, she continuing with the same care and thrift and innocence, so long as I keep her from occasions of being otherwise, as ever she was in her life, and keeps the house well.

3RD. To my Lord Sandwich, from whom I receive every day more and more signs of his confidence and esteem of me. Here I met with Pierce the chyrurgeon, who tells me that my Lady Castlemaine is with child; but though it be the King's yet her Lord being still in town, and sometimes seeing of her, though never to eat or lie together, it will be laid to him. He tells me also how the Duke of York is smitten in love with my Lady Chesterfield (a virtuous lady, daughter to my Lord of Ormond); and so much, that the duchess of York hath complained to the King and her father about it, and my Lady Chesterfield is gone into the country for it. At all which I am sorry; but it is the effect of idleness, and having nothing else to employ their great spirits upon. At night to my office, and did business; and there came to me Mr. Wade and Evett, who have been again with their prime intelligencer, a woman, I perceive: and though we have missed twice, yet they bring such an account of the probability of the truth of the thing, though we are not certain of the place, that we shall set upon it once more; and I am willing and hopefull in it. So we resolved to set upon it again on Wednesday morning; and the woman herself will be there in a disguise, and confirm us in the place.

7TH. Up and being by appointment called upon by Mr. Lee, he and I to the Tower, to make our third attempt upon the cellar. And now privately the woman, Barkestead's great confident, is brought, who do positively say that this is the place which he did say the money was hid in, and where he and she did put up the £50,000 in butter firkins; and the very day that he went out of England did say that neither he nor his would be the better for that money, and therefore wishing that she and hers might. And so left us, and we full of hope did resolve to dig all over the cellar, which by seven o'clock at night we performed. At noon we sent for a dinner, and upon the head of a barrel dined very merrily, and to work again. But at last we saw we were mistaken; and after digging the cellar quite through, and removing the barrels from one side to the other, we were forced to pay our porters, and give over our expectations, though I do believe there must be money hid somewhere by him, or else he did delude this woman in hopes to oblige her to further serving him, which I am apt to believe.

13TH. Then to my office late, and this afternoon my wife in her discontent sent me a letter, which I am in a quandary what to do, whether to read it or not, but I purpose not, but to burn it before her face, that I may put a stop to more of this nature. But I must think of some way, either to find her some body to keep her company, or to set her to work, and by employment to take up her thoughts and time. After doing what I had to do I went home to supper, and there was very sullen to my wife, and so went to bed and to sleep (though with much ado, my mind being troubled) without speaking one word to her.

14TH. She began to talk in the morning and to be friends, believing all this while that I had read her letter, which I perceive by her discourse was full of good counsel, and relating the reason of her desiring a woman, and how little charge she did intend it to be to me, so I begun and argued it as full and plain to her, and she to reason it highly to me, to put her away, and take one of the Bowyers if I did dislike her, that I did resolve when the house is ready she shall try her for a while; the truth is, I having a mind to have her come for her musique and dancing.

21ST. At night to supper and to bed; this night having first put up a spitting sheet, which I find very convenient. This day come the King's pleasure-boats from Calais, with the Dunkirk money, being 400,000 pistolles.

22ND. This day I bought the book of country dances against my wife's woman Gosnell comes, who dances finely; and there meeting Mr. Playford he did give me his Latin songs of Mr. Deering's, which he lately printed.

24TH. Sir J. Minnes, Sir W. Batten, and I, going forth toward White Hall, we hear that the King and Duke are come this morning to the Tower to see the Dunkirk money. So we by coach to them, and there went up and down all the magazines with them; but methought it was but poor discourse and frothy that the King's companions (young Killigrew among the rest) about the cod pieces of some of the men in armour there to be seen, had with him. We saw none of the money, but Mr. Slingsby did show the King, and I did see, the stamps of the new money that is now to be made by Blondeau's fashion, which are very neat, and like the King.

25TH. All day long till twelve o'clock at night getting my house in order, my wife putting up the red hangings and bed in her woman's chamber, and I my books and all other matters in my chamber and study, which is now very pretty. So to bed.

27TH. At my waking, I found the tops of the houses covered with snow, which is a rare sight, that I have not seen these three years. We all went to the next house upon Tower Hill, to see the coming by of the Russian Embassador; for whose reception all the City trained-bands do attend in the streets, and the King's life-guards, and most of the wealthy citizens in their black velvet coats, and gold chains. I could not see the Embassador in his coach; but his attendants in their habits and fur caps very handsome, comely men, and most of them with hawkes upon their fists to present to the King. But Lord! to see the absurd nature of Englishmen, that cannot forbear laughing and jeering at everything that looks strange.

30TH (LORD'S DAY). To church in the morning, and Mr. Mills made a pretty good sermon. It is a bitter cold frost to-day. This day I first did wear a muffe, being my wife's last year's muffe, and now I have bought her a new one, this serves me very well. Thus ends this month; in great frost; myself and family all well.

DECEMBER 5TH. So home, and there I find Gosnell come, who, my wife tells me, is like to prove a pretty companion, of which I am glad. In the evening by Gosnell's coming I do put off these thoughts to entertain myself with my wife and her, who sings exceeding well, and I shall take great delight in her, and so merrily to bed.

6TH. Up and to the office, and there sat all the morning, Mr. Coventry and I alone, the rest being paying off of ships. Dined at home with my wife and Gosnell, my mind much pleased with her, and after dinner sat with them a good while, till my wife seemed to take notice of my being at home now more than at other times. I went away to my office again, and doing my business there, I went home, and after a song by Gosnell we to bed.

9TH. Lay long with my wife, contenting her about the business of Gosnell's going, and I perceive she will be contented as well as myself. After dinner staid within all the afternoon, being vexed in my mind about the going away of Sarah this afternoon, who cried mightily, and so was I ready to do, and Jane did also, and then anon went Gosnell away, which did trouble me too; though upon many considerations, it is better that I am rid of the charge. All together makes my house appear to me very lonely, which troubles me much, and in a melancholy humour I went to the office, then home and to supper, and my wife and I melancholy to bed.

15TH. Up and to my Lord's and thence to the Duke, and followed him into the Park, where, though the ice was broken and dangerous, yet he would go slide upon his scates, which I did not like, but he slides very well. Thence walked a good while up and down the gallerys; and among others, met with Dr. Clerke, who in discourse tells me, for all this, that the King is very kind to the Queen: who, he says, is one of the best women in the world. Strange how the King is bewitched to this pretty Castle-maine.

19TH. Up and by appointment with Mr. Lee, Wade, Evett, and workmen to the Tower, and with the Lieutenant's leave set them to work in the garden, in the corner against the mayne-guard, a most unlikely place. Is being cold, Mr. Lee and I did sit all the day till three o'clock by the fire in the Governor's house; I reading a play of Fletcher's, being "A Wife for a Month," wherein no great wit or language. Having done we went to them at work, and having wrought below the bottom of the foundation of the wall, I bid them give over, and so all our hopes ended.

22ND. My wife and I to read "Ovid's Metamorphoses," which I brought her home from Paul's Churchyard to-night, having called for it by the way, and so to bed.

26TH. Up, my wife to the making of Christmas pies all day, being now pretty well again. Hither come Mr. Battersby; and we falling into a discourse of a new book of drollery in verse called Hudebras, I would needs go find it out, and met with it at the Temple: cost me 2s. 6d. But when I came to read it, it is so silly an abuse of the Presbyter Knight going to the warrs, that I am ashamed of it; and by and by meeting at Mr. Townsend's at dinner, I sold it to him for 18d.

29TH. Hither came Jack Spicer to me, and I took him to the Swan. He told me of the great vast trade of the goldsmiths in supplying the King with money at dear rates. Thence to White Hall, and got up to the top gallerys in the Banquetting House, to see the audience of the Russia Embassadors; and very hand-some it was. After they were come in, I went down and got through the croude almost as high as the King and the Embas-sadors, where I saw all the presents, being rich furs, hawks, car-pets, cloths of tissue, and sea-horse teeth. The King took two or three hawks upon his fist, having a glove on, wrought with gold, given him for the purpose. The son of one of the Embassadors was in the richest suit for pearl and tissue, that ever I did see, or shall, I believe. After they and all the company had kissed the King's hand, then the three Embassadors and the son, and no more, did kiss the Queen's. One thing more I did observe, that the chief Embassador did carry up his master's letters in state before him on high; and as soon as he had delivered them, he did fall down to the ground and lay there a great while.

30TH. After dinner drinking five or six glasses of wine, which liberty I now take till I begin my oath again, I went home and took my wife into coach, and carried her to Westminster; thence to White Hall, where I carried my wife to see the Queen in her presence-chamber; and the maydes of honour and the young Duke of Monmouth playing at cards. Some of them, and but a few, were very pretty; though all well dressed in velvet gowns.

31ST. Thence merry back, Mr. Povy and I, to White Hall; he carrying me thither on purpose to carry me into the ball this night before the King. All the way he talking very ingeniously, and I find him a fine gentleman, and one that loves to live nobly and neatly, as I perceive by his discourse of his house, pictures, and horses. He brought me first to the Duke's chamber, where I saw him and the Duchess at supper; and thence into the room where the ball was to be, crammed with fine ladies, the greatest of the Court. By and by comes the King and Queen, the Duke and Duchess and all the great ones; and after seating themselves, the King takes out the Duchess of York; and the Duke, the Duchess of Buckingham; the Duke of Monmouth, my Lady Castlemaine; and so other lords other ladies; and they danced the Bransle. After that, the King led a lady a single Coranto; and then the rest of the lords, one after another, other ladies; very noble it was, and great pleasure to see. Then to country dances; the King leading the first, which he called for; which was, says he, "Cuckolds all awry," the old dance of England. Of the ladies that danced, the Duke of Monmouth's mistress, and my Lady Castlemaine, and a daughter of Sir

Harry de Vicke's, were the best. The manner was, when the King dances, all the ladies in the room, and the Queen herself, stand up; and indeed he dances rarely, and much better than the Duke of York.

Thus ends this year with great mirth to me and my wife. Our condition being thus:—we are at present spending a night or two at my Lord's lodgings at White Hall. Our home at the Navy office, which is and hath a pretty while been in good condition, finished and made very convenient. My purse is worth about £650, besides my goods of all sorts, which yet might have been more but for my late layings out upon my house and public assessment, and yet would not have been so much if I had not lived a very orderly life all this year by virtue of the oaths that God put into my heart to take against wine, plays, and other expenses, and to observe for these last twelve months, and which I am now going to renew, I under God owing my present content thereunto. My family is myself and wife, William, my clerk; Jane, my wife's upper mayde, but, I think, growing proud and negligent upon it: we must part, which troubles me; Susan, our cook-mayde, a pretty willing wench, but no good cook; and Wayneman, my boy, who I am now turning away for his naughty tricks. We have had from the beginning our healths to this day, very well, blessed be God! Publique matters stand thus: The King is bringing, as is said, his family, and Navy, and all other his charges, to a less expence. In the mean time, himself following his pleasures more than with good advice he would do; at least, to be seen to all the world to do so. His dalliance with my Lady Castlemaine being publique, every day, to his great reproach; and his favouring of none at Court so much as those that are the confidants of his pleasure, as Sir H. Bennet and Sir Charles Barkeley; which, good God! put it into his heart to mend, before he makes himself too much contemned by his people for it! The Duke of Monmouth is in so great splendour at Court, and so dandled by the King, that some doubt, if the King should have no child by the Queen (which there is yet no appearance of), whether he would not be acknowledged for a lawful son; and that there will be a difference follow upon it between the Duke of York and him; which

God prevent! My Lord Chancellor is threatened by people to be questioned, the next sitting of the Parliament, by some spirits that do not love to see him so great; but certainly he is a good servant to the King. My Lord Sandwich is still in good esteem, and now keeping his Christmas in the country; and I in good esteem, I think, as any man can be, with him. In fine, for the good condition of myself, wife, family, and estate, in the great degree that it is, and for the public state of the nation, so quiett as it is, the Lord God be praised!

1663

JANUARY 1ST. To my wife, and found Mrs. Sarah with us in the chamber we lay in. Among other discourse, Mrs. Sarah tells us how the King sups at least four or [five] times every week with my Lady Castlemaine; and most often stays till the morning with her, and goes home through the garden all alone privately, and that so as the very centrys take notice of it and speak of it.

6TH (TWELFTH DAY). Up and Mr. Creed brought a pot of chocolate ready made for our morning draft, and then he and I to the Duke's. This night making an end wholly of Christmas, with a mind fully satisfied with the great pleasures we have had by being abroad from home, and I do find my mind so apt to run to its old want of pleasures, that it is high time to betake myself to my late vows, which I will to-morrow, God willing, perfect and bind myself to, that so I may, for a great while, do my duty, as I have well begun, and increase my good name and esteem in the world, and get money, which sweetens all things, and whereof I have much need.

9TH. Waking in the morning, my wife I found also awake, and begun to speak to me with great trouble and tears. At last we are pretty good friends, and my wife begun to speak again of the necessity of her keeping somebody to bear her company; for her familiarity with her other servants is it that spoils them all, and other company she hath none, which is too true, and called for Jane to reach her out of her trunk, giving her the keys to that purpose, a bundle of papers, and pulls out a paper, a copy of what, a pretty while since, she had wrote in a discontent to me, which I would not read, but burnt. She now read it, and it was so piquant, and wrote in English, and most of it true, of the retiredness of her life, and how unpleasant it was; that being wrote in English, and so in danger of being met with and read by others, I was vexed at it, and desired her and then commanded her to tear it. When she desired to be excused it, I forced it from her, and tore it, and withal took her other bundle of papers from her, and leapt out of the bed and in my shirt clapped them into the pocket of my breeches, that she might not get them from me, and having got on my stockings and breeches and gown, I pulled them out one by one and tore them all before her face, though it went against my heart to do it, she crying and desiring me not to do it, but such was my passion and trouble to see the letters of my love to her, and my Will wherein I had given her all I have in the world, when I went to sea with my Lord Sandwich, to be joyned with a paper of so much disgrace to me and dishonour, if it should have been found by any body. Having torn them all, saving a bond of my uncle Robert's, which she hath long had in her hands, and our marriage license, and the first letter that ever I sent her when I was her servant, I took up the pieces and carrying them into my chamber, and there, after many disputes with myself whether I should burn them or no, and having picked up the pieces of the paper she read to-day, and of my Will which I tore, I burnt all the rest, and so went out to my office troubled in mind. I home to dinner. And to see my folly, as discontented as I am, when my wife came I could not forbear smiling all dinner till she began to speak bad words again, and then I began to be angry again, and so to my office. My wife and I to friends again, though I and she never were so heartily angry in our lives as to-day almost, and I doubt the heart-burning will not [be] soon over, and the truth is I am sorry for the tearing of so many poor loving letters of mine from sea and elsewhere to her.

12TH. To my Lord's lodging.

17TH. Waked early with my mind troubled about our law matters, but it came into my mind that [saying] of Epictetus about his ἐφ' ἡμῖν χαὶ οὐχ, &c., ("Some things are in our power, others are not"), which did put me to a great deal of ease, it being a saying of great reason.

30TH. A solemn fast for the King's murther, and we were forced to keep it more than we would have done, having forgot to take any victuals into the house.

FEBRUARY 1ST (LORD'S DAY). This day Creed and I walking in White Hall garden did see the King coming privately from my Lady Castlemaine's; which is a poor thing for a prince to do.

6TH. And so to a Bookseller's in the Strand, and there bought Hudibras again, it being certainly some ill humour to be so against that which all the world cries up to be the example of wit; for which I am resolved once again to read him, and see whether I can find it or no.

27TH. About 11 o'clock, Commissioner Pett and I walked to Chyrurgeon's Hall (we being all invited thither, and promised to dine there); where we were led into the Theatre; and by and by comes the reader, Dr. Tearne, with the Master and Company, in a very handsome manner: and all being settled, he begun his lecture, this being the second upon the kidneys, ureters, &c., which was very fine; and his discourse being ended, we walked into the Hall, and there being great store of company, we had a fine dinner and good learned company, many Doctors of Physique, and we used with extraordinary great respect. After dinner Dr. Scarborough took some of his friends, and I went along with them, to see the body alone, which we did, which was a lusty fellow, a seaman, that was hanged for a robbery. I did touch the dead body with my bare hand: it felt cold, but methought it was a very unpleasant sight. It seems one Dillon, of a great family, was, after much endeavours to have saved him, hanged with a silken halter this Sessions (of his own preparing), not for honour only, but it seems, it being soft and sleek, it do slip close and kills, that is, strangles presently: whereas, a stiff one do not come so close together, and so the party may live the longer before killed. But all the Doctors at table conclude, that there is no pain at all in hanging, for that it do stop the circulation of the blood; and so stops all sense and motion in an instant.

MARCH 10TH. Up and to my office all the morning, and great pleasure it is to be doing my business betimes.

APRIL 3RD. Going out of White Hall, I met Captain Grove, who did give me a letter directed to myself from himself. I discerned money to be in it, and took it, knowing, as I found it to be, the proceed of the place I have got him to be, the taking up of vessels for Tangier. But I did not open it till I came home to my office, and there I broke it open, not looking into it till all the money was out, that I might say I saw no money in the paper, if ever I should be questioned about it. There was a piece in gold and £4 in silver.

4TH. Home to dinner, whither by and by comes Roger Pepys, Mrs. Turner her daughter, Joyce Norton, and a young lady, a daughter of Coll. Cockes, my uncle Wight, his wife and Mrs. Anne Wight. This being my feast, in lieu of what I should have had a few days ago for my cutting of the stone, for which the Lord make me truly thankful. Very merry at, before, and after dinner, and the more for that my dinner was great, and most neatly dressed by our own only maid. We had a fricasee of rabbits and chickens, a leg of mutton boiled, three carps in a dish, a great dish of a side of lamb, a dish of roasted pigeons, a dish of four lobsters, three tarts, a lamprey pie (a most rare pie), a dish of anchovies, good wine of several sorts, and all things mighty noble and to my great content. After dinner to Hide Park. At the Park was the King, and in another coach my Lady Castlemaine, they greeting one another at every tour.

5TH (LORD'S DAY). Then to church again, where a simple bawling young Scot preached.

12TH (LORD'S DAY). Coming home to-night, a drunken boy was carrying by our constable to our new pair of stocks to handsel them, being a new pair and very handsome.

14TH. Sir G. Carteret tells me to-night that he perceives the Parliament is likely to make a great bustle before they will give the King any money; will call all things into question; and, above all, the expences of the Navy; and do enquire into the King's expences everywhere.

19TH (EASTER DAY). Up and this day put on my close-kneed coloured suit, which, with new stockings of the colour, with belt, and new gilt-handled sword, is very handsome.

20TH. This day the little Duke of Monmouth was marryed at White Hall, in the King's chamber; and to-night is a great supper and dancing at his lodgings, near Charing Cross. I observed his coat at the tail of his coach: he gives the arms of England, Scotland, and France, quartered upon some other fields, but what it is that speaks his being a bastard I know not.

23RD. At cards till late, and being at supper, my boy being sent for some mustard to a neat's tongue, the rogue staid half an hour in the streets, it seems at a bonfire, at which I was very angry, and resolve to beat him tomorrow.

24TH. Up betimes, and with my salt eel went down in the parler and there got my boy and did beat him till I was fain to take breath two or three times, yet for all I am afeard it will make the boy never the better, he is grown so hardened in his tricks, which I am sorry for, he being capable of making a brave man, and is a boy that I and my wife love very well. After dinner all the afternoon fiddling upon my viallin (which I have not done many a day), while Ashwell danced above in my upper best chamber, which is a rare room for musique.

25TH. So in the evening home, and after supper (my father at my brother's) and merrily practising to dance, which my wife hath begun to learn this day of Mr. Pembleton, but I fear will hardly do any great good at it, because she is conceited that she do well already, though I think no such thing. So to bed. Lastly I did hear that the Queen is much grieved of late at the King's neglecting her, he having not supped once with her this quarter of a year, and almost every night with my Lady Castlemaine; who hath been with him this St. George's feast at Windsor, and came home with him last night; and, which is more, they say is removed as to her bed from her own home to a chamber in White Hall, next to the King's own; which I am sorry to hear, though I love her much.

26TH (LORD'S DAY). In the evening (my father being gone to my brother's to lie to-night) my wife, Ashwell, and the boy and I, and the dogg, over the water and walked to Half-way house, and beyond into the fields, gathering of cowslipps, and so to Half-way house, with some cold lamb we carried with us, and there supped, and had a most pleasant walk back again.

MAY 1ST. In my way, in Leadenhall Street, there was morris-dancing which I have not seen a great while.

4TH. By and by the dancing-master came, whom standing by, seeing him instructing my wife, when he had done with her, he would needs have me try the steps of a coranto, and what with his desire and my wife's importunity, I did begin, and then was obliged to give him entry-money 10s., and am become his scholler. The truth is, I think it a thing very useful for a gentleman, and sometimes I may have occasion of using it.

11TH. To St. James's, where we attended the Duke of York: and, among other things, Sir G. Carteret and I had a great dispute about the different value of the pieces of eight rated by Mr. Creed at 4s. and 5d., and by Pitts at 4s. and 9d., which was the greatest husbandry to the King? he persisting that the greatest sum was; which is as ridiculous a piece of ignorance as could be imagined.

12TH. Up between four and five, and after dressing myself then to my office to prepare business against the afternoon, where all the morning, and dined at noon at home, where a little angry with my wife for minding nothing now but the dancing-master, having him come twice a day, which is folly.

13TH. God mend all, for I am sure we are but in an ill condition in the Navy, however the King is served in other places. Home to supper, to cards, and to bed.

15TH. It is made very doubtful whether the King do not intend the making of the Duke of Monmouth legitimate; but surely the Commons of England will never do it, nor the Duke of York suffer it, whose lady, I am told, is very troublesome to him by her jealousy. Home, where I found it almost night, and my wife and the dancing-master alone above, not dancing but talking. Now so deadly full of jealousy I am that my heart and head did so cast about and fret that I could not do any business possibly, but went out to my office, and anon late home again and ready to chide at every thing, and then suddenly to bed and could hardly sleep. But it is a deadly folly and plague that I bring upon myself to be so jealous and by giving myself such an occasion more than my wife desired of giving her another month's dancing. Which however shall be ended as soon as I can possibly. But I am ashamed to think what a course I did take by lying to see whether my wife did wear drawers to-day as she used to do, and other things to raise my suspicion of her, but I found no true cause of doing it.

16TH. Up with my mind disturbed and with my last night's doubts upon me, for which I deserve to be beaten if not really served as I am fearful of being, especially since God knows that I do not find honesty enough in my own mind but that upon a small temptation I could be false to her, and therefore ought not to expect more justice from her, but God pardon both my sin and my folly herein.

2OTH. So that I fear without great discretion I shall go near to lose too my command over her, and nothing do it more than giving her this occasion of dancing and other pleasures, whereby her mind is taken up from her business and finds other sweets besides pleasing of me, and so makes her that she begins not at all to take pleasure in me or study to please me as heretofore.

23RD. Waked this morning between four and five by my blackbird, which whistles as well as ever I heard any; only it is the beginning of many tunes very well, but there leaves them, and goes no further.

26TH. Lay long in bed talking and pleasing myself with my wife. So up and to my office a while and then home, where I found Pembleton, and by many circumstances I am led to conclude that there is something more than ordinary between my wife and him.

27TH. At home where we danced country dances, and single, my wife and I; and my wife paid him [Pembleton] off for this month also, and so he is cleared. After dancing we took him down to supper, and were very merry, and I made myself so, and kind to him as much as I could, to prevent his discourse, though I perceive to my trouble that he knows all, and may do me the disgrace to publish it as much as he can.

29TH. To the Duke's house, and there saw "The Slighted Mayde," wherein Gosnell acted Pyramena, a great part, and did it very well, and I believe will do it better and better, and prove a good actor. So home, and in my way did take two turns forwards and backwards through the Fleete Ally to see a couple of pretty [strumpets] that stood off the doors there, and God forgive me I could scarce stay myself from going into their houses with them, so apt is my nature to evil after once, as I have these two days, set upon pleasure again.

30TH. So to my brother's, and there I found my aunt James, a poor, religious, well-meaning, good soul, talking of nothing but God Almighty, and that with so much innocence that mightily pleased me. Here was a fellow that said grace so long like a prayer; I believe the fellow is a cunning fellow, and yet I by my brother's desire did give him a crown, he being in great want, and, it seems, a parson among the fanatiques, and a cozen of my poor aunt's.

JUNE 1ST. I with Sir J. Minnes to the Strand Maypole; and there 'light out of his coach, and walked to the New Theatre, which, since the King's players are gone to the Royal one, is this day begun to be employed by the fencers to play prizes at. And here I came and saw the first prize I ever saw in my life; and it was between one Mathews, who did beat at all weapons, and one Westwicke, who was soundly cut several times both in the head and legs, that he was all over blood; and other deadly blows they did give and take in very good earnest, till Westwicke was in a most sad pickle. They fought at eight weapons, three bouts at each weapon. It was very well worth seeing, because I did till this day think that it has only been a cheat; but this being upon a private quarrel, they did it in good earnest; and I felt one of their swords, and found it be very little, if at all blunter on the edge, than the common swords are. Strange to see what a deal of money is flung to them both upon the stage between every bout. But a woful rude rabble there was, and such noises, made my head ake all this evening.

4TH. In the Hall to-day Dr. Pierce tells me that the Queen begins to be brisk, and play like other ladies, and is quite another woman from what she was, of which I am glad. It may be, it may make the King like her the better, and forsake his two mistresses, my Lady Castlemaine and Stewart.

12TH. Abroad with my wife by water to the Royall Theatre; and there saw "The Committee," a merry but indifferent play, only Lacey's part, an Irish footman, is beyond imagination. Here I saw my Lord Falconbridge, and his Lady, my Lady Mary Cromwell, who looks as well as I have known her, and well clad; but when the House began to fill she put on her vizard, and so kept it on all the play; which of late is become a great fashion among the ladies, which hides their whole face. So to the Exchange, to buy things with my wife; among others, a vizard for herself.

13TH. So home to dinner, where I found my wife's brother, and thence after dinner by water to the Royall Theatre, where I resolve to bid farewell, as shall appear by my oaths to-morrow against all plays either at publique houses or Court till Christmas be over.

14TH (LORD's DAY). My wife and I did even out reckonings, and had a great deal of serious talk. I did give her 40s. to carry into the country to-morrow with her, whereof 15s. is to go for the coach-hire for her and Ashwell, there being 20s. paid here already in earnest. In the evening our discourse turned to great content and love, and I hope that after a little forgetting our late differences, and being a while absent one from another, we shall come to agree as well as ever. By and by in comes Sir J. Minnes and Sir W. Batten, and so we sat talking. Among other things, Sir J. Minnes brought many fine expressions of Chaucer, which he doats on mightily, and without doubt he is a very fine poet.

15TH. Up betimes, and anon my wife rose and did give me her keys, and put other things in order and herself against going this morning into the country. I was forced to go to Thames Street and strike up a bargain for some tarr. Thence home, but finding my wife gone, I took coach and after her to her inn, where I am troubled to see her forced to sit in the back of the coach, though pleased to see her company none but women and one parson; she I find is not troubled at all, and I seemed to make a promise to get a horse and ride after them; and so, kissing her often, and Ashwell once, I bid them adieu. That done, by water, I in the barge with the Maister, to the Trinity House at London; where, among others, I found my Lords Sandwich and Craven, and my cousin Roger Pepys, and Sir Wm. Wheeler. Anon we sat down to dinner, which was very great, as they always have. Great variety of talk. Both at and after dinner we had great discourses of the nature and power of spirits, and whether they can animate dead bodies; in all which, as of the general appearance of spirits, my Lord Sandwich is very scepticall. He says the greatest warrants that ever he had to believe any, is the present appearing of the Devil in Wilt-shire, much of late talked of, who beats a drum up and down. There are books of it, and, they say, very true; but my Lord ob-serves, that though he do answer to any tune that you will play to him upon another drum, yet one tune he tried to play and could not; which makes him suspect the whole; and I think it is a good argument. Sometimes they talked of handsome women, and Sir J. Minnes saying that there was no beauty like what he sees in the country-markets, and specially at Bury, in which I will agree with him that there is a prettiest woman I ever saw. My Lord replied thus: "Sir John, what do you think of your neighbour's wife?" looking upon me. "Do you not think that he hath a great beauty to his wife? Upon my word he hath." Which I was not a little proud of. Thence by barge with my Lord to Blackfriars, where we landed and I thence walked home. I up to my wife's closett, and there played on my viallin a good while, and without supper anon to bed, sad for want of my wife, whom I love with all my heart, though of late she has given me some troubled thoughts.

17TH. Up before 4 o'clock, which is the hour I intend now to rise at, and to my office a while, and with great pleasure I fell to my business again.

19TH. Thence to Wilkinson's after a good walk in the Park, where we met on horseback Captain Ferrers; who tells us that the King of France is well again, and that he saw him train his Guards, all brave men, at Paris; and that when he goes to his mistress, Madame la Valiere, a pretty little woman, now with child by him, he goes with his guards with him publiquely, and his trumpets and kettle-drums with him, who stay before the house while he is with her; and yet he says that, for all this, the Queen do not know of it, for that nobody dares to tell her; but that I dare not believe.

21ST (LORD'S DAY). Up betimes, and fell to reading my Latin grammar, which I perceive I have great need of, having lately found it by my calling Will to the reading of a chapter in Latin, and I am resolved to go through it. So to church, and slept all the sermon, the Scot, to whose voice I am not to be reconciled, preaching.

29TH. Met Mr. Creed in the Park, and after a walk or two, discoursing his business, took leave of him in Westminster Hall, whither we walked, and then came again to the Hall and fell to talk with Mrs. Lane, and after great talk that she never went abroad with any man as she used heretofore to do, I with one word got her to go with me and to meet me at the further Rhenish wine-house, where I did give her a Lobster. . . . When weary I did give over and somebody, having seen some of our dalliance, called aloud in the street, "Sir! why do you kiss the gentlewoman so?" and flung a stone at the window, which vexed me. So home and up to my lute long, and then, after a little Latin chapter with Will, to bed. But I have used of late, since my wife went, to make a bad use of my fancy with whatever woman I have a mind to, which I am ashamed of, and shall endeavour to do so no more. So to sleep.

30TH. Thus, by God blessing's, ends this book of two years; I being in all points in good health and a good way to thrive and do well. Some money I do and can lay up, but not much, being worth now about £700, besides goods of all sorts. My wife in the country with Ashwell, her woman, with my father; myself at home with W. Hewer and my cooke-maid Hannah, my boy Wayneman being lately run away from me.

July 1st. By water with Sir W. Batten to Trinity House, there to dine with him, which we did; and after dinner we fell talking, Sir J. Minnes, Mr. Batten and I; Mr. Batten telling us of a late triall of Sir Charles Sydly the other day, before my Lord Chief Justice Foster and the whole bench, for his debauchery a little while since at Oxford Kate's, coming in open day into the Balcone and showed his nakedness, ... and abusing of scripture and as it were from thence preaching a mountebank sermon from the pulpit, saying that there he had to sell such a powder as should make all the [women] in town run after him, 1,000 people standing underneath to see and hear him, and that being done he took a glass of wine ... and then drank it off, and then took another and drank the King's health. It seems my Lord and the rest of the Judges did all of them round give him a most high reproof; my Lord Chief Justice saying, that it was for him, and such wicked wretches as he was, that God's anger and judgments hung over us, calling him sirrah many times. It's said they have bound him to his good behaviour (there being no law against him for it) in £5,000.

4th. With Creed to the King's Head ordinary; but, coming late, dined at the second table very well for 12d.; and a pretty gentleman in our company, who confirms my Lady Castle-maine's being gone from Court, but knows not the reason; he told us of one wipe the Queen a little while ago did give her, when she came in and found the Queen under the dresser's hands, and had been so long: "I wonder your Majesty," says she, "can have the patience to sit so long a-dressing?"—"I have so much reason to use patience," says the Queen, "that I can very well bear with it." He thinks that it may be the Queen hath commanded her to retire, though that is not likely. Thence with Creed to hire a coach to carry us to Hide Park, to-day there being a general muster of the King's Guards, horse and foot. Yet methought all these gay men are not the soldiers that must do the King's business, it being such as these that lost the old King all he had, and were beat by the most ordinary fellows that could be.

8TH. In the evening I received letters out of the country, among others from my wife, who methinks writes so coldly that I am much troubled at it, and I fear shall have much ado to bring her to her old good temper. So home to supper and musique, which is all the pleasure I have of late given myself, or is fit I should, others spending too much time and money.

9TH. Up. Sir W. Batten and I sat a little this afternoon at the office, and thence I by water to Deptford, and there mustered the Yard, purposely, God forgive me, to find out Bagwell, a carpenter, whose wife is a pretty woman, that I might have some occasion of knowing him and forcing her to come to the office again, which I did so luckily that going thence he and his wife did of themselves meet me in the way to thank me for my old kindness, but I spoke little to her, but shall give occasion for her coming to me.

12TH. J. Minnes being gone to bed, I took Mr. Whitfield, one of the clerks, and walked to the Dock about eleven at night, and there got a boat and a crew, and rowed down to the guard-ships, it being a most pleasant moonshine evening that ever I saw almost. The guardships were very ready to hail us, being no doubt commanded thereto by their Captain, who remembers how I surprised them the last time I was here. However, I found him ashore, but the ship in pretty good order, and the arms well fixed, charged, and primed. Thence to the Soveraign, where I found no officers aboard, no arms fixed, nor any powder to prime their few guns, which were charged, without bullet though. So to the London, where neither officers nor any body awake; I boarded her, and might have done what I would, and at last could find but three little boys; and so spent the whole night in visiting all the ships, in which I found, for the most part, neither an officer aboard, nor any man so much as awake, which I was grieved to find, specially so soon after a great Larum, as Commissioner Pett brought us word that he [had] provided against, and put all in a posture of defence but a week ago, all which I am resolved to represent to the Duke.

13TH. By water to Whitehall, and so walked to St. James's, but missed Mrs. Coventry. I met the Queen-Mother walking in the Pell Mell, led by my Lord St. Alban's. And finding many coaches at the Gate, I found upon enquiry that the Duchess is brought to bed of a boy; and hearing that the King and Queen are rode abroad with the Ladies of Honour to the Park, and seeing a great crowd of gallants staying here to see their return, I also staid walking up and down. By and by the King and Queen, who looked in this dress (a white laced waistcoat and a crimson short pettycoat, and her hair dressed *à la negligence*) mighty pretty; and the King rode hand in hand with her. Here was also my Lady Castlemaine rode among the rest of the ladies; but the King took, methought, no notice of her; nor when they 'light did any body press (as she seemed to expect, and staid for it) to take her down, but was taken down by her own gentleman. She looked mighty out of humour and had a yellow plume in her hat (which all took notice of), and yet is very handsome, but very melancholy: nor did any body speak to her, or she so much as smile or speak to any body. I followed them up into White Hall, and into the Queen's presence, where all the ladies walked, talking and fiddling with their hats and feathers, and changing and trying one another's by one another's heads, and laughing. But it was the finest sight to me, considering their great beautys and dress, that ever I did see in all my life. But, above all, Mrs. Stewart in this dress, with her hat cocked and a red plume, with her sweet eye, little Roman nose, and excellent taille, is now the greatest beauty I ever saw, I think, in my life; and, if ever woman can, do exceed my Lady Castlemaine, at least in this dress; nor do I wonder if the King changes, which I verily believe is the reason of his coldness to my Lady Castlemaine. So home to supper and to bed, before I sleep fancying myself to sport with Mrs. Stewart with great pleasure.

27TH. By water to Westminster, and there came most luckily to the Lords' House as the House of Commons were going
into the Lords' House, and there I crowded in along with the
Speaker, and got to stand close behind him, where he made his
speech to the King (who sat with his crown on and robes, and
so all the Lords in their robes, a fine sight); wherein he told his
Majesty what they have done this Parliament, and now offered
for his royal consent. After the bills passed, the King, sitting on
his throne, with his speech writ in a paper which he held in his
lap, and scarce looked off of it, I thought, all the time he made
his speech to them, giving them thanks for their subsidys, of
which, had he not need, he would not have asked or received
them; and that need, not from any extravagancys of his, he was
sure, in any thing, but the disorders of the times compelling
him to be at greater charge than he hoped for the future, by
their care in their country, he should be: and that for his family
expenses and others, he would labour however to retrench in
many things convenient, and would have all others to do so too.
He desired that nothing of old faults should be remembered, or
severity for the same used to any in the country, it being his desire to have all forgot as well as forgiven. His speech was very
plain, nothing at all of spirit in it, nor spoke with any; but rather
on the contrary imperfectly, repeating many times his words
though he read all; which I was sorry to see, it having not been
hard for him to have got all the speech without book.

31ST. Before I went to the office I went to the Coffee House,
where Sir J. Cutler and Mr. Grant were, and there Mr. Grant
showed me letters of Sir William Petty's, wherein he says, that
his vessel which he hath built upon two keeles (a modell
whereof, built for the King, he showed me) hath this month
won a wager of £50 in sailing between Dublin and Holyhead
with the pacquett-boat, the best ship or vessel the King hath
there; and he offers to lay with any vessel in the world. It is
about thirty ton in burden, and carries thirty men, with good
accommodation (as much more as any ship of her burden), and
so any vessel of this figure shall carry more men, with better
accommodation by half, than any other ship. This carries also

ten guns, of about five tons weight. Strange things are told of this vessel, and he concludes his letter with this position, "I only affirm that the perfection of sayling lies in my principle, finde it out who can."

AUGUST 4TH. This day I received a letter from my wife, which troubles me mightily, wherein she tells me how Ashwell did give her the lie to her teeth, and that thereupon my wife giving her a box on the eare, the other struck her again, and a deal of stir which troubles me, and that my Lady has been told by my father or mother something of my wife's carriage, which altogether vexes me.

9TH (LORD'S DAY). Home, and staid up a good while examining Will in his Latin below, and my brother along with him in his Greeke, and so to prayers and to bed.

10TH. Hither came W. Howe about business, and he and I had a great deal of discourse about my Lord Sandwich, and I find by him that my Lord do dote upon one of the daughters of Mrs. [Becke] where he lies, so that he spends his time and money upon her. He tells me she is a woman of a very bad fame and very imprudent, and has told my Lord so, yet for all that my Lord do spend all his evenings with her, though he be at court in the day time, and that the world do take notice of it. In fine, I perceive my Lord is dabbling with this wench, for which I am sorry, though I do not wonder at it, being a man amorous enough, and now begins to allow himself the liberty that he says every body else at Court takes. Yesterday, I am told also, that Sir J. Lenthall, in Southwarke, did apprehend about one hundred Quakers, and other such people, and hath sent some of them to the gaole at Kingston, it being now the time of the Assizes. Hence home and examined a piece of Latin of Will's with my brother, and so to prayers and to bed.

12TH. By water to my brother's, and there I hear my wife is come and gone home, and my father is come to town also, at which I wondered. I home, where methought I found my wife strange, not knowing, I believe, in what temper she could expect me to be in, but I fell to kind words, and so we were very kind only she could not forbear telling me how she had been used by them and her mayde, Ashwell, in the country, but I find it will be best not to examine it, for I doubt she's in fault too, and therefore I seek to put it off from my hearing, and so to bed and there entertained her with great content, and so to sleep.

13TH. Before going to bed Ashwell began to make her complaint, and by her I do perceive that she has received most base usage from my wife, which my wife sillily denies, but it is impossible the wench could invent words and matter so particularly, against which my wife has nothing to say but flatly to deny.

14TH. Awake, and to chide my wife again, and I find that my wife has got too great head to be brought down soon, nor is it possible with any convenience to keep Ashwell longer, my wife is so set and convinced, as she was in Sarah, to make her appear a Lyer in every small thing that we shall have no peace while she stays.

16TH (LORD's DAY). Up and with my wife to church, and finding her desirous to go to church, I did suspect her meeting of Pembleton, but he was not there, and so I thought my jealousy in vain, and treat the sermon with great quiet.

20TH. Up betimes and to my office (having first been angry with my brother John, and in the heat of my sudden passion called him Asse and coxcomb, for which I am sorry, it being but for leaving the key of his chamber with a spring lock within side of his door). This evening the girle that was brought to me to-day for so good a one, being cleansed of lice this day by my wife, and good, new clothes put on her back, she run away from Goody Taylour that was shewing her the way to the bakehouse, and we heard no more of her. So to supper and to bed.

21st. To my brother's, and there told him how my girl has served us which he sent me, and directed him to get my clothes again, and get the girl whipped.

25th. This noon going to the Exchange, I met a fine fellow with trumpets before him in Leadenhall-street, and upon enquiry I find that he is the clerk of the City Market; and three or four men carried each of them an arrow of a pound weight in their hands. It seems this Lord Mayor begins again an old custome, that upon the three first days of Bartholomew Fayre, the first, there is a match of wrestling, which was done, and the Lord Mayor there and Aldermen in Moorefields yesterday: to-day, shooting; and to-morrow, hunting. And this officer of course is to perform this ceremony of riding through the city, I think to proclaim or challenge any to shoot.

31st. This noon came Jane Gentleman to serve my wife as her chamber mayde. I wish she may prove well. So ends this month, with my mind pretty well in quiett, and in good disposition of health since my drinking at home of a little wine with my beer; but no where else do I drink any wine at all.

September 7th. And so I to my Lord Crew's, thinking to have dined there, but it was too late, and so back and called at my brother's and Mr. Holden's about several businesses, and went all alone to the Black Spread Eagle in Bride Lane, and there had a chopp of veale and some bread, cheese, and beer, cost me a shilling to my dinner, and so through Fleet Ally, God forgive me, out of an itch to look upon the sluts there, against which when I saw them my stomach turned.

8th. Up and to my viall a while. Dined at home with my wife. It being washing day, we had a good pie baked of a leg of mutton; and then to my office, and then abroad, and among other places to Moxon's, and there bought a payre of globes cost me £3 10s., with which I am well pleased, I buying them principally for my wife, who has a mind to understand them, and I shall take pleasure to teach her.

9TH. Met with Ned Pickering, with whom I walked 3 or 4 hours till evening, he telling me the whole business of my Lord's folly with this Mrs. Becke, at Chelsey, of all which I am ashamed to see my Lord so grossly play the beast and fool, to the flinging off of all honour, friends, servants, and every thing and person that is good; but believe it to no purpose for me to meddle with it, but let him go on till God Almighty and his own conscience and thoughts of his lady and family do it.

11TH. This morning, about two or three o'clock, knocked up in our back yard, and rising to the window, being moonshine, I found it was the constable and his watch, who had found our back yard door open, and so came in to see what the matter was. So I desired them to shut the door, and bid them good night, and so to bed again, and at 6 o'clock up and a while to my vyall.

21ST. So home, and by and by comes my wife by coach well home, and having got a good fowl ready for supper against her coming, we eat heartily, and so with great content and ease to our own bed, there nothing appearing so to our content as to be at our own home, after being abroad awhile.

22ND. Every day brings newes of the Turke's advance into Germany, to the awakeing of all the Christian Princes thereabouts, and possessing himself of Hungary.

24TH. In the afternoon telling my wife that I go to Deptford, I went by water to Westminster Hall, and there finding Mrs. Lane, took her over to Lambeth, where we were lately.... But, trust in the Lord, I shall never do so again while I live. After being tired with her company I landed her at White Hall, and so home and at my office writing letters till 12 at night almost, and then home to supper and bed, and there found my poor wife hard at work, which grieved my heart to see that I should abuse so good a wretch, and that is just with God to make her bad with me for my wronging of her, but I do resolve never to do the like again. So to bed.

27TH (LORD'S DAY). So home to dinner, being a little troubled to see Pembleton out again, but I do not discern in my wife the least memory of him.

OCTOBER 6TH. Slept pretty well, and my wife waked to ring the bell to call up our mayds to the washing about 4 o'clock, and I was and she angry that our bell did not wake them sooner, but I will get a bigger bell.

14TH. Thence home and after dinner my wife and I by Mr. Rawlinson's conduct, to the Jewish Synagogue; where the men and boys in their vayles, and the women behind a lattice out of sight; and some things stand up, which I believe is their Law, in a press to which all coming in do bow; and at the putting on their vayles do say something, to which others that hear him do cry Amen, and the party do kiss his vayle. Their service all in a singing way, and in Hebrew. And anon their Laws that they take out of the press are carried by several men, four or five several burthens in all, and they do relieve one another; and whether it is that every one desires to have the carrying of it, I cannot tell, thus they carried it round about the room while such a service is singing. And in the end they had a prayer for the King, which they pronounced his name in Portugall; but the prayer, like the rest, in Hebrew. But, Lord! to see the disorder, laughing, sporting, and no attention, but confusion in all their service, more like brutes than people knowing the true God, would make a man forswear ever seeing them more: and indeed I never did see so much, or could have imagined there had been any religion in the whole world so absurdly performed as this.

19TH. Waked with a very high wind, and said to my wife, "I pray God I hear not of the death of any great person, this wind is so high!" fearing that the Queen might be dead. So up; and going by coach with Sir W. Batten and Sir J. Minnes to St. James's, they tell me that Sir W. Compton died yesterday: at which I was most exceedingly surprised, he being, and so all the world saying that he was, one of the worthyest men and best officers of State now in England. Coming to St. James's, I hear that the Queen did sleep five hours pretty well to-night, and that she waked and gargled her mouth, and to sleep again; but that her pulse beats fast, beating twenty to the King's, or my Lady Suffolk's eleven; but not so strong as it was. It seems she was so ill as to be shaved and pidgeons put to her feet, and to have the extreme unction given her by the priests, who were so long about it that the doctors were angry. The King, they all say, is most fondly disconsolate for her, and weeps by her, which makes her weep; which one this day told me he reckons a good sign, for that it carries away some rheume from the head. After being a little with the Duke, and being invited to dinner to my Lord Barkeley's, and so, not knowing how to spend our time till noon, Sir W. Batten and I took coach, and to the Coffee-house in Cornhill; where much talk about the Turk's proceedings, and that the plague is got to Amsterdam, brought by a ship from Argier; and it is also carried to Hambrough. The Duke says the King purposes to forbid any of their ships coming into the river.

2OTH. At Paul's Churchyard, and while I was in Kirton's shop, a fellow came to offer kindness or force to my wife in the coach, but she refusing, he went away, after the coachman had struck him, and he the coachman. So I being called, went thither, and the fellow coming out again of a shop, I did give him a good cuff or two on the chops, and seeing him not oppose me, I did give him another; at last found him drunk, of which I was glad, and so left him, and home, and so to my office awhile, and so home to supper and to bed. This evening, at my Lord's lodgings, Mrs. Sarah talking with my wife and I how the Queen do, and how the King tends her being so ill. She tells us that the Queen's sickness is the spotted fever; that she was as full of the spots as a leopard; which is very strange that it should be no more known; but perhaps it is not so. And that the King do seem to take it much to heart, for that he hath wept before her; but, for all that, that he hath not missed one night since she was sick, of supping with my Lady Castlemaine.

22ND. This morning, hearing that the Queen grows worse again, I sent to stop the making of my velvet cloake, till I see whether she lives or dies.

24TH. Up to my office, where busy all the morning about Mr. Gauden's account, and at noon to dinner with him at the Dolphin, where mighty merry by pleasant stories of Mr. Coventry's and Sir J. Minnes's, which I have put down some of in my book of tales.

27TH. Mr. Coventry tells me to-day that the Queen had a very good night last night; but yet it is strange that still she raves and talks of little more than of her having of children, and fancys now that she hath three children, and that the girle is very like the King. And this morning about five o'clock waked (the physician feeling her pulse, thinking to be better able to judge, she being still and asleep, waked her) and the first word she said was, "How do the children?"

31ST. The Queene continues light-headed, but in hopes to recover. The plague is much in Amsterdam, and we in fears of it here, which God defend. The Turke goes on mightily in the Emperor's dominions, and the Princes cannot agree among themselves how to go against him.

NOVEMBER 2ND. Up, and by coach to White Hall, and there in the long Matted Gallery I find Sir G. Carteret, Sir J. Minnes, and Sir W. Batten; and by and by comes the King to walk there with three or four with him; and soon as he saw us, says he, "Here is the Navy Office," and there walked twenty turns the length of the gallery, talking, methought, but ordinary talke. By and by came the Duke, and he walked, and at last they went into the Duke's lodgings. The King staid so long that we could not discourse with the Duke, and so we parted. I heard the Duke say that he was going to wear a perriwigg; and they say the King also will. I never till this day observed that the King is mighty gray.

3RD. By and by comes Chapman, the periwigg-maker, and upon my liking it, without more ado, I went up, and there he cut off my haire, which went a little to my heart at present to part with it; but, it being over, and my periwigg on, I paid him £3 for it; and away went he with my owne haire to make up another of, and I by and by, after I had caused all my mayds to look upon it; and they conclude it do become me; though Jane was mightily troubled for my parting of my own haire, and so was Besse.

4TH. Up to my office, shewing myself to Sir W. Batten, and Sir J. Minnes, and no great matter made of my periwigg, as I was afeard there would be.

6TH. This morning waking, my wife was mighty earnest with me to persuade me that she should prove with child since last night, which if it be, let it come, and welcome.

8TH (LORD'S DAY). Up, and it being late, to church without my wife. I found that my coming in a perriwigg did not prove so strange to the world as I was afeard it would, for I thought that all the church would presently have cast their eyes all upon me, but I found no such thing.

9TH. Up and found myself very well, and so by coach to White Hall and there met all my fellow officers, and so to the Duke, where, when we came into his closett, he told us that Mr. Pepys was so altered with his new perriwigg that he did not know him. Thence to Westminster Hall, where I met with Mr. Pierce, chyrurgeon. He told me also how loose the Court is, nobody looking after business, but every man his lust and gain: and how the King is now become besotted upon Mrs. Stewart, that he gets into corners, and will be with her half an houre together kissing her to the observation of all the world; and she now stays by herself and expects it, as my Lady Castlemaine did use to do; to whom the King, he says, is still kind, so as now and then he goes to have a chat with her as he believes; but with no such fondness as he used to do. But yet it is thought that this new wench is so subtle, that she lets him not do any thing that is not safe to her, but yet his doting is so great that, Pierce tells me, it is verily thought if the Queene had died, he would have married her. Mr. Blackburne and I fell to talk of many things, wherein I did speak so freely to him in many things agreeing with his sense that he was very open to me: first, in that of religion, he makes it great matter of prudence for the King and Council to suffer liberty of conscience; and imputes the losse of Hungary to the Turke from the Emperor's denying them this liberty of their religion. He says that many pious ministers of the word of God, some thousands of them, do now beg their bread: and told me how highly the present clergy carry themselves every where, so as that they are hated and laughed at by every body; among other things, for their excommunications, which they send upon the least occasion almost that can be. And I am convinced in my judgment, not only from his discourse, but my thoughts in general, that the present clergy will never heartily go down with the generality of the commons of England; they have been so used to liberty and freedom, and they are so acquainted with the pride and debauchery of the present clergy. He tells me that the King by name, with all his dignities, is prayed for by them that they call Fanatiques, as heartily and powerfully as in any of the other churches that are thought better: and that, let the King think what he will, it is them that must helpe him in the day of warr. For as they are the most, so generally they are the most substantiall sort of people, and the soberest; and did desire me to observe it to my Lord Sandwich, among other things, that of all the old army now you cannot see a man begging about the street; but what? You shall have this captain turned a shoemaker, the lieutenant, a baker; this a brewer; that a haberdasher; this common soldier, a porter; and every man in his apron and frock, &c., as if they never had done anything else: whereas the others go with their belts and swords, swearing and cursing, and stealing; running into people's houses, by force oftentimes, to carry away something; and this is the difference between the temper of one and the other; and concludes (and I think with some reason) that the spirits of the old parliament soldiers are so quiett and contented with God's providences, that the King is safer from any evil meant him by them one thousand times more than from his own discontented Cavalier.

10TH. The Queene, I hear, is now very well again, and that she hath bespoke herself a new gowne.

18TH. After dinner came Sir W. Batten, and I left him to pay off another ship, and I walked home again reading of a little book of new poems of Cowley's, given me by his brother. Abraham do lie, it seems, very sicke still, but like to recover. This morning I sent Will with my great letter of reproof to my Lord Sandwich, who did give it into his owne hand. I pray God give a blessing to it, but confess I am afeard what the consequence may be to me of good or bad, which is according to the ingenuity that he do receive it with. However, I am satisfied that it will do him good, and that he needs it.

22ND (LORD'S DAY). Up pretty early, and having last night bespoke a coach, which failed me this morning, I walked as far as the Temple, and there took coach, and to my Lord's lodgings, whom I found ready to go to chappell; but I coming, he begun, with a very serious countenance, to tell me that he had received my late letter, wherein first he took notice of my care of him and his honour, and did give me thanks for that part of it where I say that from my heart I believe the contrary of what I do there relate to be the discourse of others; but since I intended it not a reproach, but matter of information, and for him to make a judgment of it for his practice, it was necessary for me to tell him the persons of whom I have gathered the several particulars which I there insist on. I would have made excuses in it; but, seeing him so earnest in it, I found myself forced to it, and so did tell him Mr. Pierce, the chyrurgeon, in that of his Lordship's living being discoursed of at Court; a mayd servant that I kept, that lived at Chelsy school; and also Mr. Pickering, about the report touching the young woman; and also Mr. Hunt, in Axe Yard, near whom she lodged. I told him the whole city do discourse concerning his neglect of business; and so I many times asserting my dutifull intention in all this, and he owning his accepting of it as such. I find him, though he cannot but owne his opinion of my good intentions, and so he did again and again profess it, that he is troubled in his mind at it; and I confess, I think I may have done myself an injury for his good, which, were it to do again, and that I believed he would take it no better, I think I should sit quietly without taking any notice of it, for I doubt there is no medium between his taking it very well or very ill. I could not forbear weeping before him at the latter end, which, since, I am ashamed of, though I cannot see what he can take it to proceed from but my tenderness and good will to him.

26TH. The plague, it seems, grows more and more at Amsterdam; and we are going upon making of all ships coming from thence and Hambrough, or any other infected places, to perform their Quarantine.

28TH. I have been told two or three times, but to-day for certain I am told how in Holland publickly they have pictured our King with reproach. One way is with his pockets turned the wrong side outward, hanging out empty; another with two courtiers picking of his pockets; and a third, leading two ladies, while others abuse him; which amounts to great contempt.

DECEMBER 10TH. To St. Paul's Church Yard, to my bookseller's, and having gained this day in the office by my stationer's bill to the King about 40s. or £3, I did here sit two or three hours calling for twenty books to lay this money out upon, and found myself at a great losse where to choose, and do see how my nature would gladly return to laying out money in this trade. I could not tell whether to lay out my money for books of pleasure, as plays, which my nature was most earnest in; but at last, after seeing Chaucer, Dugdale's History of Paul's, Stow's London, Gesner, History of Trent, besides Shakespeare, Jonson, and Beaumont's plays, I at last chose Dr. Fuller's Worthys, the *Cabbala* or Collections of Letters of State, and a little book, *Delices de Hollande,* with another little book or two, all of good use or serious pleasure: and Hudibras, both parts, the book now in greatest fashion for drollery, though I cannot, I confess, see enough where the wit lies.

12TH. To the Exchange, where I had sent Luellin word I would come to him, and thence brought him home to dinner with me. Then he began to tell me that Mr. Deering had been with him to desire to speak to me that if I would get him off with these goods upon his hands, he would give me 50 pieces, and further that if I would stand his friend to helpe him to the benefit of his patent as the King's merchant, he could spare me £200 per annum out of his profits. I was glad to hear both of these, but answered him no further than that as I would not by any thing be bribed to be unjust in my dealings, so I was not so squeamish as not to take people's acknowledgment where I had the good fortune by my pains to do them good and just offices, and so I would not come to be at any agreement with him, but I would labour to do him this service and to except his consideration thereof afterwards as he thought fit. So I expect to hear more of it. I did make very much of Luellin in hopes to have some good by this business. I spent a little time walking in the garden, and in the mean time, while I was walking Mrs. Pen's pretty maid came by my side, and went into the office, but finding nobody there I went in to her, being glad of the occasion. She told me as she was going out again that there was nobody there, and that she came for a sheet of paper. So I told her I would supply her, and left her in the office and went into my office and opened my garden door, thinking to have got her in, and there to have caressed her, and seeming looking for paper, I told her this way was as near a way for her, but she told me she had left the door open and so did not come to me. So I carried her some paper and kissed her, leading her by the hand to the garden door and there let her go. But, Lord! to see how much I was put out of order by this surprisal, and how much I could have subjected my mind to have treated and been found with this wench, and how afterwards I was troubled to think what if she should tell this and whether I had spoke or done any thing that might be unfit for her to tell. But I think there was nothing more passed than just what I here write.

15TH. So to White Hall, and there by order found some of the Commissioners of Tangier met, and my Lord Sandwich among the rest, to whom I bowed, but he shewed me very little if any countenance at all, which troubles me mightily. Home and to my office, and there very late with Sir W. Warren upon very serious discourse, telling him how matters passed to-day, and in the close he and I did fall to talk very openly of the business of this office. He did particularly run over every one of the officers and commanders, and shewed me how I had reason to mistrust every one of them, either for their falseness or their overgreat power, being too high to fasten a real friendship in, and did give me a common but a most excellent [saying] to observe in all my life. He did give it in rhyme, but the sense was this, that a man should treat every friend in his discourse and opening his mind to him as of one that may hereafter be his foe.

21ST. I to my Lord's, but he not being within, took coach, and, being directed by sight of bills upon the walls, I did go to Shoe Lane to see a cocke-fighting at a new pit there, a sport I was never at in my life; but, Lord! to see the strange variety of people, from Parliament-man (by name Wildes, that was Deputy Governor of the Tower when Robinson was Lord Mayor) to the poorest 'prentices, bakers, brewers, butchers, draymen, and what not; and all these fellows one with another in swearing, cursing, and betting. I soon had enough of it, and yet I would not but have seen it once, it being strange to observe the nature of these poor creatures, how they will fight till they drop down dead upon the table, and strike after they are ready to give up the ghost, not offering to run away when they are weary or wounded past doing further, whereas where a dunghill brood comes he will, after a sharp stroke that pricks him, run off the stage, and then they wring off his neck without more ado, whereas the other they preserve, though their eyes be both out, for breed only of a true cock of the game. Sometimes a cock that has had ten to one against him will by chance give an unlucky blow, will strike the other starke dead in a moment, that he never stirs more; but the common rule is, that though a cock neither runs nor dies, yet if any man will bet £10 to a crowne, and nobody take the bet, the game is given over, and not sooner. One thing more it is strange to see how people of this poor rank, that look as if they had not bread to put in their mouths, shall bet three or four pounds at one bet, and lose it, and yet bet as much the next battle (so they call every match of two cocks), so that one of them will lose £10 or £20 at a meeting. Thence, having enough of it, by coach to my Lord Sandwich's.

25TH (CHRISTMAS DAY). Lay long talking pleasantly with my wife, but among other things she begun, I know not whether by design or chance, to enquire what she should do if I should by any accident die, to which I did give her some slight answer; but shall make good use of it to bring myself to some settlement for her sake, by making a will as soon as I can.

28TH. Up and by coach to my Lord's lodgings, but he was gone abroad, so I lost my pains, but, however, walking through White Hall I heard the King was gone to play at Tennis, so I down to the new Tennis Court, and saw him and Sir Arthur Slingsby play against my Lord of Suffolke and my Lord Chesterfield. The King beat three, and lost two sets, they all, and he particularly playing well, I thought. Thence went and spoke with the Duke of Albemarle about his wound at Newhall, but I find him a heavy dull man, methinks, by his answers to me.

29TH. After dinner Luellin took me up to my chamber to give me £50 for the service I did him, though not so great as he expected and I intended. But I told him that I would not sell my liberty to any man. I did also tell him that neither this nor any thing should make me to do any thing that should not be for the King's services besides.

1664

JANUARY 2ND. After dinner I took my wife out, for I do find that I am not able to conquer myself as to going to plays till I come to some new vowe concerning it, and that I am now come, that is to say, that I will not see above one in a month at any of the publique theatres till the sum of 50s. be spent, and then none before New Year's Day next, unless that I do become worth £1,000 sooner than then, and then am free to come to some other terms.

6TH. This morning I began a practice which I find by the ease I do it with that I shall continue, it saving me money and time; that is, to trimme myself with a razer: which pleases me mightily.

9TH. I home to dinner, and by discourse with my wife thought upon inviting my Lord Sandwich to a dinner shortly. It will cost me at least ten or twelve pounds; but, however, some arguments of prudence I have, which however I shall think again upon before I proceed to that expence.

11TH. This morning I stood by the King arguing with a pretty Quaker woman, that delivered to him a desire of hers in writing. The King showed her Sir J. Minnes, as a man the fittest for her quaking religion, saying that his beard was the stiffest thing about him, and again merrily said, looking upon the length of her paper, that if all she desired was of that length she might lose her desires; she modestly saying nothing till he begun seriously to discourse with her, arguing the truth of his spirit against hers; she replying still with these words: "O King!" and thou'd him all along.

20TH. Then my Lord Sandwich came upon me, to speak with whom my business of coming again to-night to this ende of the town chiefly was, in order to the seeing in what manner he received me, in order to my inviting him to dinner to my house, but as well in the morning as now, though I did wait upon him home and there offered occasion to talk with him, yet he treated me, though with respect, yet as a stranger, without any of the intimacy or friendship which he used to do, and which I fear he will never, through his consciousness of his faults, ever do again.

21ST. Up, and after sending my wife to my aunt Wight's to get a place to see Turner hanged, I to the office, where we sat all the morning, and at noon going to the 'Change; and seeing people flock in the City, I enquired, and found that Turner was not yet hanged. And so I went among them to Leadenhall Street, at the end of Lyme Street, near where the robbery was done; and to St. Mary Axe, where he lived. And there I got for a shilling to stand upon the wheel of a cart, in great pain, above an houre before the execution was done; he delaying the time by long discourses and prayers one after another, in hopes of a reprieve; but none came, and at last was flung off the ladder in his cloake. A comely-looked man he was, and kept his countenance to the end: I was sorry to see him. It was believed there were at least 12 or 14,000 people in the street. After that I had good discourse with a pretty young merchant with mighty content.

27TH. He [Sir William Petty] shewed finely whence it happens that good writers are not admired by the present age; because there are but few in any age that do mind anything that is abstruse and curious; and so longer before any body do put the true praise, and set it on foot in the world, the generality of mankind pleasing themselves in the easy delights of the world, as eating, drinking, dancing, hunting, fencing, which we see the meanest men do the best, those that profess it. A gentleman never dances so well as the dancing master, and an ordinary fiddler makes better musique for a shilling than a gentleman will do after spending forty, and so in all the delights of the world almost.

30TH. This evening, being in a humour of making all things even and clear in the world, I tore some old papers; among others, a romance which (under the title of "Love a Cheate") I begun ten years ago at Cambridge; and at this time reading it over to-night I liked it very well, and wondered a little at myself at my vein at that time when I wrote it, doubting that I cannot do so well now if I would try.

FEBRUARY 1ST. I took Strutt by coach with me to White Hall. Here I hear how two men last night, justling for the wall about the New Exchange, did kill one another, each thrusting the other through; one of them of the King's Chappell, one Cave, and the other a retayner of my Lord Generall Middleton's. Thence to White Hall; where, in the Duke's chamber, the King came and stayed an hour or two laughing at Sir W. Petty, who was there about his boat; and at Gresham College in general. Gresham College he mightily laughed at, for spending time only in weighing of ayre, and doing nothing else since they sat. Here I met with Mr. Pierce, who tells me of several passages at Court, among others how the King, coming the other day to his Theatre to see "The Indian Queene" (which he commends for a very fine thing), my Lady Castlemaine was in the next box before he came; and leaning over other ladies awhile to whisper to the King, she rose out of the box and went into the King's, and set herself on the King's right hand between the King and the Duke of York; which, he swears, put the King himself, as well as every body else, out of countenance; and believes that she did it only to show the world that she is not out of favour yet, as was believed.

2ND. Then to the 'Change again, and thence off to the Sun Taverne with Sir W. Warren, and with him discoursed long, and had good advice, and hints from him, and among other things he did give me a payre of gloves for my wife wrapt up in paper, which I would not open, feeling it hard; but did tell him that my wife should thank him, and so went on in discourse. When I came home, Lord! in what pain I was to get my wife out of the room without bidding her go, that I might see what these gloves were; and, by and by, she being gone, it proves a payre of white gloves for her and forty pieces in gold, which did so cheer my heart, that I could eat no victuals almost for dinner for joy to think how God do bless us every day more and more.

3RD. This night late coming in my coach, coming up Ludgate Hill, I saw two gallants and their footmen taking a pretty wench, which I have much eyed, lately set up shop upon the hill, a seller of riband and gloves. They seek to drag her by some force, but the wench went, and I believe had her turn served, but, God forgive me! what thoughts and wishes I had of being in their place. In Covent Garden to-night, going to fetch home my wife, I stopped at the great Coffee-house there, where I never was before; where Dryden the poet (I knew at Cambridge), and all the wits of the town, and Harris the player, and Mr. Hoole of our College.

9TH. Great talke of the Dutch proclaiming themselves in India, Lords of the Southern Seas, and deny traffick there to all ships but their owne, upon pain of confiscation; which makes our merchants mad.

10TH. Up, and by coach to my Lord Sandwich, to his new house, a fine house, but deadly dear, in Lincoln's Inne Fields, where I found and spoke a little to him. He is high and strange still, but did ask me how my wife did, and at parting remembered him to his cozen, which I thought was pretty well, being willing to flatter myself that in time he will be well again.

15TH. This afternoon Sir Thomas Chamberlin came to the office to me, and showed me several letters from the East Indys, showing the height that the Dutch are come to there, showing scorn to all the English, even in our only Factory there of Surat, beating several men, and hanging the English Standard St. George under the Dutch flagg in scorn; saying, that whatever their masters do or say at home, they will do what they list, and will be masters of all the world there; and have so proclaimed themselves Soveraigne of all the South Seas; which certainly our King cannot endure, if the Parliament will give him money.

22ND. This evening came Mr. Alsopp the King's brewer, with whom I spent an houre talking and bewailing the posture of things at present; the King led away by half-a-dozen men, that none of his serious servants and friends can come at him. He loves not the Queen at all, but is rather sullen to her; and she, by all reports, incapable of children. He is so fond of the Duke of Monmouth, that every body admires it; and he says the Duke hath said, that he would be the death of any man that says the King was not married to his mother: though Alsopp says, it is well known that she was a common whore before the King lay with her. But it seems, he says, that the King is mighty kind to these his bastard children; and at this day will go at midnight to my Lady Castlemaine's nurses, and take the child and dance it in his arms.

26TH. So rode home and there found my uncle Wight. 'Tis an odd thing as my wife tells me his caressing her and coming on purpose to give her visits, but I do not trouble myself for him at all, but hope the best and very good effects of it.

27TH. Up, but weary, and to the office, where we sat all morning. Before I went to the office there came Bagwell's wife to me to speak for her husband. I liked the woman very well and stroked her under the chin, but could not find in my heart to offer anything uncivil to her, she being, I believe, a very modest woman.

28TH (LORD'S DAY). Walked in the garden by brave moonshine with my wife about two hours, till past 8 o'clock, then to supper, and after prayers to bed.

MARCH 2ND. I by coach endeavoured to have waited on my Lord Sandwich, but meeting him in Chancery Lane going towards the City I stopped and so fairly walked home again, calling at St. Paul's Churchyarde and there looked upon a pretty burlesque poem, called "Scarronides, or Virgile Travesty;" extraordinary good. At home to the office till dinner, and after dinner my wife cut my hair short, which is growne pretty long again, and then to the office, and there till 9 at night doing business.

8TH. Up with some little discontent with my wife upon her saying that she had got and used some puppy-dog water, being put upon it by a desire of my aunt Wight to get some for her, who hath a mind, unknown to her husband, to get some for her ugly face.

14TH. So to the 'Change, and thence home, where my wife and I fell out about my not being willing to have her have her gowne laced, but would lay out the same money and more on a plain new one. At this she flounced away in a manner I never saw her, nor which I could ever endure. So I away to the office, though she had dressed herself to go see my Lady Sandwich. She by and by in a rage follows me, and coming to me tells me in a spiteful manner like a vixen and with a look full of rancour that she would go buy a new one and lace it and make me pay for it, and then let me burn it if I would after she had done it, and so went away in a fury.

15TH. After dinner we took coach and to my brother's, where contrary to my expectation he continues as bad or worse, talking idle, and now not at all knowing any of us as before. Here we staid a great while, I going up and down the house looking after things. About 8 o'clock my brother began to fetch his spittle with more pain, and to speak as much but not so distinctly, till at last the phlegm getting the mastery of him, and he beginning as we thought to rattle, I had no mind to see him die, as we thought he presently would, and so withdrew and led Mrs. Turner home, but before I came back, which was in half a quarter of an hour, my brother was dead. I went up and found the nurse holding his eyes shut, and he poor wretch lying with his chops fallen, a most sad sight, and that which put me into a present very great transport of grief and cries, and indeed it was a most sad sight to see the poor wretch lie now still and dead, and pale like a stone. I staid till he was almost cold, while Mrs. Croxton, Holden, and the rest did strip and lay him out, they observing his corpse, as they told me afterwards, to be as clear as any they ever saw, and so this was the end of my poor brother, continuing talking idle and his lips working even to his last that his phlegm hindered his breathing, and at last his breath broke out bringing a flood of phlegm and stuff out with it, and so he died. This evening he talked among other talk a great deal of French very plain and good, as, among others: *quand un homme boit quand il n'a poynt d'inclination a boire il ne luy fait jamais de bien.* I once begun to tell him something of his condition, and asked him whither he thought he should go. He in distracted manner answered me—"Why, whither should I go? there are but two ways: If I go to the bad way I must give God thanks for it, and if I go the other way I must give God more thanks for it; and I hope I have not been so undutifull and unthankfull in my life but I hope I shall go that way." This was all the sense, good or bad, that I could get of him this day. I left my wife to see him laid out, and I by coach home carrying my brother's papers, all I could find, with me, and having wrote a letter to my father telling him what hath been said I returned by coach, it being very late, and dark, to my brother's, but all being gone, the corpse laid out, and my wife at Mrs. Turner's, I thither, and there after an hour's talk, we up to bed, my wife and I in the little blue chamber, and I lay close to my wife, being full of disorder and grief for my brother that I could not sleep nor wake with satisfaction, at last I slept till 5 or 6 o'clock.

18TH. Up betimes, and walked to my brother's, where a great while putting things in order against anon; then to Madam Turner's and eat a breakfast there, and so to Wotton, my shoemaker, and there got a pair of shoes blacked on the soles against anon for me; so to my brother's and to church, and with the grave-maker chose a place for my brother to lie in, just under my mother's pew. But to see how a man's tombes are at the mercy of such a fellow, that for sixpence he would (as his owne words were), "I will justle them together but I will make room for him;" speaking of the fulness of the middle isle, where he was to lie; and that he would, for my father's sake, do my brother that is dead all the civility he can; which was to disturb other corps that are not quite rotten, to make room for him; and methought his manner of speaking it was very remarkable; as of a thing that now was in his power to do a man a courtesy or not; and so to my brother's again; whither, though invited, as the custom is, at one or two o'clock, they came not till four or five. But at last one after another they come, many more than I bid: and my reckoning that I bid was one hundred and twenty; but I believe there was nearer one hundred and fifty. Their service was six biscuits a-piece, and what they pleased of burnt claret. My cosen Joyce Norton kept the wine and cakes above; and did give out to them that served, who had white gloves given them. But above all, I am beholden to Mrs. Holden, who was most kind, and did take mighty pains not only in getting the house and every thing else ready, but this day in going up and down to see the house filled and served, in order to mine, and their great content, I think; the men sitting by themselves in some rooms, and women by themselves in others, very close, but yet room enough. Anon to church, walking out into the streete to the Conduit, and so across the streete, and had a very good company along with the corps. And being come to the grave as above, Dr. Pierson, the minister of the parish, did read the service for buriall: and so I saw my poor brother laid into the grave; and so all broke up; and I and my wife and Madam Turner and her family to my brother's, and by and by fell to a barrell of oysters, cake, and cheese, of Mr. Honiwood's, with him, in his chamber and below, being too merry for so late a sad work. But, Lord! to see how the world makes nothing of the memory of a man, an houre after he is dead! And, indeed, I must blame myself; for though at the sight of him dead and dying, I had real grief for a while, while he was in my sight; yet presently after, and ever since, I have had very little grief indeed for him. By and by, it beginning to be late, I put things in some order in the house, and so took my wife and Besse (who hath done me very good service in cleaning and getting ready every thing and serving the wine and things to-day, and is indeed a most excellent good-natured and faithful wench, and I love her mightily), by coach home, and so after being at the office to set down the day's work home to supper and to bed.

25TH (LADY-DAY). Up and by water to White Hall, and there to chappell; where it was most infinite full to hear Dr. Critton. It was the worst sermon I ever heard him make, I must confess; and yet it was good, and in two places very bitter, advising the King to do as the Emperor Severus did, to hang up a Presbyter John (a short coat and a long gowne interchangeably) in all the Courts of England. He told the King and the ladies plainly, speaking of death and of the skulls and bones of dead men and women, how there is no difference; that nobody could tell that of the great Marius or Alexander from a pyoneer; nor, for all the pains the ladies take with their faces, he that should look in a charnell-house could not distinguish which was Cleopatra's, or fair Rosamond's, or Jane Shoare's. Thence by water home.

26TH. This morning in discourse Sir W. Rider [said] that he hath kept a journall of his life for almost these forty years, even to this day and still do, which pleases me mightily. So home, and there found Madam Turner, her daughter The., Joyce Norton, my father and Mr. Honywood, and by and by come my uncle Wight and aunt. This being my solemn feast for my cutting of the stone, it being now, blessed be God! this day six years since the time; and I bless God I do in all respects find myself free from that disease or any signs of it. After dinner Sir W. Batten sent to speak with me. . . . He tells me also, how, upon occasion of some 'prentices being put in the pillory to-day for beating of their masters, or some such like thing, in Cheapside, a company of 'prentices came and rescued them, and pulled down the pillory; and they being set up again, did the like again. So that the Lord Mayor and Major Generall Browne was fain to come and stay there, to keep the peace.

APRIL 1ST. This day Mrs. Turner did lend me, as a rarity, a manuscript of one Mr. Wells, writ long ago, teaching the method of building a ship, which pleases me mightily. I was at it to-night, but durst not stay long at it, I being come to have a great pain and water in my eyes after candlelight.

2ND. At noon to the Coffee-house, where excellent discourse with Sir W. Petty, who proposed it as a thing that is truly questionable, whether there really be any difference between waking and dreaming, that it is hard not only to tell how we know when we do a thing really or in a dream, but also to know what the difference [is] between one and the other.

5TH. Anon comes the King [to the House of Commons] and passed the Bill for repealing the Triennial Act, and another about Writs of Errour. I crowded in and heard the King's speech to them; but he speaks the worst that ever I heard man in my life; worse than if he read it all, and he had it in writing in his hand. Home myself, where I find my wife dressed as if she had been abroad, but I think she was not, but she answering me some way that I did not like I pulled her by the nose, indeed to offend her, though afterwards to appease her I denied it, but only it was done in haste. The poor wretch took it mighty ill, and I believe besides wringing her nose she did feel pain, and so cried a great while, but by and by I made her friends, and so after supper to my office a while, and then home to bed.

12TH. Thence a little to the 'Change, and thence to my uncle Wight's, where dined my father, poor melancholy man, that used to be as full of life as anybody. So home, and find my father come to lie at our house, and so supped, and saw him, poor man, to bed, my heart never being fuller of love to him, nor admiration of his prudence and pains heretofore in the world than now.

13TH. Though late, past 12, before we went to bed, yet I heard my poor father up, and so I rang up my people, and I rose and got something to eat and drink for him, and so abroad, it being a mighty foul day, by coach, setting my father down in Fleet Streete and I to St. James's.

18TH. To Hide Parke, where I have not been since last year; where I saw the King with his periwigg, but not altered at all; and my Lady Castlemayne in a coach by herself, in yellow satin and a pinner on; and many brave persons. And myself being in a hackney and full of people, was ashamed to be seen by the world, many of them knowing me.

22ND. Having directed it last night, I was called up this morning before four o'clock. It was full light enough to dress myself, and so by water against tide, it being a little coole, to Greenwich; and thence, only that it was somewhat foggy till the sun got to some height, walked with great pleasure to Woolwich, in my way staying several times to listen to the nightingales.

MAY 2ND. And to my office, whither comes Mr. Bland and pays me the debt he acknowledged he owed me for my service in his business of the Tangier Merchant, twenty pieces of new gold, a pleasant sight. It cheered my heart; and he being gone, I home to supper, and shewed them my wife; and she, poor wretch, would fain have kept them to look on, without any other design but a simple love to them; but I thought it not convenient, and so took them into my own hand. So, after supper, to bed.

11TH. My uncle Wight came to me to my office this afternoon to speak with me about Mr. Maes's business again, and from me went to my house to see my wife, and strange to think that my wife should by and by send for me after he was gone to tell me that he should begin discourse of her want of children and his also, and how he thought it would be best for him and her to have one between them, and he would give her £500 either in money or jewells beforehand, and make the child his heir. He commended her body, and discoursed that for all he knew the thing was lawful. She says she did give him a very warm answer, such as he did not excuse himself by saying that he said this in jest, but told her that since he saw what her mind was he would say no more to her of it, and desired her to make no words of it. It seemed he did say all this in a kind of counterfeit laugh, but by all words that passed, which I cannot now so well set down, it is plain to me that he was in good earnest, and that I fear all his kindness is but only his lust to her. What to think of it of a sudden I know not, but I think not to take notice yet of it to him till I have thought better of it.

23RD. So to Deptford, did some business there; but, Lord! to see how in both places the King's business, if ever it should come to a warr, is likely to be done, there not being a man that looks or speaks like a man that will take pains, or use any forecast to serve the King, at which I am heartily troubled.

JUNE 1ST. Thence to W. Joyce's, where by appointment I met my wife (but neither of them at home), and she and I to the King's house, and saw "The Silent Woman"; but methought not so well done or so good a play as I formerly thought it to be, or else I am now-a-days out of humour. Before the play was done, it fell such a storm of hayle, that we in the middle of the pit were fain to rise; and all the house in a disorder, and so my wife and I out and got into a little alehouse, and staid there an hour after the play was done before we could get a coach.

3RD. At the Committee for Tangier all the afternoon, where a sad consideration to see things of so great weight managed in so confused a manner as it is, so as I would not have the buying of an acre of land bought by—the Duke of York and Mr. Coventry, for aught I see, being the only two that do anything like men; Prince Rupert do nothing but swear and laugh a little, with an oathe or two, and that's all he do.

4TH. And then up to the Duke, and was with him giving him an account how matters go, and of the necessity there is of a power to presse seamen, without which we cannot really raise men for this fleete of twelve sayle, besides that it will assert the King's power of pressing, which at present is somewhat doubted, and will make the Dutch believe that we are in earnest. Mr. Coventry discoursing this noon about Sir W. Batten (what a sad fellow he is!) told me how the King told him the other day how Sir W. Batten, being in the ship with him and Prince Rupert when they expected to fight with Warwick, did walk up and down sweating with a napkin under his throat to dry up his sweat; and that Prince Rupert being a most jealous man, and particularly of Batten, do walk up and down swearing bloodily to the King, that Batten had a mind to betray them to-day, and that the napkin was a signal; "but, by God," says he, "if things go ill, the first thing I will do is to shoot him." He discoursed largely and bravely to me concerning the different sort of valours, the active and passive valour. For the latter he brought as an instance General Blake, who, in the defending of Taunton and Lime for the Parliament, did through his stubborn sort of valour defend it the most *opiniastrément* that ever any man did any thing; and yet never was the man that ever made any attaque by land or sea, but rather avoyded it on all, even fair occasions. On the other side, Prince Rupert, the boldest attaquer in the world for personal courage; and yet, in the defending of Bristol, no man ever did anything worse, he wanting the patience and seasoned head to consult and advise for defence, and to bear with the evils of a siege. The like he says is said of my Lord Tiviott, who was the boldest adventurer of his person in the world, and from a mean man in a few years was come to this greatness of command and repute only by the death of all his officers, he many times having the luck of being the only survivor of them all, by venturing upon services for the King of France that nobody else would; and yet no man upon a defence, he being all fury and no judgment in a fight. He tells me above all of the Duke of Yorke, that he is more himself and more of judgment is at hand in him in the middle of a desperate service, than at other times, as appeared in the business of Dunkirke, wherein no man ever did braver things, or was in hotter service in the close of that day, being surrounded with enemies; and then, contrary to the advice of all about him, his counsel carried himself and the rest through them safe, by advising that he might make his passage with but a dozen with him, "For," says he, "the enemy cannot move after me so fast with a great body, and with a small one we shall be enough to deal with them;" and though he is a man naturally martiall to the highest degree, yet a man that never in his life talks one word of himself or service of his owne; but only that he saw such or such a thing, and lays it down for a maxime that a Hector can have no courage. He told me also, as a great instance of some men, that the Prince of Condé's excellence is, that there not being a more furious man in the world, danger in fight never disturbs him more than just to make him civill, and to command in words of great obligation to his officers and men; but without any the least disturbance in his judgment or spirit.

13TH. Thence walked with Mr. Coventry to St. James's, and there spent by his desire the whole morning reading of some old Navy books given him of old Sir John Cooke's by the Archbishop of Canterbury that now is. We did also talk of a History of the Navy of England, how fit it were to be writ; and he did say that it hath been in his mind to propose to me the writing of the History of the late Dutch warr, which I am glad to hear, it being a thing I much desire, and sorts mightily with my genius; and, if well done, may recommend me much. So he says he will get me an order for making of searches to all records, &c., in order thereto, and I shall take great delight in doing of it.

22ND. At noon to the 'Change and Coffee-house, where great talke of the Dutch preparing of sixty sayle of ships. The plague grows mightily among them, both at sea and land.

24TH. After dinner to White Hall; and there met with Mr. Pierce, and he showed me the Queene's bed-chamber, and her closett, where she had nothing but some pretty pious pictures, and books of devotion; and her holy water at her head as she sleeps, with her clock by her bed-side, wherein a lamp burns that tells her the time of the night at any time. Thence with him to the Parke, and there met the Queene coming from Chappell, with her Mayds of Honour, all in silver-lace gowns again: which is new to me, and that which I did not think would have been brought up again. Thence he carried me to the King's closett: where such variety of pictures, and other things of value and rarity, that I was properly confounded and enjoyed no pleasure in the sight of them; which is the only time in my life that ever I was so at a loss for pleasure, in the greatest plenty of objects to give it me.

JULY 4TH. After dinner I walked homeward, still doing business by the way, and at home find my wife this day of her owne accord to have lain out 25s. upon a pair of pendantes for her eares, which did vex me and brought both me and her to very high and very foule words from her to me, such as trouble me to think she should have in her mouth, and reflecting upon our old differences, which I hate to have remembered. I vowed to breake them, or that she should go and get what she could for them again. I went with that resolution out of doors; the poor wretch afterwards in a little while did send out to change them for her money again. I followed Besse her messenger at the 'Change, and there did consult and sent her back; I would not have them changed, being satisfied that she yielded. So went home, and friends again as to that business; but the words I could not get out of my mind, and so went to bed at night discontented, and she came to bed to me, but all would not make me friends, but sleep and rise in the morning angry.

7TH. To the New Exchange to drink some creame, but missed it and so parted, and I home, calling by the way for my new bookes, viz., Sir H. Spillman's "Whole Glossary," "Scapula's Lexicon," and Shakespeare's plays, which I have got money out of my stationer's bills to pay for.

8TH. So to Paul's Churchyarde about my books, and to the binder's and directed the doing of my Chaucer, though they were not full neate enough for me, but pretty well it is; and thence to the clasp-maker's to have it clasped and bossed.

15TH. Then with Creed to St. James's, and missing Mr. Coventry, to White Hall; where, staying for him in one of the galleries, there comes out of the chayre-room Mrs. Stewart, in a most lovely form, with her hair all about her eares, having her picture taking there. There was the King and twenty more, I think, standing by all the while, and a lovely creature she in this dress seemed to be.

18TH. To Westminster to my barber's, to have my Periwigg he lately made me cleansed of its nits, which vexed me cruelly that he should put such a thing into my hands. Here meeting his mayd Jane, that has lived with them so long, I talked with her, and sending her of an errand to Dr. Clerk's, did meet her, and took her into a little alehouse in Brewers Yard, and there did sport with her, without any knowledge of her though, and a very pretty innocent girl she is. Thence home and Creed with me, and there he took occasion to owne his obligations to me, and did lay down twenty pieces in gold upon my shelf in my closett, which I did not refuse, but wish and expected should have been more. But, however, this is better than nothing, and now I am out of expectation, and shall henceforward know how to deal with him.

20TH. Dined together with a good pig, and then out by coach to White Hall, to the Committee for Fishing; but noth-ing done, it being a great day to-day there upon drawing at the

Lottery of Sir Arthur Slingsby. I got in and stood by the two Queenes and the Duchesse of Yorke, and just behind my Lady Castlemayne, whom I do heartily adore; and good sport it was to see how most that did give their ten pounds did go away with a pair of globes only for their lot, and one gentlewoman, one Mrs. Fish, with the only blanke. And one I staid to see drew a suit of hangings valued at £430, and they say are well worth the money, or near it. One other suit there is better than that; but very many lots of three and four-score pounds. I observed the King and Queenes did get but as poor lots as any else. But the wisest man I met with was Mr. Cholmley, who insured as many as would, from drawing of the one blank for 12d.; in which case there was the whole number of persons to one, which I think was three or four hundred. And so he insured about 200 for 200 shillings, so that he could not have lost if one of them had drawn it, for there was enough to pay the £10; but it happened another drew it, and so he got all the money he took. This evening being moonshine I played a little late upon my flageo-lette in the garden. But being at Westminster Hall I met with great news that Mrs. Lane is married to one Martin, one that serves Captain Marsh. She is gone abroad with him to-day, very fine. I must have a bout with her very shortly to see how she finds marriage.

21ST. This morning to the office comes Nicholas Osborne, Mr. Gauden's clerke, to desire of me what piece of plate I would choose to have a £100, or thereabouts, bestowed upon me in, he having order to lay out so much; and, out of his free-dom with me, do of himself come to make this question. I a great while urged my unwillingness to take any, not knowing how I could serve Mr. Gauden, but left it wholly to himself; so at noon I find brought home in fine leather cases a pair of the noblest flaggons that ever I saw all the days of my life; whether I shall keepe them or no I cannot tell; for it is to oblige me to him in the business of the Tangier victualling, wherein I doubt I shall not; but glad I am to see that I shall be sure to get some-thing on one side or other, have it which will: so, with a merry heart, I looked upon them, and locked them up.

23RD. From thence walked toward Westminster, and being in an idle and wanton humour, walked through Fleet Alley, and there stood a most pretty wench at one of the doors, so I took a turn or two, but what by sense of honour and conscience I would not go in, but much against my will took coach and away, and away to Westminster Hall, and there 'light of Mrs. Lane, and plotted with her to go over the water. So met at White's stairs in Chanel Row, and over to the old house at Lambeth Marsh, and there eat and drank. After an hour's stay and more back again and set her ashore there again, and I forward to Fleet Street, and called at Fleet Alley, not knowing how to command myself, and went in and there saw what formerly I have been acquainted with, the wickedness of these houses, and the forcing a man to present expense. The woman indeed is a most lovely woman, but I had no courage to meddle with her. So to my office writing letters, and then home and to bed, weary of the pleasure I have had to-day, and ashamed to think of it.

25TH. Thence back again homewards, and Sir W. Batten and I to the Coffee-house, but no news, only the plague is very hot still, and encreases among the Dutch.

26TH. Great discourse of the fray yesterday in Moorefields, how the butchers at first did beat the weavers (between whom there hath been ever an old competition for mastery), but at last the weavers rallied and beat them. At first the butchers knocked down all for weavers that had green or blue aprons, till they were fain to pull them off and put them in their breeches. At last the butchers were fain to pull off their sleeves, that they might not be known, and were soundly beaten out of the field, and some deeply wounded and bruised; till at last the weavers went out tryumphing, calling £100 for a butcher. I to Mr. Reeves to see a microscope, he having been with me to-day morning, and there chose one which I will have.

27TH. This afternoon came my great store of Coles in, being 10 Chaldron, so that I may see how long they will last me.

28TH. My present posture is thus: my wife in the country and my mayde Besse with her and all quiett there. I am endeavouring to find a woman for her to my mind, and above all one that understands musique, especially singing. I am the willinger to keepe one because I am in good hopes to get 2 or £300 per annum extraordinary by the business of the victualling of Tangier.

AUGUST 7TH (LORD'S DAY). So I walked homeward and met with Mr. Spong, and he with me as far as the Old Exchange talking of many ingenuous things, musique, and at last of glasses, and I find him still the same ingenuous man that ever he was. While we were talking came by several poor creatures carried by, by constables, for being at a conventicle. They go like lambs, without any resistance. I would to God they would either conform, or be more wise, and not be catched!

20TH. I forth to bespeak a case to be made to keep my stone in, which will cost me 25s.

SEPTEMBER 3RD. I have had a bad night's rest to-night, not sleeping well, as my wife observed, and once or twice she did wake me, and I thought myself to be mightily bit with fleas, and in the morning she chid her mayds for not looking the fleas a-days. But, when I rose, I found that it is only the change of the weather from hot to cold, which, as I was two winters ago, do stop my pores, and so my blood tingles and itches all day all over my body, and so continued to-day all the day long just as I was then.

5TH. Up and to St. James's, and there did our business with the Duke; where all our discourse of warr in the highest measure. Prince Rupert was with us; who is fitting himself to go to sea in the Heneretta. And afterwards in White Hall I met him and Mr. Gray, and he spoke to me, and in other discourse, says he, "God damn me, I can answer but for one ship, and in that I will do my part; for it is not in that as in an army, where a man can command every thing."

6TH. So home, having called upon Doll, our pretty Change woman, for a pair of gloves trimmed with yellow ribbon, to [match the] petticoate my wife bought yesterday, which cost me 20s.; but she is so pretty, that, God forgive me! I could not think it too much—which is a strange slavery that I stand in to beauty, that I value nothing near it.

9TH. So back again home, and there my wife and Mercer and Tom and I sat till eleven at night, singing and fiddling, and a great joy it is to see me master of so much pleasure in my house, that it is and will be still. I hope, a constant pleasure to me to be at home. The girle plays pretty well upon the harpsicon, but only ordinary tunes, but hath a good hand; sings a little, but hath a good voyce and eare. My boy, a brave boy, sings finely, and is the most pleasant boy at present, while his ignorant boy's tricks last, that ever I saw. So to supper, and with great pleasure to bed.

10TH. Up and to the office, where we sate all the morning, and I much troubled to think what the end of our great sluggishness will be, for we do nothing in this office like people able to carry on a warr. We must be put out, or other people put in.

12TH. By coach to St. James's, and there did our business as usual with the Duke; and saw him with great pleasure play with his little girle, like an ordinary private father of a child. Thence walked to Jervas's, where I took Jane in the shop alone, and there heard of her, her master and mistress were going out. So I went away and came again half an hour after. In the meantime went to the Abbey, and there went in to see the tombs with great pleasure. Back again to Jane, and there upstairs and drank with her, and staid two hours with her kissing her, but nothing more.

24TH. We were told to-day of a Dutch ship of 3 or 400 tons, where all the men were dead of the plague, and the ship cast ashore at Gottenburgh.

OCTOBER 3RD. I to my barber's, and there only saw Jane and stroked her under the chin, and away to the Exchange, and there long about several businesses, hoping to get money by them, and thence home to dinner and there found Hawly. But meeting Bagwell's wife at the office before I went home I took her into the office and there kissed her only. She rebuked me for doing it, saying that did I do so much to many bodies else it would be a stain to me. But I do not see but she takes it well enough, though in the main I believe she is very honest. So after some kind discourse we parted, and I home to dinner, and after dinner down to Deptford.

4TH. Up and to the office, where we sat all the morning. Thence after dinner to a play, to see "The Generall;" which is so dull and so ill-acted, that I think it is the worst I ever saw or heard in all my days. I happened to sit near to Sir Charles Sidly; who I find a very witty man, and he did at every line take notice of the dullness of the poet and badness of the action, that most pertinently; which I was mightily taken with. To-morrow they told us should be acted, or the day after, a new play, called "The Parson's Dreame," acted all by women.

5TH. So to the Coffee-house, and there fell in discourse with the Secretary of the Virtuosi of Gresham College, and had very fine discourse with him. He tells me of a new invented instrument to be tried before the College anon, and I intend to see it. So to Trinity House, and there I dined among the old dull fellows, and so home and to my office a while. Thence to the Musique-meeting at the Post-office, where I was once before. And thither anon come all the Gresham College and a great deal of noble company: and the new instrument was brought called the Arched Viall, where being tuned with lute-strings, and played on with kees like an organ, a piece of parchment is always kept moving; and the strings, which by the kees are pressed down upon it, are grated in imitation of a bow, by the parchment; and so it is intended to resemble several vyalls played on with one bow, but so basely and harshly, that it will never do. But after three hours' stay it could not be fixed in tune; and so they were fain to go to some other musique of instruments.

9TH (LORD'S DAY). To our owne church, and there staid wholly privately at the great doore to gaze upon a pretty lady, and from church dogged her home, whither she went to a house near Tower hill, and I think her to be one of the prettiest women I ever saw.

10TH. This day, by the blessing of God, my wife and I have been married nine years: but my head being full of business, I did not think of it to keep it in any extraordinary manner. But bless God for our long lives and loves and health together, which the same God long continue, I wish, from my very heart!

11TH. My wife tells me the sad news of my Lady Castlemayne's being now become so decayed, that one would not know her; at least far from a beauty, which I am sorry for.

25TH. It seems the City did last night very freely lend the King £100,000 without any security but the King's word, which was very noble.

NOVEMBER 3RD. At noon to the 'Change, and thence by appointment was met with Bagwell's wife, and she followed me into Moorfields, and there into a drinking house, and all alone eat and drank together. I didn't there caress her, but though I did make some offer did not receive any compliance from her in what was bad, but very modestly she denied me, which I was glad to see and shall value her the better for it, and I hope never tempt her to any evil more.

21ST. I to the 'Change and there staid long doing business, and this day for certain newes is come that Teddiman hath brought in eighteen or twenty Dutchmen, merchants, their Bourdeaux fleete, and two men of warr to Portsmouth. And I had letters this afternoon, that three are brought into the Downes and Dover; so that the warr is begun: God give a good end to it!

DECEMBER 6TH. Up, and in Sir W. Batten's coach to White Hall, but the Duke being gone forth, I to Westminster Hall, and there spent much time till towards noon to and fro with people. So by and by Mrs. Lane comes and plucks me by the cloak to speak to me, and I was fain to go to her shop, and pretending to buy some bands made her go home, and by and by followed her.

14TH. Up, and after a while at the office, I abroad in several places, among others to my bookseller's, and there spoke for several books against New Year's day, I resolving to lay out about £7 or £8, God having given me some profit extraordinary of late; and bespoke also some plate, spoons, and forks. I pray God keep me from too great expenses, though these will still be pretty good money. To-night spoke for some fruit for the country for my father against Christmas, and where should I do it, but at the pretty woman's, that used to stand at the doore in Fanchurch Streete, I having a mind to know her.

18TH (LORD'S DAY). To church, where, God forgive me! I spent most of my time in looking [on] my new Morena at the other side of the church, an acquaintance of Pegg Pen's. So home to dinner, and then to my chamber to read Ben Johnson's Cataline, a very excellent piece.

19TH. Going to bed betimes last night we waked betimes, and from our people's being forced to take the key to go out to light a candle, I was very angry and begun to find fault with my wife for not commanding her servants as she ought. Thereupon she giving me some cross answer I did strike her over her left eye such a blow as the poor wretch did cry out and was in great pain, but yet her spirit was such as to endeavour to bite and scratch me. But I coying with her made her leave crying, and sent for butter and parsley, and friends presently one with another, and I up, vexed at my heart to think what I had done, for she was forced to lay a poultice or something to her eye all day, and is black, and the people of the house observed it. But I was forced to rise, and up and with Sir J. Minnes to White Hall, and there we waited on the Duke. Thence home, and not finding Bagwell's wife as I expected, I to the 'Change and there walked up and down, and then home, and she being come I bid her go and stay at Mooregate for me, and after going up to my wife (whose eye is very bad, but she is in very good temper to me), and after dinner I to the place and walked round the fields again and again, but not finding her I to the 'Change, and there found her waiting for me and took her away, and to an alehouse, and there made I much of her, and then away thence and to another and endeavoured to caress her, but *elle me voulait pas*, which did vex me.

2OTH. Up and walked to Deptford, where after doing something at the yard I walked, without being observed, with Bagwell home to his house, and there was very kindly used, and the poor people did get a dinner for me in their fashion, of which I also eat very well. After dinner I found occasion of sending him abroad. . . . By and by he coming back again I took leave and walked home.

22ND. I to a barber's shop to have my hair cut, and there met with a copy of verses, mightily commended by some gentlemen there, of my Lord Mordaunt's, in excuse of his going to sea this late expedition, with the Duke of Yorke. But, Lord! they are but sorry things; only a Lord made them.

28TH. I abroad with Sir W. Batten to the Council Chamber, where all of us to discourse about the way of measuring ships and the freight fit to give for them by the tun, where it was strange methought to hear so poor discourses among the Lords themselves, and most of all to see how a little empty matter delivered gravely by Sir W. Pen was taken mighty well, though nothing in the earth to the purpose. But clothes, I perceive more and more every day, is a great matter.

31st. At the office all the morning, and after dinner there again, dispatched first my letters, and then to my accounts, not of the month but of the whole yeare also, and was at it till past twelve at night, it being bitter cold; but yet I was well satisfied with my worke, and, above all, to find myself, by the great blessing of God, worth £1,349, by which, as I have spent very largely, so I have laid up above £500 this yeare above what I was worth this day twelvemonth. The Lord make me for ever thankful to his holy name for it! Thence home to eat a little and to bed. Soon as ever the clock struck one, I kissed my wife in the kitchen by the fireside, wishing her a merry new yeare, observing that I believe I was the first proper wisher of it this year, for I did it as soon as ever the clock struck one.

I bless God I never have been in so good plight as to my health. But I am at a great losse to know whether it be my hare's foote, or taking every morning of a pill of turpentine, or my having left off the wearing of a gowne. This Christmas I judged it fit to look over all my papers and books; and to tear all that I found either boyish or not to be worth keeping, or fit to be seen, if it should please God to take me away suddenly. Among others, I found these two or three notes, which I thought fit to keep—

Charmes

1. FOR STENCHING OF BLOOD

Sanguis mane in te,
Sicut Christus fuit in se;
Sanguis mane in tuâ venâ
Sicut Christus in suâ pœnâ;
Sanguis mane fixus,
Sicut Christus quando fuit crucifixus.

2. A THORNE.

Jesus, that was of a Virgin born,
Was pricked both with nail and thorn;
It neither wealed nor belled, rankled, nor boned;
In the name of Jesus no more shall this.

Or, thus:—

Christ was of a Virgin born,
And he was pricked with a thorn;
And it did neither bell, nor swell;
And I trust in Jesus this never will.

3. A CRAMP.

Cramp be thou faintless,
As our Lady was sinless,
When she bare Jesus.

4. A BURNING.

There came three Angells out of the East;
The one brought fire, the other brought frost—
Out fire; in frost.
In the name of the Father, and Son, and Holy Ghost.

AMEN.

1665

JANUARY 2ND. So back again home, where thinking to be merry was vexed with my wife's having looked out a letter in Sir Philip Sidney about jealousy for me to read, which she industriously and maliciously caused me to do, and the truth is my conscience told me it was most proper for me, and therefore was touched at it, but tooke no notice of it, but read it out most frankly, but it stucke in my stomach.

4TH. Lay long, and then up and to my Lord of Oxford's, but his Lordshipp was in bed at past ten o'clock; and Lord helpe us! so rude a dirty family I never saw in my life. He sent me out word my business was not done, but should against the afternoon.

11TH. Up, and very angry with my boy for lying long a bed and forgetting his lute. To my office all the morning. This evening, by a letter from Plymouth, I hear that two of our ships, the Leopard and another, in the Straights, are lost by running aground; and that three more had like to have been so, but got off, whereof Captain Allen one: and that a Dutch fleete are gone thither; which if they should meet with our lame ships, God knows what would become of them. This I reckon most sad newes; God make us sensible of it! This night, when I come home, I was much troubled to hear my poor canary bird, that I have kept these three or four years, is dead.

15TH (LORD'S DAY). Up, and after a little at my office to prepare a fresh draught of my vows for the next yeare, I to church, where a most insipid young coxcomb preached.

18TH. Up and by and by to my bookseller's, and there did give thorough direction for the new binding of a great many of my old books, to make my whole study of the same binding, within very few.

20TH. Up and to Westminster, where having spoke with Sir Ph. Warwicke, I to Jervas', and there I find them all in great disorder about Jane, her mistress telling me secretly that she was sworn not to reveal anything, but she was undone. At last for all her oath she told me that she had made herself sure to a fellow that comes to their house that can only fiddle for his living, and did keep him company, and had plainly told her that she was sure to him never to leave him for anybody else. Now they were this day contriving to get her presently to marry one Hayes that was there, and I did seem to persuade her to it. And at last got them to suffer me to advise privately, and by that means had her company and think I shall meet her next Sunday, but I do really doubt she will be undone in marrying this fellow. But I did give her my advice, and so let her do her pleasure, so I have now and then her company.

21ST. To my office till past 12, and then home to supper and to bed, being now mighty well, and truly I cannot but impute it to my fresh hare's foote. Before I went to bed I sat up till two o'clock in my chamber reading of Mr. Hooke's *Microscopicall Observations*, the most ingenious book that ever I read in my life.

24TH. Home to dinner and then to the office, where all the afternoon and at night till very late and then home to supper and bed, having a great cold, got on Sunday last, by sitting too long with my head bare, for Mercer to comb my hair and wash my eares.

FEBRUARY 3RD. Up, and walked with my boy (whom, because of my wife's making him idle I dare not leave at home) walked first to Salsbury court, there to excuse my not being at home at dinner to Mrs. Turner. She was dressing herself by the fire in her chamber, and there took occasion to show me her leg, which indeed is the finest I ever saw, and she is not a little proud of it.

10TH. Up and abroad to Paul's Churchyard, there to see the last of my books new bound: among others, my "Court of King James," and "The Rise and Fall of the Family of the Stewarts;" and much pleased I am now with my study; it being, methinks, a beautiful sight.

18TH. My Lord Sandwich and his fleete of twenty-five ships in the Downes, returned from cruising, but could not meet with any Dutchmen.

19TH. Lay in bed, it being Lord's day, all the morning talking with my wife, sometimes pleased, sometimes displeased, and then up and to dinner. At supper hearing by accident of my mayds their letting in a rogueing Scotch woman that haunts the office, to helpe them to washe and scoure in our house, and that very lately, I fell mightily out, and made my wife, to the disturbance of the house and neighbours, to beat our little girle, and then we shut her down into the cellar, and there she lay all night. So we to bed.

20TH. At my office my wife comes and tells me that she hath hired a chamber mayde, one of the prettiest maydes that ever she saw in her life, and that she is really jealous of me for her, but hath ventured to hire her month to month, but I think she means merrily. So to supper and to bed.

28TH. Come home, I to the taking my wife's kitchen accounts at the latter end of the month, and there find 7s. wanting, which did occasion a very high falling out between us, I indeed too angrily insisting upon so poor a thing, and did give her very provoking high words, calling her beggar, and reproaching her friends, which she took very stomachfully and reproached me justly with mine, and I confess, being myself, I cannot see what she could have done less. We parted after many high words very angry, and I to my office to my month's accounts, and find myself worth £1,270, for which the Lord God be praised!

MARCH 4TH. This day was proclaimed at the 'Change the war with Holland.

6TH. Up, and with Sir J. Minnes by coach, being a most lamentable cold day as any this year, to St. James's, and there did our business with the Duke. Great preparations for his speedy return to sea. I saw him try on his buff coat and hat-piece covered with black velvet. It troubles me more to think of his venture, than of anything else in the whole warr. So home, and there find our new chamber-mayde, Mary, come, which instead of handsome, as my wife spoke and still seems to reckon, is a very ordinary wench, I think, and therein was mightly disappointed.

9TH. This night my wife had a new suit of flowered ash-coloured silke, very noble.

13TH. This day my wife begun to wear light-coloured locks, quite white almost, which, though it makes her look very pretty, yet not being natural, vexes me, that I will not have her wear them.

16TH. This afternoon Mr. Harris, the sayle-maker, sent me a noble present of two large silver candlesticks and snuffers, and a slice to keep them upon, which indeed is very handsome. At night come Mr. Andrews with £36, the further fruits of my Tangier contract, and so to bed late and weary with business, but in good content of mind, blessing God for these his benefits.

17TH. Up and to my office, and then with Sir W. Batten to St. James's, where many come to take leave, as was expected, of the Duke, but he did not go till Monday. The Duke did give us some commands, and so broke up, not taking leave of him. But the best piece of newes is, that instead of a great many troublesome Lords, the whole business is to be left with the Duke of Albemarle to act as Admirall in his stead; which is a thing that do cheer my heart. For the other would have vexed us with attendance, and never done the business.

20TH. The Duke did direct Secretary Bennet, who was there, to declare his mind to the Tangier Committee, that he approves of me for Treasurer; and with a character of me to be a man whose industry and discretion he would trust soon as any man's in England: and did the like to my Lord Sandwich. So to White Hall to the Committee of Tangier. Whereupon, Secretary Bennet did deliver the Duke's command, which was received with great content and allowance beyond expectation; the Secretary repeating also the Duke's character of me. And I could discern my Lord Fitz-Harding was well pleased with me, and signified full satisfaction, and whispered something seriously of me to the Secretary. And there I received their constitution under all their hands presently; so that I am already confirmed their Treasurer, and put into a condition of striking of tallys; and all without one harsh word or word of dislike, but quite the contrary; which is a good fortune beyond all imagination.

21ST. By coach to the Mewes, but Creed was not there. In our way the coach drove through a lane by Drury Lane, where

abundance of loose women stood at the doors, which, God forgive me, did put evil thoughts in me, but proceeded no further,
blessed be God. So home, and late at my office, then home and
there found a couple of state cups, very large, coming, I suppose, each to about £6 a piece, from Burrows the slopseller.

APRIL 1ST. All the morning very busy at the office preparing
a last half-year's account for my Lord Treasurer. Thence home,
vexed mightily to see how simply our greatest ministers do
content themselves to understand and do things, while the
King's service in the meantime lies a-bleeding.

3RD. Up and to the Duke of Albemarle and White Hall,
where much business. Thence home and to dinner, and then
with Creed, my wife, and Mercer to a play at the Duke's, of my
Lord Orrery's, called "Mustapha." All the pleasure of the play
was, the King and my Lady Castlemayne were there; and pretty
Witty Nell, at the King's house, and the younger Marshall sat
next us; which pleased me mightily.

4TH. All the morning at the office busy, at noon to the
'Change, and then went up to the 'Change to buy a pair of cot-
ton stockings, which I did at the husband's shop of the most
pretty woman there, who did also invite me to buy some linnen
of her, and I was glad of the occasion, and bespoke some bands
of her, intending to make her my seamstress, she being one of
the prettiest and most modest looked women that ever I did
see.

6TH. I also went to Jervas's, my barber, for my periwigg that
was mending there, and there do hear that Jane is quite undone,
taking the idle fellow for her husband yet not married, and lay
with him several weeks that had another wife and child, and
she is now going into Ireland.

12TH. And there I did give them a large account of the
charge of the Navy, and want of money. But strange to see how
they held up their hands crying, "What shall we do?" Says my

Lord Treasurer, "Why, what means all this, Mr. Pepys? This is true, you say; but what would you have me to do? I have given all I can for my life. Why will not people lend their money? Why will they not trust the King as well as Oliver? Why do our prizes come to nothing, that yielded so much heretofore?" And this was all we could get, and went away without other answer, which is one of the saddest things that, at such a time as this, with the greatest action on foot that ever was in England, nothing should be minded, but let things go on of themselves do as well as they can. So home, vexed, and going to my Lady Batten's, there found a great many women with her, in her chamber merry, my Lady Pen and her daughter, among others; where my Lady Pen flung me down upon the bed, and herself and others, one after another, upon me, and very merry we were, and thence I home and called my wife with my Lady Pen to supper, and very merry as I could be, being vexed as I was. So home to bed.

17TH. Up and to the Duke of Albermarle's, where he shewed me Mr. Coventry's letters, how three Dutch privateers are taken, in one whereof Everson's son is captaine. But they have killed poor Captaine Golding in The Diamond. Two of them, one of 32 and the other of 20 odd guns, did stand stoutly up against her, which hath 46, and the Yarmouth that hath 52 guns, and as many more men as they. So that they did more than we could expect, not yielding till many of their men were killed. And Everson, when he was brought before the Duke of Yorke, and was observed to be shot through the hat, answered, that he wished it had gone through his head, rather than been taken. Thence to White Hall; where the King seeing me, did come to me, and calling me by name, did discourse with me about the ships in the River; and this is the first time that ever I knew the King did know me personally; so that hereafter I must not go thither, but with expectation to be questioned, and to be ready to give good answers.

2OTH. Up, and all the morning busy at the office. At noon dined, and Mr. Povy by agreement with me (where his boldness with Mercer, poor innocent wench, did make both her and me blush, to think how he were able to debauch a poor girl if he had opportunity) at a dish or two of plain meat of his own choice.

22ND. This day I have newes from Mr. Coventry that the fleete is sailed yesterday from Harwich to the coast of Holland to see what the Dutch will do. God go along with them!

24TH. To the Cockepitt, and there walked an houre with my Lord Duke of Albemarle alone in his garden, where he expressed in great words his opinion of me; that I was the right hand of the Navy here, nobody but I taking care of any thing therein; so that he should not know what could be done without me. At which I was (from him) not a little proud.

26TH. Up very betimes, my cold continuing and my stomach sick with the buttered ale that I did drink the last night in bed, which did lie upon me till I did this morning vomitt it up.

30TH (LORD'S DAY). The fleete, with about 106 ships upon the coast of Holland, in sight of the Dutch, within the Texel. Great fears of the sicknesse here in the City, it being said that two or three houses are already shut up. God preserve us all!

MAY 5TH. After dinner to Mr. Evelyn's; he being abroad, we walked in his garden, and a lovely noble ground he hath indeed. And among other rarities, a hive of bees, so as being hived in glass, you may see the bees making their honey and combs mighty pleasantly. This day, after I had suffered my owne hayre to grow long, in order to wearing it, I find the convenience of periwiggs is so great, that I have cut off all short again, and will keep to periwiggs.

7TH (LORD'S DAY). Yesterday begun my wife to learn to limn of one Browne, which Mr. Hill helps her to, and, by her beginning upon some eyes, I think she will [do] very fine things, and I shall take great delight in it.

12TH. To the 'Change and thence to my watchmaker, where he has put it [i.e. the watch] in order, and a good and brave piece it is, and he tells me worth £14, which is a greater present than I valued it.

13TH. So home and late at my office. But, Lord! to see how much of my old folly and childishnesse hangs upon me still that I cannot forbear carrying my watch in my hand in the coach all this afternoon, and seeing what o'clock it is one hundred times, and am apt to think with myself, how could I be so long without one; though I remember since, I had one, and found it a trouble, and resolved to carry one no more about me while I lived.

14TH (LORD's DAY). Up, and with my wife to church, it being Whitsunday; my wife very fine in a new yellow bird's-eye hood, as the fashion is now.

15TH. Our victualling ships to set them agoing, and so home, and after dinner to the King's playhouse, all alone, and saw "Love's Maistresse." Some pretty things and good variety in it, but no or little fancy in it. Thence to the Swan at Herbert's, and there the company of Sarah a little while, and so away and called at the Harp and Ball, where the mayde, Mary, is very *formosa;* but, Lord! to see in what readiness I am, upon the expiring of my vowes this day, to begin to run into all my pleasures and neglect of business. Thence home, and being sleepy to bed.

18TH. Up, and with Sir J. Minnes to the Duke of Albemarle, where we did much business, and I with good content to myself; among other things we did examine Nixon and Stanesby, about their late running from two Dutchmen; for which they are committed to a vessel to carry them to the fleete to be tried. A most fowle unhandsome thing as ever was heard, for plain cowardice on Nixon's part. To the office, and dined, and then to the office again, and abroad to speak with Sir G. Carteret; but, Lord! to see how fraile a man I am, subject to my vanities, that

I can hardly forbear, though pressed with never so much business, my pursuing of pleasure, but home I got, and there very busy very late.

24TH. All the newes is of the Dutch being gone out, and of the plague growing upon us in this towne; and of remedies against it; some one thing, some another.

28TH (LORD'S DAY). By water to the Duke of Albemarle, where I hear that Nixon is condemned to be shot to death for his cowardice, by a Council of War. Thence to my Lady Sandwich's, where, to my shame, I had not been a great while before. Here, upon my telling her a story of my Lord Rochester's running away on Friday night last with Mrs. Mallett, the great beauty and fortune of the North, who had supped at White Hall with Mrs. Stewart, and was going home to her lodgings with her grandfather, my Lord Haly, by coach; and was at Charing Cross seized on by both horse and foot men, and forcibly taken from him, and put into a coach with six horses, and two women, provided to receive her, and carried away. Upon immediate pursuit, my Lord of Rochester (for whom the King had spoke to the lady often, but with no successe) was taken at Uxbridge; but the lady is not yet heard of, and the King mighty angry, and the Lord sent to the Tower. Hereupon my Lady, did confess to me, as a great secret, her being concerned in this story.

JUNE 1ST. I took coach and to Westminster Hall, where I took the fairest flower, and by coach to Tothill Fields for the ayre till it was dark. I 'light, and in with the fairest flower to eat a cake, and there did do as much as was safe with my flower, and that was enough on my part. Broke up, and away without any notice, and, after delivering the rose where it should be, I to the Temple and 'light, and come to the middle door, and there took another coach, and so home to write letters, but very few, God knows, being by my pleasure made to forget everything that is. The coachman that carried [us] cannot know me again, nor the people at the house where we were. Home to bed, certain news being come that our fleete is in sight of the Dutch ships.

2ND. Up and to the Duke of Albemarle, but missed him. Thence to the Harp and Ball and to Westminster Hall, where I visited "the flowers" in each place, and so met with Mr. Creed, and he and I to Mrs. Croft's to drink and did, but saw not her daughter Borroughes.

3RD. All this day by all people upon the River, and almost every where else hereabout were heard the guns, our two fleets for certain being engaged; which was confirmed by letters from Harwich, but nothing particular: and all our hearts full of concernment for the Duke, and I particularly for my Lord Sandwich and Mr. Coventry after his Royall Highnesse.

4TH (SUNDAY). Newes being come that our fleete is pursuing the Dutch, who, either by cunning, or by being worsted, do give ground, but nothing more for certain.

5TH. Thence home to dinner, after 'Change, where great talke of the Dutch being fled and we in pursuit of them, and that our ship Charity is lost upon our Captain's, Wilkinson, and Lieutenant's yielding, but of this there is no certainty.

7TH. This day, much against my will, I did in Drury Lane see two or three houses marked with a red cross upon the doors, and "Lord have mercy upon us" writ there; which was a sad sight to me, being the first of the kind that, to my remembrance, I ever saw. It put me into an ill conception of myself and my smell, so that I was forced to buy some roll-tobacco to smell to and chaw, which took away the apprehension.

8TH. Alone at home to dinner, my wife, mother, and Mercer dining at W. Joyce's; I giving her a caution to go round by the Half Moone to his house, because of the plague. I to my Lord Treasurer's by appointment of Sir Thomas Ingram's, to meet the Goldsmiths; where I met with the great news at last newly come, brought by Bab May from the Duke of Yorke, that we have totally routed the Dutch; that the Duke himself, the Prince, my Lord Sandwich and Mr. Coventry are all well which did put me into such joy, that I forgot almost all other thoughts. Admirall Opdam blown up, Trump killed, and said by Holmes; all the rest of their admiralls, as they say, but Everson are killed: we having taken and sunk, as is believed, about 24 of their best ships; killed and taken near 8 or 10,000 men, and lost, we think, not above 700. A great[er] victory never known in the world. They are all fled, some 43 got into the Texell, and others elsewhere, and we in pursuit of the rest. Thence, when my heart full of joy, home, and to my office a little; then to my Lady Pen's, where they are all joyed and not a little puffed up at the good successe of their father; and good service indeed is said to have been done by him. Had a great bonfire at the gate; and I with my Lady Pen's people and others to Mrs. Turner's great room, and then down into the streete. I did give the boys 4s. among them, and mighty merry. So home to bed, with my heart at great rest and quiett, saving that the consideration of the victory is too great for me presently to comprehend.

9TH. Lay long in bed, my head akeing with too much thoughts I think last night.

10TH. In the evening home to supper; and there, to my great trouble, hear that the plague is come into the City (though it hath these three or four weeks since its beginning been wholly out of the City); but where should it begin but in my good friend and neighbour's, Dr. Burnett, in Fanchurch Street: which in both points troubles me mightily. To the office to finish my letters and then home to bed, being troubled at the sicknesse, and my head filled also with other business enough, and particularly how to put my things and estate in order, in case it should please God to call me away, which God dispose of to his glory.

11TH (LORD'S DAY). Up, and expected long a new suit; but, coming not, dressed myself in my late new black silke camelott suit; and, when fully ready, comes my new one of coloured ferrandin, which my wife puts me out of love with, which vexes me, but I think it is only my not being used to wear colours which makes it look a little unusual upon me. To my chamber and there spent the morning reading. I out of doors a little, to shew, forsooth, my new suit, and back again, and in going I saw poor Dr. Burnett's door shut; but he hath, I hear, gained great goodwill among his neighbours; for he discovered it himself first, and caused himself to be shut up of his own accord: which was very handsome.

15TH. The towne grows very sickly, and people to be afeard of it; there dying this last week of the plague 112, from 43 the week before, whereof but [one] in Fanchurch-streete, and one in Broad-streete, by the Treasurer's office.

16TH. I to White Hall, where the Court is full of the Duke and his courtiers returned from sea. All fat and lusty, and ruddy by being in the sun.

17TH. It struck me very deep this afternoon going with a hackney coach from my Lord Treasurer's down Holborne, the coachman I found to drive easily and easily, at last stood still, and come down hardly able to stand, and told me that he was suddenly struck very sicke, and almost blind, he could not see; so I 'light and went into another coach, with a sad heart for the poor man and trouble for myself, lest he should have been struck with the plague, being at the end of the towne that I took him up; but God have mercy upon us all!

20TH. This day I informed myself that there died four or five at Westminster of the plague in one alley in several houses upon Sunday last, Bell Alley, over against the Palace-gate; yet people do think that the number will be fewer in the towne than it was the last weeke.

21ST. So homewards and to the Cross Keys at Cripplegate, where I find all the towne almost going out of towne, the coaches and waggons being all full of people going into the country. Here I had some of the company of the tapster's wife a while, and so home to my office, and then home to supper and to bed.

23RD. So home by hackney coach, which is become a very dangerous passage now-a-days, the sickness increasing mightily, and to bed.

26TH. The plague encreases mightily, I this day seeing a house, at a bitt-maker's over against St. Clement's Church, in the open street, shut up; which is a sad sight.

29TH. Up and by water to White Hall, where the Court full of waggons and people ready to go out of towne. To the Harp and Ball, and there drank and talked with Mary, she telling me in discourse that she lived lately at my neighbour's, Mr. Knightly, which made me forbear further discourse. This end of the towne every day grows very bad of the plague. The Mortality Bill is come to 267; which is about ninety more than the last: and of these but four in the City, which is a great blessing to us.

30TH. Thus this book of two years ends. Myself and family in good health, consisting of myself and wife, Mercer, her woman, Mary, Alice, and Susan our maids, and Tom my boy. In a sickly time of the plague growing on. Having upon my hands the troublesome care of the Treasury of Tangier, with great sums drawn upon me, and nothing to pay them with: also the business of the office great. Consideration of removing my wife to Woolwich; she lately busy in learning to paint, with great pleasure and successe. All other things well; especially a new interest I am making, by a match in hand between the eldest son of Sir G. Carteret, and my Lady Jemimah Montagu.

JULY 1ST. To Westminster, where I hear the sicknesse encreases greatly. Sad at the newes that seven or eight houses in Bazing Hall street, are shut up of the plague.

3RD. Resolving from this night forwards to close all my letters, if possible, and end all my business at the office by daylight, and I shall go near to do it and put all my affairs in the world in good order, the season growing so sickly, that it is much to be feared how a man can escape having a share with others in it, for which the good Lord God bless me, or to be fitted to receive it. So after supper to bed, and mightily troubled in my sleep all night with dreams of Jacke Cole, my old schoolfellow, lately dead, who was born at the same time with me, and we reckoned our fortunes pretty equal. God fit me for his condition!

7TH. Up, and having set my neighbour, Mr. Hudson, wine coopers, at work drawing out a tierce of wine for the sending of some of it to my wife, I abroad, only taking notice to what a condition it hath pleased God to bring me that at this time I have two tierces of Claret, two quarter casks of Canary, and a smaller vessel of Sack; a vessel of Tent, another of Malaga, and another of white wine, all in my wine cellar together; which, I believe, none of my friends of my name now alive ever had of his owne at one time.

1OTH. Up, and with great pleasure looking over a nest of puppies of Mr. Sheldon's, with which my wife is most extraordinary pleased, and one of them is promised her.

12TH. After doing what business I could in the morning, it being a solemn fast-day for the plague growing upon us, I took boat and down to Deptford, where I stood with great pleasure an houre or two by my Lady Sandwich's bedside, talking to her (she lying prettily in bed).

18TH. I was much troubled this day to hear at Westminster how the officers do bury the dead in the open Tuttle-fields, pretending want of room elsewhere; whereas the New Chappell church-yard was walled-in at the publick charge in the last plague-time, merely for want of room and now none, but such as are able to pay dear for it, can be buried there.

21ST. So home and late at my chamber, setting some papers in order; the plague growing very raging, and my apprehensions of it great. So very late to bed.

26TH. Up, and after doing a little business, down to Deptford with Sir W. Batten, and there left him, and I to Greenwich to the Park, where I hear the King and Duke are come by water this morn from Hampton Court. They asked me several questions. The King mightily pleased with his new buildings there. Down to Woolwich (and there I just saw and kissed my wife, and saw some of her painting, which is very curious; and away again to the King) and back again with him in the barge, hearing him and the Duke talk, and seeing and observing their manner of discourse. And God forgive me! though I admire them with all the duty possible, yet the more a man considers and observes them, the less he finds of difference between them and other men, though (blessed be God!) they are both princes of great nobleness and spirits. Duke of Monmouth is the most skittish leaping gallant that ever I saw, always in action, vaulting or leaping, or clambering. The sicknesse is got into our parish this week, and is got, indeed, every where; so that I begin to think of setting things in order, which I pray God enable me to put both as to soul and body.

28TH. Up betimes, and down to Deptford, where, after a little discourse with Sir G. Carteret. Set out with my Lady all alone with her with six horses to Dagenhams; going by water to the Ferry. And a pleasant going, and good discourse; and when there, very merry, and the young couple now well acquainted. But, Lord! to see in what fear all the people here do live would make one mad, they are afeard of us that come to them, insomuch that I am troubled at it, and wish myself away. But some cause they have; for the chaplin, with whom but a week or two ago we were here mighty high disputing, is since fallen into a fever and dead, being gone hence to a friend's a good way off. A sober and a healthful man. These considerations make us all hasten the marriage, and resolve it upon Monday next, which is three days before we intended it. Mighty merry all of us, and in the evening with full content took coach again and home by daylight with great pleasure, and thence I down to Woolwich, where find my wife well, and after drinking and talking a little we to bed.

3OTH (LORD'S DAY). It was a sad noise to hear our bell to toll and ring so often to-day, either for deaths or burials; I think five or six times. At night weary with my day's work, but full of joy at my having done it, I to bed, being to rise betimes to-morrow to go to the wedding at Dagenhams.

31ST. Up, and very betimes by six o'clock at Deptford, and there find Sir G. Carteret, and my Lady ready to go: I being in my new coloured silk suit, and coat trimmed with gold buttons and gold broad lace round my hands, very rich and fine. By water to the Ferry, where, when we come, no coach there; and tide of ebb so far spent as the horse-boat could not get off on the other side the river to bring away the coach. So we were fain to stay there in the unlucky Isle of Doggs, in a chill place, the morning cool, and wind fresh, above two if not three hours to our great discontent. Yet being upon a pleasant errand, and seeing that it could not be helped, we did bear it very patiently. Anon the coach comes. We, fearing the canonicall hour would be past before we got thither, did with a great deal of unwill-ingness send away the license and wedding ring. So that when we come, though we drove hard with six horses, yet we found them gone from home; and going towards the church, met them coming from church, which troubled us. The young lady mighty sad, which troubled me; but yet I think it was only her gravity in a little greater degree than usual. All saluted her, but I did not till my Lady Sandwich did ask me whether I had saluted her or no. So to dinner, and very merry we were; but yet in such a sober way as never almost any wedding was in so great families; but it was much better. After dinner company divided, some to cards, others to talk. At night to supper, and so to talk; and which, methought, was the most extraordinary thing, all of us to prayers as usual, and the young bride and bridegroom too: and so after prayers, soberly to bed; only I got into the bridegroom's chamber while he undressed himself, and there was very merry, till he was called to the bride's cham-ber, and into bed they went. I kissed the bride in bed, and so the curtaines drawne with the greatest gravity that could be, and so good night. But the modesty and gravity of this business was so decent, that it was to me indeed ten times more delightfull than if it had been twenty times more merry and joviall. Whereas I feared I must have sat up all night, we did here all get good beds. Thus I ended this month with the greatest joy that ever I did any in my life, because I have spent the greatest part of it with abundance of joy and honour, and pleasant journeys, and brave entertainments, and without cost of money; and at last live to see the business ended with great content on all sides. This evening with Mr. Brisband, speaking of enchantments and spells, I telling him some of my charms; he told me this of his own knowledge, at Bourdeaux in France. The words these:

> *Voyci un Corps mort,*
> *Royde come un Baston,*
> *Froid comme Marbre,*
> *Leger come un esprit,*
> *Levons te au nom de Jesus Christ.*

He saw four little girles, very young ones, all kneeling, each of them, upon one knee; and one begun the first line, whispering in the eare of the next, and the second to the third, and the third to the fourth, and she to the first. Then the first begun the second line, and so round quite through, and putting each one finger only to a boy that lay flat upon his back on the ground, as if he was dead; at the end of the words, they did with their four fingers raise this boy as high as they could reach, and he [Mr. Brisband] being there, and wondering at it, as also being afeared to see it, for they would have had him to have bore a part in saying the words, in the roome of one of the little girles that was so young that they could hardly make her learn to repeat the words, did, for feare there might be some sleight used in it by the boy, or that the boy might be light, call the cook of the house, a very lusty fellow, as Sir G. Carteret's cook, who is very big, and they did raise him in just the same manner. This is one of the strangest things I ever heard, but he tells it me of his owne knowledge, and I do heartily believe it to be true. I enquired of him whether they were Protestant or Catholique girles; and he told me they were Protestant, which made it the more strange to me.

AUGUST 1ST. Slept, and lay long; then up and my Lord [Crew] and Sir G. Carteret being gone abroad, I first to see the bridegroom and bride, and found them both up, and he gone to dress himself. Both red in the face, and well enough pleased this morning with their night's lodging.

2ND. Up, it being a publique fast, as being the first Wednesday of the month, for the plague; I within doors all day, and upon my monthly accounts late, I did find myself really worth £1,900, for which the great God of Heaven and Earth be praised!

5TH. In the morning up, and my wife showed me several things of her doing, especially one fine woman's Persian head mighty finely done beyond what I could expect of her; and so away by water, having ordered in the yarde six or eight bargemen to be whipped, who had last night stolen some of the King's cordage from out of the yarde.

10TH. By and by to the office, where we sat all the morning; in great trouble to see the Bill this week rise so high, to above 4,000 in all, and of them above 3,000 of the plague. And an odd story of Alderman Bence's stumbling at night over a dead corps in the street, and going home and telling his wife, she at the fright, being with child, fell sicke and died of the plague. Thence to the office and, after writing letters, home, to draw over anew my will, which I had bound myself by oath to dispatch by to-morrow night; the town growing so unhealthy, that a man cannot depend upon living two days to an end.

11TH. Up, and all day long finishing and writing over my will twice, for my father and my wife, only in the morning a pleasant rencontre happened in having a young married woman brought me by her father, old Delkes, that carries pins always in his mouth, to get her husband off that he should not go to sea, *une contre pouvait avoir* done any *cose cum elle,* but I did nothing, *si ni baisser* her. After they were gone my mind run upon having them called back again, and I sent a messenger to Blackwall, but he failed. So I lost my expectation.

12TH. The people die so, that now it seems they are fain to carry the dead to be buried by day-light, the nights not sufficing to do it in. And my Lord Mayor commands people to be within at nine at night all, as they say, that the sick may have liberty to go abroad for ayre.

14TH. This night I did present my wife with the dyamond ring, awhile since given me by Mr. Dicke Vines's brother, for helping him to be a purser, valued at about £10, the first thing of that nature I did ever give her. Great fears we have that the plague will be a great Bill this weeke.

15TH. Up by 4 o'clock and walked to Greenwich, where called at Captain Cocke's and to his chamber, he being in bed, where something put my last night's dream into my head, which I think is the best that ever was dreamt, which was that I had my Lady Castlemayne in my armes and was admitted to use all the dalliance I desired with her, and then dreamt that this could not be awake, but that it was only a dream; but that since it was a dream, and that I took so much real pleasure in it, what a happy thing it would be if when we are in our graves (as Shakespeere resembles it) we could dream, and dream but such dreams as this, that then we should not need to be so fearful of death, as we are this plague time. It was dark before I could get home, and so land at Churchyard stairs, where, to my great trouble, I met a dead corps of the plague, in the narrow ally just bringing down a little pair of stairs. But I thank God I was not much disturbed at it. However, I shall beware of being late abroad again.

19TH. Our fleete is come home to our great grief with not above five weeks' dry, and six days' wet provisions: however, must out again. Having read all this news, and received commands of the Duke with great content, he giving me the words which to my great joy he hath several times said to me that his greatest reliance is upon me. And my Lord Craven also did come out to talk with me, and told me that I am in mighty esteem with the Duke, for which I bless God.

28TH. Up, and being ready I out to Mr. Colvill, the goldsmith's, having not for some days been in the streets; but now how few people I see, and those looking like people that had taken leave of the world.

30TH. Up betimes and to my business of settling my house and papers, and then abroad and met with Hadley, our clerke, who, upon my asking how the plague goes, he told me it encreases much, and much in our parish; for, says he, there died nine this week, though I have returned but six: which is a very ill practice, and makes me think it is so in other places; and therefore the plague much greater than people take it to be. Thence, walked towards Moorefields to see (God forbid my presumption!) whether I could see any dead corps going to the grave; but, as God would have it, did not. But, Lord! how every body's looks, and discourse in the street is of death, and nothing else, and few people going up and down, that the towne is like a place distressed and forsaken.

31ST. Up; and, after putting several things in order to my removal, to Woolwich; the plague having a great encrease this week, beyond all expectation of almost 2,000, making the general Bill 7,000, odd 100; and the plague above 6,000. Thus this month ends with great sadness upon the publick, through the greatness of the plague every where through the kingdom almost. Every day sadder and sadder news of its encrease. In the City died this week 7,496, and of them 6,102 of the plague. But it is feared that the true number of the dead this week is near 10,000; partly from the poor that cannot be taken notice of, through the greatness of the number, and partly from the Quakers and others that will not have any bell ring for them. Our fleete gone out to find the Dutch, we having about 100 sail in our fleete, and in them the Soveraigne one; so that it is a better fleete than the former with the Duke was.

SEPTEMBER 3RD (LORD's DAY). Up; and put on my coloured silk suit very fine, and my new periwigg, bought a good while since, but durst not wear, because the plague was in Westminster when I bought it; and it is a wonder what will be the fashion after the plague is done, as to periwiggs, for nobody will dare to buy any haire, for fear of the infection, that it had been cut off of the heads of people dead of the plague.

6TH. Busy all the morning writing letters to several, so to dinner, to London, to pack up more things thence; and there I looked into the street and saw fires burning in the street, as it is through the whole City, by the Lord Mayor's order.

15TH. Up, it being a cold misling morning. I by water to Deptford, thinking to have seen my valentine, but I could not, and so come back again, and to the office, where a little business, and thence with Captain Cocke, and there drank a cup of good drink, which I am fain to allow myself during this plague time, by advice of all, and not contrary to my oathe, my physician being dead, and chyrurgeon out of the way, whose advice I am obliged to take.

19TH. But, Lord! what a sad time it is to see no boats upon the River; and grass grows all up and down White Hall court, and nobody but poor wretches in the streets!

OCTOBER 5TH. The Bill, blessed be God! is less this week by 740 of what it was the last week. Being come to my lodging I got something to eat, having eat little all the day, and so to bed, having this night renewed my promises of observing my vowes as I used to do; for I find that, since I left them off, my mind is run a' wool-gathering and my business neglected.

7TH. Did business, though not much, at the office; because of the horrible crowd and lamentable moan of the poor seamen that lie starving in the streets for lack of money. Which do trouble and perplex me to the heart; and more at noon when we were to go through them, for then a whole hundred of them followed us; some cursing, some swearing, and some praying to us.

15TH (LORD'S DAY). Up, and while I staid for the barber, tried to compose a duo of counterpoint, and I think it will do very well, it being by Mr. Berckenshaw's rule.

16TH. Thence I walked to the Tower; but, Lord! how empty the streets are and melancholy, so many poor sick people in the streets full of sores; and so many sad stories overheard as I walk, every body talking of this dead, and that man sick, and so many in this place, and so many in that. And they tell me that, in Westminster, there is never a physician and but one apothecary left, all being dead; but that there are great hopes of a great decrease this week: God send it!

26TH. The 'Change pretty full, and the town begins to be lively again, though the streets very empty, and most shops shut.

NOVEMBER 3RD. Was called up about four o'clock and in the darke by lanthorne took boat and to the Ketch and set sayle, sleeping a little in the Cabbin till day and then up and fell to reading of Mr. Evelyn's book about Paynting, which is a very pretty book. We after this talked of some other little things and so to dinner, where my Lord infinitely kind to me, and after dinner I rose and left him with some Commanders at the table taking tobacco and I took the Bezan back with me, and with a brave gale and tide reached up that night to the Hope, taking great pleasure in learning the seaman's manner of singing when they sound the depths, and then to supper and to sleep, which I did most excellently all night, it being a horrible foule night for wind and raine.

5TH (LORD'S DAY). I to the Swan, thinking to have seen Sarah but she was at church, and so I by water to Deptford, and there made a visit to Mr. Evelyn, who, among other things, showed me most excellent painting in little; in distemper, Indian incke, water colours: graveing; and, above all, the whole secret of mezzo-tinto, and the manner of it which is very pretty, and good things done with it. He read to me very much also of his discourse, he hath been many years and now is about, about Guardenage; which will be a most noble and pleasant piece. He read me part of a play or two of his making, very good, but not as he conceits them, I think, to be. He showed me his Hortus Hyemalis; leaves laid up in a book of several plants kept dry, which preserve colour, however, and look very finely, better than any Herball. In fine, a most excellent person he is, and must be allowed a little for a little conceitedness; but he may well be so, being a man so much above others. He read me, though with too much gusto, some little poems of his own, that were not transcendant, yet one or two very pretty epigrams; among others, of a lady looking in at the grate, and being pecked at by an eagle that was there. Here comes in, in the middle of our discourse Captain Cocke, as drunk as a dogg, but could stand, and talk and laugh. He did so joy himself in a brave woman that he had been with all the afternoon, and who should it be but my Lady Robinson, but very troublesome he is with his noise and talke, and laughing, though very pleasant.

13TH. Up, and to my office, where busy all the morning, and at noon to Captain Cocke's to dinner as we had appointed in order to settle our business of accounts. So he and I to Glanville's, and there he and I sat talking and playing with Mrs. Penington, whom we found undrest in her smocke and petticoats by the fireside, and there we drank and laughed, and she willingly suffered me to put my hand in her bosom very wantonly, and keep it there long. Which methought was very strange, and I looked upon myself as a man mightily deceived in a lady, for I could not have thought she could have suffered it, by her former discourse with me; so modest she seemed and I know not what.

15TH. The plague, blessed be God! is decreased 400; making the whole this week but 1,300 and odd, for which the Lord be praised!

16TH. Up, and fitted myself for my journey down to the fleete. So I on board my Lord Bruncker; and there he and Sir Edmund Pooly carried me down into the hold of the India shipp, and there did show me the greatest wealth lie in confusion that a man can see in the world. Pepper scattered through every chink, you trod upon it; and in cloves and nutmegs, I walked above the knees; whole rooms full. And silk in bales, and boxes of copper-plate, one of which I saw opened.

17TH. Sailed all night, and got down to Quinbrough water, where all the great ships are now come, and there on board my Lord, and was soon received with great content. And there spent an houre, my Lord playing upon the gittarr, which he now commends above all musique in the world, because it is base enough for a single voice, and is so portable and manageable without much trouble.

24TH. After dinner Captain Cocke and I about some business, and then with my other barrel of oysters home to Greenwich, sent them by water to Mrs. Penington, while he and I landed, and visited Mr. Evelyn, where most excellent discourse with him; among other things he showed me a ledger of a Treasurer of the Navy, his great grandfather, just 100 years old; which I seemed mighty fond of, and he did present me with it, which I take as a great rarity; and he hopes to find me more, older than it. He also shewed us several letters of the old Lord of Leicester's, in Queen Elizabeth's time, under the very handwriting of Queen Elizabeth, and Queen Mary, Queen of Scotts; and others, very venerable names. But, Lord! how poorly, methinks, they wrote in those days, and in what plain uncut paper.

28TH. Up before day, and Cocke and I took a hackney coach appointed with four horses to take us up, and so carried us over London Bridge. But there, thinking of some business, I did 'light at the foot of the bridge, and by helpe of a candle at a stall, where some pavers were at work, I wrote a letter to Mr. Hater, and never knew so great an instance of the usefulness of carrying pen and ink and wax about one.

30TH. Great joy we have this week in the weekly Bill, it being come to 544 in all, and but 333 of the plague; so that we are encouraged to get to London soon as we can. And my father writes as great news of joy to them, that he saw Yorke's waggon go again this week to London, and was full of passengers.

DECEMBER 6TH. I spent the afternoon upon a song of Soly-man's words to Roxalana that I have set, and so with my wife walked and Mercer to Mrs. Pierce's. Here the best company for musique I ever was in, in my life, and wish I could live and die in it, both for musique and the face of Mrs. Pierce, and my wife and Knipp, who is pretty enough; but the most excellent, mad-humoured thing, and sings the noblest that ever I heard in my life, and Rolt, with her, some things together most excellently. I spent the night in extasy almost.

15TH. Away toward the office and in my way met with Sir James Bunce; and after asking what newes, he cried "Ah!" says he (I know [not] whether in earnest or jest), "this is the time for you," says he, "that were for Oliver heretofore; you are full of employment, and we poor Cavaliers sit still and can get noth-ing;" which was a pretty reproach, I thought, but answered nothing to it, for fear of making it worse.

20TH. After dinner I to the Exchange to see whether my pretty seamstress be come again or no, and I find she is, so I to her, saluted her over her counter in the open Exchange above, and mightily joyed to see her, poor pretty woman! I must con-fess I think her a great beauty.

25TH (CHRISTMAS-DAY). To church in the morning, and there saw a wedding in the church, which I have not seen many a day; and the young people so merry one with another, and strange to see what delight we married people have to these poor fools decoyed into our condition, every man and woman gazing and smiling at them. Here I saw again my beauty Lethulier.

31st. I have never lived so merrily (besides that I never got so much) as I have done this plague time, by my Lord Bruncker's and Captain Cocke's good company, and the acquaintance of Mrs. Knipp, Coleman and her husband, and Mr. Laneare, and great store of dancings we have had at my cost (which I was willing to indulge myself and wife) at my lodgings. My whole family hath been well all this while, and all my friends I know of, saving my aunt Bell, who is dead, and some children of my cozen Sarah's, of the plague. But many of such as I know very well, dead; yet, to our great joy, the town fills apace, and shops begin to be open again. Pray God continue the plague's decrease! for that keeps the Court away from the place of business, and so all goes to rack as to publick matters, they at this distance not thinking of it.

1666

JANUARY 5TH. I with my Lord Bruncker and Mrs. Williams by coach with four horses to London, to my Lord's house in Covent-Guarden. But, Lord! what staring to see a nobleman's coach come to town. And porters every where bow to us; and such begging of beggars. And a delightful thing it is to see the towne full of people again as now it is; and shops begin to open, though in many places seven or eight together, and more, all shut; but yet the towne is full, compared with what it used to be. I mean the City end; for Covent-Guarden and Westminster are yet very empty of people, no Court nor gentry being there. By and by comes my Lord, and did take me up and so to Greenwich, and after sitting with them a while at their house, home, thinking to get Mrs. Knipp, but could not, she being busy with company, but sent me a pleasant letter, writing herself "Barbary Allen." So home and to my papers for lacke of company, but by and by comes little Mrs. Tooker and sat and supped with me, and I kept her very late talking and making her comb my head.

6TH. With Lord Bruncker to Greenwich by water to a great dinner and much company; Mr. Cottle and his lady and others and I went, hoping to get Mrs. Knipp to us, having wrote a letter to her in the morning, calling myself "Dapper Dicky," in answer to her's of "Barbary Allen," but could not, and am told by the boy that carried my letter, that he found her crying; but I fear she lives a sad life with that ill-natured fellow her husband: so we had a great, but a melancholy dinner, having not her there, as I hoped. After dinner to cards, and then comes notice that my wife is come unexpectedly to me to towne. So I to her. It is only to see what I do, and why I come not home; and she is in the right that I would have a little more of Mrs. Knipp's company before I go away.

7TH (LORD'S DAY). Up, and being trimmed I was invited by Captain Cocke, so I left my wife, having a mind to some discourse with him, and dined with him. So with my wife and Mercer took boat and away home; but in the evening, before I went, comes Mrs. Knipp, just to speake with me privately, to excuse her not coming to me yesterday, complaining how like a devil her husband treats her, but will be with us in towne a weeke hence, and so I kissed her and parted.

9TH. Up, and then to the office, where we met first since the plague, which God preserve us in! After dinner Pierce and I up to my chamber, where he tells me how a great difference hath been between the Duke and Duchesse, he suspecting her to be naught with Mr. Sidney. He tells me that my Lord Sandwich is lost there at Court, though the King is particularly his friend. But people do speak every where slightly of him; which is a sad story to me, but I hope it may be better again. And that Sir G. Carteret is neglected, and hath great enemies at work against him. That matters must needs go bad, while all the town, and every boy in the streete, openly cries, "The King cannot go away till my Lady Castlemaine be ready to come along with him;" she being lately put to bed.

20TH. To the office, I sent my boy home for some papers, where, he staying longer than I would have him, I become angry, and boxed my boy when he came, that I do hurt my thumb so much, that I was not able to stir all the day after, and in great pain.

22ND. I back presently to the Crowne taverne behind the Exchange by appointment, and there met the first meeting of Gresham College since the plague. Dr. Goddard did fill us with talke, in defence of his and his fellow physicians going out of towne in the plague-time; saying that their particular patients were most gone out of towne, and they left at liberty; and a great deal more, &c.

26TH. Up, and pleased mightily with what my poor wife hath been doing these eight or ten days with her owne hands, like a drudge in fitting the new hangings of our bedchamber of blue, and putting the old red ones into my dressing-room, and so by coach to White Hall.

28TH. After dinner took coach and to Court, where we find the King, and Duke, and Lords, all in council; so we walked up and down: there being none of the ladies come, and so much the more business I hope will be done. The Council being up, out comes the King, and I kissed his hand, and he grasped me very kindly by the hand. The Duke also, I kissed his, and he mighty kind, and Sir W. Coventry. I found my Lord Sandwich there, poor man! I see with a melancholy face, and suffers his beard to grow on his upper lip more than usual. I took him a little aside to know when I should wait on him, and where: he told me, and that it would be best to meet at his lodgings, without being seen to walk together. I went down into one of the Courts, and there met the King and Duke; and the Duke called me to him. And the King come to me of himself, and told me, "Mr. Pepys," says he, "I do give you thanks for your good service all this year, and I assure you I am very sensible of it."

30TH. This is the first time I have been in this church since I left London for the plague, and it frighted me indeed to go through the church more than I thought it could have done, to see so [many] graves lie so high upon the churchyards where people have been buried of the plague.

FEBRUARY 12TH. Up, and very busy to perform an oathe in finishing my Journall this morning for 7 or 8 days past. Then comes Mr. Caesar, my boy's lute-master, whom I have not seen since the plague before, but he hath been in Westminster all this while very well; and tells me in the height of it, how bold people there were, to go in sport to one another's burials; and in spite too, ill people would breathe in the faces (out of their windows) of well people going by.

13TH. Up, and all the morning at the office. At noon to the 'Change, and thence after business dined at the Sheriffe's [Hooker], being carried by Mr. Lethulier, where to my heart's content I met with his wife, a most beautiful fat woman.

MARCH 3RD. By coach to Hales's, and there saw my wife sit; and I do like her picture mightily, and very like it will be, and a brave piece of work. But he do complain that her nose hath cost him as much work as another's face, and he hath done it finely indeed.

9TH. By water down to Deptford, where I met my Lord Bruncker and Sir W. Batten by agreement, and to measuring Mr. Castle's new third-rate ship, which is to be called the Defyance. And here I had my end in saving the King some money and getting myself some experience in knowing how they do measure ships. Anon, all home to Sir W. Batten's and there Mrs. Knipp coming we did spend the evening together very merry. She and I singing, and, God forgive me! I do still see that my nature is not to be quite conquered, but will esteem pleasure above all things, though yet in the middle of it, it has reluctances after my business, which is neglected by my following my pleasure. However musique and women I cannot but give way to, whatever my business is.

1OTH. The truth is, I do indulge myself a little the more in pleasure, knowing that this is the proper age of my life to do it; and out of my observation that most men that do thrive in the world, do forget to take pleasure during the time that they are getting their estate, but reserve that till they have got one, and then it is too late for them to enjoy it with any pleasure.

12TH. The King is come this noon to towne from Audly End, with the Duke of Yorke and a fine train of gentlemen.

14TH. To Hales's, to see my wife's picture, which I like mighty well, and there had the pleasure to see how suddenly he draws the Heavens, laying a darke ground and then lightening it when and where he will. Thence to walk all alone in the fields behind Grayes Inne, making an end of reading over my dear "Faber fortunae," of my Lord Bacon's, and thence, it growing dark, took two or three wanton turns about the idle places and lanes about Drury Lane, but to no satisfaction, but a great fear of the plague among them.

19TH. Sir J. Minnes come to us, and after dinner we walked to the King's play-house, all in dirt, they being altering of the stage to make it wider. But God knows when they will begin to act again; but my business here was to see the inside of the stage and all the tiring-rooms and machines; and, indeed, it was a sight worthy seeing. But to see their clothes, and the various sorts, and what a mixture of things there was; here a wooden-leg, there a ruff, here a hobby-horse, there a crown, would make a man split himself to see with laughing; and particularly Lacy's wardrobe, and Shotrell's. But then again, to think how fine they show on the stage by candlelight, and how poor things they are to look now too near hand is not pleasant at all. The machines are fine, and the paintings very pretty.

26TH. My Lord Bruncker and I to the Tower, to see the fa-mous engraver, to get him to grave a seale for the office. And did see some of the finest pieces of work in embossed work, that ever I did see in my life, for fineness and smallness of the images thereon, and I will carry my wife thither to shew them her. Here I also did see bars of gold melting, which was a fine sight.

29TH. All the morning hard at the office. This day, poor Jane, my old, little Jane, came to us again, to my wife's and my great content, and we hope to take mighty pleasure in her, she having all the marks and qualities of a good and loving and honest servant, she coming by force away from the other place, where she hath lived ever since she went from us, and at our desire, her late mistresse having used all the stratagems she could to keepe her.

30TH. My wife and I mighty pleased with Jane's coming to us again. Up, and away goes Alice, our cooke-mayde, a good servant, whom we loved and did well by her, and she an excellent servant, but would not bear being told of any faulte in the fewest and kindest words.

APRIL 3RD. After dinner I to my accounts hard all the afternoon till it was quite darke, and I thank God I do come to bring them very fairly to make me worth £5,000 stocke in the world, which is a great mercy to me.

6TH. I home, where all things, methinks, melancholy in the absence of my wife.

8TH. The Court full this morning of the newes of Tom Cheffin's death, the King's closett-keeper. He was well last night as ever playing at tables in the house, and not very ill this morning at six o'clock, yet dead before seven: they think, of an imposthume in his breast. But it looks fearfully among people now-a-days, the plague, as we hear, encreasing every where again. To the Chappell, but could not get in to hear well. But I had the pleasure once in my life to see an Archbishop (this was of Yorke) in a pulpit. At night had Mercer comb my head and so to supper, sing a psalm, and to bed.

13TH. Called upon an old woman in Pannier Ally to agree for ruling of some paper for me and she will do it pretty cheap. Here I found her have a very comely black mayde to her servant, which I liked very well.

15TH (EASTER DAY). Walked into the Park to the Queene's chappell, and there heard a good deal of their mass, and some of their musique, which is not so contemptible, I think, as our people would make it, it pleasing me very well; and, indeed, better than the anthem I heard afterwards at White Hall, at my coming back. I staid till the King went down to receive the Sacrament, and stood in his closett with a great many others, and there saw him receive it, which I did never see the manner of before. But I do see very little difference between the degree of the ceremonies used by our people in the administration thereof, and that in the Roman church, saving that methought our Chappell was not so fine, nor the manner of doing it so glorious, as it was in the Queene's chappell. Thence walked to Mr. Pierce's, and there dined, I alone with him and her and their children: very good company and good discourse, they being able to tell me all the businesses of the Court; the amours and the mad doings that are there; how for certain Mrs. Stewart do do everything with the King that a mistress should do; and that the King hath many bastard children that are known and owned, besides the Duke of Monmouth. With a linke, it being about 10 o'clock, walked home and after singing a Psalm or two and supped to bed.

17TH. This day I am told that Moll Davis, the pretty girle, that sang and danced so well at the Duke's house, is dead.

18TH. Coming home called at my paper ruler's and there found black Nan, which pleases me mightily, and having saluted her again and again away home and to bed. . . . In all my ridings in the coach and intervals my mind hath been full these three weeks of setting in musique "It is decreed, &c."

19TH. Anon comes home my wife from Brampton, not looked for till Saturday, which will hinder me of a little pleasure, but I am glad of her coming.

20TH. Up, and after an houre or two's talke with my poor wife, who gives me more and more content every day than other, I abroad by coach to Westminster, and there met with Mrs. Martin, and she and I over the water to Stangold, and after a walke in the fields to the King's Head, and there spent an houre or two with pleasure with her, and eat a tansy and so parted, and I to the New Exchange, there to get a list of all the modern plays which I intend to collect and to have them bound up together.

21ST. With my Lord Bruncker in his coach to Hide Parke, the first time I have been there this year. There the King was; but I was sorry to see my Lady Castlemaine, for the mourning forceing all the ladies to go in black, with their hair plain and without any spots, I find her to be a much more ordinary woman than ever I durst have thought she was; and, indeed, is not so pretty as Mrs. Stewart, whom I saw there also.

25TH. Up, and to White Hall to the Duke as usual, and did our business there. So abroad to my ruler's of my books, having, God forgive me! a mind to see Nan there, which I did, and so back again, and then out again to see Mrs. Bettons, who were looking out of the window as I come through Fenchurch Streete. So that indeed I am not, as I ought to be, able to command myself in the pleasures of my eye.

MAY 2ND. Among other stops went to my ruler's house, and there staid a great while with Nan idling away the afternoon with pleasure.

4TH. Home to the office a little and then to dinner, and had a great fray with my wife again about Browne's coming to teach her to paynt, and sitting with me at table, which I will not yield to. I do thoroughly believe she means no hurte in it; but very angry we were, and I resolved all into my having my will done, without disputing, be the reason what it will; and so I will have it. This evening, being weary of my late idle courses, and the little good I shall do the King or myself in the office, I bound myself to very strict rules till Whitsunday next.

5TH. About 11 I home, it being a fine moonshine and so my wife and Mercer come into the garden, and, my business being done, we sang till about twelve at night, with mighty pleasure to ourselves and neighbours, by their casements opening, and so home to supper and to bed.

12TH. Up to the office very betimes to draw up a letter for the Duke of Yorke relating to him the badness of our condition in this office for want of money.

13TH (LORD'S DAY). Fell by chance into St. Margett's Church, where I heard a young man play the foole upon the doctrine of purgatory. At this church I spied Betty Howlett, who indeed is mighty pretty, and struck me mightily.

14TH. I fell to examine my wife's kitchen book, and find 20s. mistake, which made me mighty angry and great difference between us, and so in the difference to bed.

29th (KING'S BIRTH-DAY AND RESTAURATION DAY). Waked with the ringing of the bells all over the towne; so up before five o'clock, and to the office.

JUNE 2ND. Up, and to the office, where certain newes is brought us of a letter come to the King this morning from the Duke of Albemarle, dated yesterday at eleven o'clock, as they were sailing to the Gunfleete, that they were in sight of the Dutch fleete, and were fitting themselves to fight them; so that they are, ere this, certainly engaged; besides, several do averr they heard the guns all yesterday in the afternoon. This put us at the Board into a tosse. Presently come orders for our sending away to the fleete a recruite of 200 soldiers. After dinner having nothing else to do till flood, I went and saw Mrs. Daniel, to whom I did not tell that the fleets were engaged, because of her husband, who is in the R. Charles. Very pleasant with her half an hour, and so away and down to Blackewall, and there saw the soldiers (who were by this time gotten most of them drunk) shipped off. But, Lord! to see how the poor fellows kissed their wives and sweethearts in that simple manner at their going off, and shouted, and let off their guns, was strange sport.

4TH. After wayting upon the Duke, Sir W. Pen (who was commanded to go to-night by water down to Harwich, to dispatch away all the ships he can) and I home, drinking two bottles of Cocke ale in the streete in his new fine coach, where no sooner come, but newes is brought me of a couple of men come to speak with me from the fleete; so I down, and who should it be but Mr. Daniel, all muffled up, and his face as black as the chimney, and covered with dirt, pitch, and tarr, and powder, and muffled with dirty clouts, and his right eye stopped with okum. He is come last night at five o'clock from the fleete, with a comrade of his that hath endangered another eye. They were set on shore at Harwich this morning, and at two o'clock, in a catch with about twenty more wounded men from the Royall Charles. They being able to ride, took post about three this morning, and were here between eleven and twelve. I went presently into the coach with them, and carried them to Somerset-House-stairs, and there took water (all the world gazing upon us, and concluding it to be newes from the fleete, and every body's face appeared expecting of newes) to the Privy-stairs, and left them at Mr. Coventry's lodging (he, though, not being there); and so I into the Parke to the King, and told him my Lord Generall was well the last night at five o'clock, and the Prince come with his fleete and joyned with his about seven. The King was mightily pleased with this newes, and so took me by the hand and talked a little of it. Giving him the best account I could; and then he bid me to fetch the two seamen to him, he walking into the house. So I went and fetched the seamen into the Vane room to him, and there he heard the whole account.

THE FIGHT

How we found the Dutch fleete at anchor on Friday half seas over, between Dunkirke and Ostend, and made them let slip their anchors. They about ninety, and we less than sixty. We fought them, and put them to the run, till they met with about sixteen sail of fresh ships, and so bore up again. The fight continued till night, and then again the next morning from five till seven at night. And so, too, yesterday morning they begun again, and continued till about four o'clock, they chasing us for the most part of Saturday and yesterday, we flying from them. The Duke himself, then those people were put into the catch, and by and by spied the Prince's fleete coming, upon which De Ruyter called a little council (being in chase at this time of us), and thereupon their fleete divided into two squadrons; forty in one, and about thirty in the other (the fleete being at first about ninety, but by one accident or another, supposed to be lessened to about seventy); the bigger to follow the Duke, the less to meet the Prince. But the Prince come up with the Generall's fleete, and the Dutch come together again and bore towards their own coast, and we with them; and now what the consequence of this day will be, at that time fighting, we know not. The Duke was forced to come to anchor on Friday, having lost his sails and rigging. No particular person spoken of to be hurt but Sir W. Clerke, who hath lost his leg, and bore it bravely. The Duke himself had a little hurt in his thigh, but signified little. The King did pull out of his pocket about twenty pieces in gold, and did give it Daniel for himself and his companion; and so parted, mightily pleased with the account he did give him of the fight, and the successe it ended with.

5TH. Thence after the Duke into the Parke, walking through to White Hall, and there every body listening for guns,

but none heard, and every creature is now overjoyed and concludes upon very good grounds that the Dutch are beaten because we have heard no guns nor no news of our fleete. By and
by walking a little further, Sir Philip Frowde did meet the Duke
with an expresse to Sir W. Coventry (who was by) from Captain
Taylor, the Storekeeper at Harwich, being the narration of
Captain Hayward of The Dunkirke; who gives a very serious
account, how upon Monday the two fleetes fought all day till
seven at night, and then the whole fleete of Dutch did betake
themselves to a very plain flight, and never looked back again.
That Sir Christopher Mings is wounded in the leg; that the
Generall is well. That it is conceived reasonably, that of all the
Dutch fleete, which, with what recruits they had, come to one
hundred sayle, there is not above fifty got home, and of them,
few if any of their flags. We were all so overtaken with this
good newes, that the Duke ran with it to the King, who was
gone to chappell, and there all the Court was in a hubbub,
being rejoiced over head and ears in this good newes. The joy
of the City was this night exceeding great.

7TH. Up betimes, and to my office about business. But my
Lord Bruncker and Sir T. H. that come from Court, tell me
quite contrary newes, which astonishes me: that is to say, that
we are beaten, lost many ships and good commanders; have not
taken one ship of the enemy's; and so can only report ourselves
a victory; nor is it certain that we were left masters of the field.
Then to my office and anon to White Hall, late, to the Duke of
York to see what commands he hath, which I did and do find
the Duke much damped in his discourse, touching the late
fight, and all the Court talk sadly of it. And as to newes, I do
find great reason to think that we are beaten in every respect,
and that we are the losers. The Duke of Albemarle writes, that
he never fought with worse officers in his life, not above twenty
of them behaving themselves as men.

10TH. This evening we hear that Sir Christopher Mings is
dead of his late wounds; and Sir W. Coventry did commend
him to me in a most extraordinary manner.

11TH. Up, and down by water to Sir W. Warren's to discourse about our lighters that he hath bought for me, and I hope to get £100 by this jobb. Having done with him I took boat again (being mightily struck with a woman in a hat, a seaman's mother, that stood on the key) and home.

12TH. Up, and to the office, where we sat all the morning. At noon to dinner, and then to White Hall. Walking here in the galleries I find the Ladies of Honour dressed in their riding garbs, with coats and doublets with deep skirts, just for all the world like mine, and buttoned their doublets up the breast, with perriwigs and with hats; so that, only for a long petticoat dragging under their men's coats, nobody could take them for women in any point whatever; which was an odde sight, and a sight did not please me.

13TH. Home, and put off Balty, and so, being invited, to Sir Christopher Mings's funeral, but find them gone to church. However I into the church (which is a fair, large church, and a great chappell) and there heard the service, and staid till they buried him, and then out. And there met with Sir W. Coventry (who was there out of great generosity, and no person of quality there but he) and went with him into his coach, and being in it with him there happened this extraordinary case—one of the most romantique that ever I heard of in my life, and could not have believed, but that I did see it; which was this:—About a dozen able, lusty, proper men come to the coachside with tears in their eyes, and one of them that spoke for the rest begun and says to Sir W. Coventry, "We are here a dozen of us that have long known and loved, and served our dead commander, Sir Christopher Mings, and have now done the last office of laying him in the ground. We would be glad we had any other to offer after him, and in revenge of him. All we have is our lives; if you will please to get His Royal Highness to give us a fireship among us all, here is a dozen of us, out of all which choose you one to be commander, and the rest of us, whoever he is, will serve him; and, if possible, do that that shall show our memory of our dead commander, and our revenge." Sir W. Coventry was herewith much moved (as well as I, who could hardly abstain from weeping), and took their names, and so parted; telling me that he would move His Royal Highness as in a thing very extraordinary, which was done.

16TH. It seems the Dutch do mightily insult of their victory, and they have great reason. Sir William Barkeley was killed before his ship taken; and there he lies dead in a sugar-chest, for every body to see, with his flag standing up by him. And Sir George Ascue is carried up and down the Hague for people to see. Home to my office, where late, and then to bed.

19TH. Home, and at my business till late at night, then with my wife into the garden and there sang with Mercer, whom I feel myself begin to love too much by handling of her breasts in a morning when she dresses me, they being the finest that ever I saw in my life, that is the truth of it. So home and to supper with beans and bacon and to bed.

25TH. Mrs. Pen carried us to two gardens at Hackny (which I every day grow more and more in love with,) Mr. Drake's one, where the garden is good, and house and the prospect admirable; the other my Lord Brooke's, where the gardens are much better, but the house not so good, nor the prospect good at all. But the gardens are excellent; and here I first saw oranges grow: some green, some half, some a quarter, and some full ripe, on the same tree, and one fruit of the same tree do come a year or two after the other. I pulled off a little one by stealth (the man being mighty curious of them) and eat it, and it was just as other little green small oranges are; as big as half the end of my little finger. Here were also great variety of other exotique plants, and several labarinths, and a pretty aviary.

27TH. My Lord is going down to his garrison to Hull, by the King's command, to put it in order for fear of an invasion: which course I perceive is taken upon the sea-coasts round; for we have a real apprehension of the King of France's invading us.

28TH. The Dutch are now known to be out, and we may expect them every houre upon our coast. But our fleete is in pretty good readiness for them.

JULY 1ST (SUNDAY). To the Tower several times, about the business of the pressed men, and late at it till twelve at night, shipping of them. But, Lord! how some poor women did cry; and in my life I never did see such natural expression of passion as I did here in some women's bewailing themselves, and running to every parcel of men that were brought, one after another, to look for their husbands, and wept over every vessel that went off, thinking that they might be there, and looking after the ship as far as ever they could by moone-light, that it grieved me to the heart to hear them. Besides, to see poor patient labouring men and housekeepers, leaving poor wives and families, taking up on a sudden by strangers, was very hard, and that without press-money, but forced against all law to be gone. It is a great tyranny.

10TH. At noon home to dinner and then to the office; the yarde being very full of women (I believe above three hundred) coming to get money for their husbands and friends that are prisoners in Holland; and they clamouring and swearing and cursing us. I do most heartily pity them, and was ready to cry to hear them, but cannot helpe them. However, when the rest were gone, I did call one to me that I heard complaine only and pity her husband and did give her some money, and she blessed me and went away.

18TH. Up in good case, and so by coach to St. James's after my fellows, and there did our business, which is mostly every day to complain of want of money, and that only will undo us in a little time.

21ST. Up and to the office, where all the morning sitting. At noon walked in the garden with Commissioner Pett (newly come to towne), who tells me how infinite the disorders are among the commanders and all officers of the fleete. No discipline: nothing but swearing and cursing, and every body doing what they please; and the Generalls, understanding no better, suffer it, to the reproaching of this Board, or whoever it will be. He himself hath been challenged twice to the field, or something as good, by Sir Edward Spragge and Captain Seymour. He tells me that captains carry, for all the late orders, what men they please; demand and consume what provisions they please; and the truth is, the gentlemen captains will undo us, for they are not to be kept in order, their friends about the King and Duke, and their own house, is so free, that it is not for any person but the Duke himself to have any command over them.

25TH. At White Hall we find [the Court] gone to Chappell, it being St. James's-day. By and by the King to dinner, and I waited there his dining; but, Lord! how little I should be pleased, I think, to have so many people crowding about me; and among other things it astonished me to see my Lord Barkeshire waiting at table, and serving the King drink, in that dirty pickle as I never saw man in my life. Here I met Mr. Williams. He would have me to dine where he was invited to dine, at the Backestayres. So after the King's meat was taken away, we thither; but he could not stay, but left me there among two or three of the King's servants, where we dined with the meat that come from his table; which was most excellent, with most brave drink cooled in ice (which at this hot time was welcome), and I drinking no wine, had metheglin for the King's owne drinking, which did please me mightily. Thence, having dined mighty nobly, I away to Mrs. Martin's new lodgings, where I find her, and was with her close. I did this afternoon call at my woman that ruled my paper to bespeak a musique card, and there did kiss Nan.

29TH (LORD'S DAY). Towards noon before sermon was done at church comes newes by a letter to Sir W. Batten, to my hand, of the late fight, which I sent to his house, he at church. But, Lord! with what impatience I staid till sermon was done, to know the issue of the fight, with a thousand hopes and fears and thoughts about the consequences of either. At last sermon is done and he come home, and the bells immediately rung as soon as the church was done. But coming to Sir W. Batten to know the newes, his letter said nothing of it; but all the towne is full of a victory. By and by a letter from Sir W. Coventry tells me that we have the victory. This is all, only we keep the sea, which denotes a victory, or at least that we are not beaten; but no great matters to brag of, God knows. So home to supper and to bed.

AUGUST 1ST. Up betimes to the settling of my last month's accounts, and I bless God I find them very clear, and that I am worth £5,700, the most that ever my book did yet make out. I to the Swan and there dined upon a rabbit, and after dinner to Mrs. Martin's, and there find Mrs. Burroughs, and by and by comes a pretty widow, one Mrs. Eastwood, and one Mrs. Fenton, a maid; and here merry kissing and looking on their breasts, and all the innocent pleasure in the world. But, Lord! to see the dissembling of this widow, how upon the singing of a certain jigg by Doll, Mrs. Martin's sister, she seemed to be sick and fainted and God knows what, because the jigg which her husband (who died this last sickness) loved. But by and by I made her as merry as is possible.

8TH. Up, and with Reeves walk as far as the Temple, doing some business in my way at my bookseller's and elsewhere, and there parted, and I took coach, having first discoursed with Mr. Hooke a little, whom we met in the streete, about the nature of sounds, and he did make me understand the nature of musicall sounds made by strings, mighty prettily; and told me that having come to a certain number of vibrations proper to make any tone, he is able to tell how many strokes a fly makes with her wings (those flies that hum in their flying) by the note that it answers to in musique during their flying. That, I suppose, is a little too much refined; but his discourse in general of sound was mighty fine.

17TH. Up and betimes with Captain Erwin down by water to Woolwich, I walking alone from Greenwich thither. Back with

Captain Erwin, discoursing about the East Indys, where he hath often been. And among other things he tells me how the King of Syam seldom goes out without thirty or forty thousand people with him, and not a word spoke, nor a hum or cough in the whole company to be heard. He tells me the punishment frequently there for malefactors is cutting off the crowne of their head, which they do very dexterously, leaving their brains bare, which kills them presently. And that he and his fellows, being strangers, were invited to see the sport of taking a wild elephant. The sport being ended, a messenger comes from the King to enquire how the strangers liked the sport. The drug-german answered that they did cry it up to be the best that ever they saw, and that they never heard of any Prince so great in every thing as this King. The messenger being gone back, Erwin and his company asked their druggerman what he had said, which he told them. "But why," say they, "would you say that without our leave, it being not true?" "It is no matter for that," says he, "I must have said it, or have been hanged, for our King do not live by meat, nor drink, but by having great lyes told him."

24TH. Up, and dispatched several businesses at home in the morning, and then comes Sympson to set up my other new presses for my books, and so he and I fell in to the furnishing of my new closett, and taking out the things out of my old, and I kept him with me all day, and he dined with me, and so all the afternoon till it was quite darke hanging things, that is my maps and pictures and draughts, and setting up my books, and as much as we could do, to my most extraordinary satisfaction; so that I think it will be as noble a closett as any man hath, and light enough—though, indeed, it would be better to have had a little more light.

SEPTEMBER 2ND (LORD'S DAY). Some of our mayds sitting up late last night to get things ready against our feast to-day, Jane called us up about three in the morning, to tell us of a great fire they saw in the City. So I rose and slipped on my night-gowne, and went to her window, and thought it to be on

the back-side of Marke-lane at the farthest; but, being unused
to such fires as followed, I thought it far enough off; and so went
to bed again and to sleep. About seven rose again to dress myself, and there looked out at the window, and saw the fire not so
much as it was and further off. By and by Jane comes and tells
me that she hears that above 300 houses have been burned
down to-night by the fire we saw, and that it is now burning
down all Fish-street, by London Bridge. So I made myself
ready presently, and walked to the Tower, and there got up
upon one of the high places, Sir J. Robinson's little son going up
with me; and there I did see the houses at that end of the bridge
all on fire, and an infinite great fire on this and the other side
the end of the bridge; which, among other people, did trouble
me for poor little Michell and our Sarah on the bridge. So
down, with my heart full of trouble, to the Lieutenant of the
Tower, who tells me that it begun this morning in the King's
baker's house in Pudding-lane, and that it hath burned St.
Magnus's Church and most part of Fish-street already. So I
down to the water-side, and there got a boat and through
bridge, and there saw a lamentable fire. Poor Michell's house, as
far as the Old Swan, already burned that way, and the fire running further, that in a very little time it got as far as the Steele-
yard, while I was there. Everybody endeavouring to remove
their goods, and flinging into the river or bringing them into
lighters that lay off; poor people staying in their houses as long
as till the very fire touched them, and then running into boats,
or clambering from one pair of stairs by the water-side to another. And among other things, the poor pigeons, I perceive,
were loth to leave their houses, but hovered about the windows
and balconys till they were, some of them burned, their wings,
and fell down. Having staid, and in an hour's time seen the fire
rage every way, and nobody, to my sight, endeavouring to
quench it, but to remove their goods, and leave all to the fire,
and having seen it get as far as the Steele-yard, and the wind
mighty high and driving it into the City; and every thing, after
so long a drought, proving combustible, even the very stones of
churches, and among other things the poor steeple by which
pretty Mrs. ———— lives, and whereof my old schoolfellow El-

borough is parson, taken fire in the very top, and there burned till it fell down: I to White Hall (with a gentleman with me who desired to go off from the Tower, to see the fire, in my boat); to White Hall, and there up to the King's closett in the Chappell, where people come about me, and I did give them an account dismayed them all, and word was carried in to the King. So I was called for, and did tell the King and Duke of Yorke what I saw, and that unless his Majesty did command houses to be pulled down nothing could stop the fire. They seemed much troubled, and the King commanded me to go to my Lord Mayor from him, and command him to spare no houses, but to pull down before the fire every way. At last met my Lord Mayor in Canning-street, like a man spent, with a handkercher about his neck. To the King's message he cried, like a fainting woman, "Lord, what can I do? I am spent: people will not obey me. I have been pulling down houses; but the fire overtakes us faster than we can do it." People all almost distracted, and no manner of means used to quench the fire. The houses, too, so very thick thereabouts, and full of matter of burning, as pitch and tarr, in Thames-street; and warehouses of oyle, and wines, and brandy, and other things. And to see the churches all filling with goods by people who themselves should have been quietly there at this time. Met with the King and Duke of York in their barge, and with them to Queen-hithe, and there called Sir Richard Browne to them. Their order was only to pull down houses apace, and so below bridge at the water-side; but little was or could be done, the fire coming upon them so fast. River full of lighters and boats taking in goods, and good goods swimming in the water, and only I observed that hardly one lighter or boat in three that had the goods of a house in, but there was a pair of Virginalls in it. So near the fire as we could for smoke; and all over the Thames, with one's face in the wind, you were almost burned with a shower of fire-drops. This is very true; so as houses were burned by these drops and flakes of fire, three or four, nay, five or six houses, one from another. When we could endure no more upon the water, we to a little ale-house on the Bankside, over against the Three Cranes, and there staid till it was dark almost, and saw the fire grow; and, as it grew darker, appeared more and more, and in corners and upon steeples, and between churches and houses, as far as we could see up the hill of the City, in a most horrid malicious bloody flame, not like the fine flame of an ordinary fire. Barbary and her husband away before us. We staid still, it being darkish, we saw the fire as only one entire arch of fire from this to the other side of the bridge, and in a bow up the hill for an arch of above a mile long: it made me weep to see it. The churches, houses, and all on fire and flaming at once; and a horrid noise the flames made, and the cracking of houses at their ruine. So home with a sad heart, and there find every body discoursing and lamenting the fire; and poor Tom Hater come with some few of his goods saved out of his house, which is burned upon Fish-streete Hill. I invited him to lie at my house, and did receive his goods, but was deceived in his lying there, the newes coming every moment of the growth of the fire; so as we were forced to begin to pack up our owne goods, and prepare for their removal; and did by moonshine (it being brave dry, and moonshine, and warm weather) carry much of my goods into the garden, and Mr. Hater and I did remove my money and iron chests into my cellar, as thinking that the safest place. And got my bags of gold into my office, ready to carry away, and my chief papers of accounts also there, and my tallys into a box by themselves.

3RD. About four o'clock in the morning, my Lady Batten sent me a cart to carry away all my money, and plate, and best things, to Sir W. Rider's at Bednall-greene. Which I did, riding myself in my night-gowne in the cart; and, Lord! to see how the streets and the highways are crowded with people running and riding, and getting of carts at any rate to fetch away things. The Duke of Yorke come this day by the office, and spoke to us, and did ride with his guard up and down the City to keep all quiet (he being now Generall, and having the care of all). At night lay down a little upon a quilt of W. Hewer's in the office, all my owne things being packed up or gone; and after me my poor wife did the like, we having fed upon the remains of yesterday's dinner, having no fire nor dishes, nor any opportunity of dressing any thing.

4TH. Up by break of day to get away the remainder of my things. Sir W. Batten not knowing how to remove his wine, did dig a pit in the garden, and laid it in there; and I took the opportunity of laying all the papers of my office that I could not otherwise dispose of. And in the evening Sir W. Pen and I did dig another, and put our wine in it; and I my Parmazan cheese, as well as my wine and some other things. Only now and then walking into the garden, and saw how horridly the sky looks, all on a fire in the night, was enough to put us out of our wits; and, indeed, it was extremely dreadful, for it looks just as if it was at us, and the whole heaven on fire. I after supper walked in the darke down to Tower-streete, and there saw it all on fire, at the Trinity House on that side, and the Dolphin Taverne on this side, which was very near us; and the fire with extraordinary vehemence. Now begins the practice of blowing up of houses in Tower-streete, those next the Tower, which at first did frighten people more than any thing; but it stopped the fire where it was done, it bringing down the houses to the ground in the same places they stood, and then it was easy to quench what little fire was in it, though it kindled nothing almost. Paul's is burned, and all Cheapside. I wrote to my father this night, but the post-house being burned, the letter could not go.

5TH. About two in the morning my wife calls me up and tells me of new cryes of fire, it being come to Barkeing Church, which is the bottom of our lane. I up, and finding it so, resolved presently to take her away, and did, and took my gold, which was about £2,350, W. Hewer, and Jane, down by Proundy's boat to Woolwich; but, Lord! what a sad sight it was by moone-light to see the whole City almost on fire, that you might see it plain at Woolwich, as if you were by it. There, when I come, I find the gates shut, but no guard kept at all, which troubled me, because of discourse now begun, that there is plot in it, and that the French had done it. I got the gates open, and to Mr. Shelden's, where I locked up my gold, and charged my wife and W. Hewer never to leave the room without one of them in it, night or day. So back again, by the way seeing my goods well in the lighters at Deptford, and watched well by people. Home, and whereas I expected to have seen our house on fire, it being now about seven o'clock, it was not. I up to the top of Barking steeple, and there saw the saddest sight of desolation that I ever saw; every where great fires, oyle-cellars, and brimstone, and other things burning. I became afeard to stay there long, and therefore down again as fast as I could, the fire being spread as far as I could see it; and to Sir W. Pen's, and there eat a piece of cold meat, having eaten nothing since Sunday, but the remains of Sunday's dinner.

6TH. It was pretty to see how hard the women did work in the cannells, sweeping of water; but then they would scold for drink, and be as drunk as devils. I saw good butts of sugar broke open in the street, and people go and take handsfull out, and put into beer, and drink it. And now all being pretty well, I took boat, and over to Southwarke, and took boat on the other side the bridge, and so to Westminster, thinking to shift myself, being all in dirt from top to bottom; but could not there find any place to buy a shirt or pair of gloves. A sad sight to see how the River looks; no houses nor church near it, to the Temple, where it stopped.

7TH. Up by five o'clock; and, blessed be God! find all well; and by water to Paul's Wharfe. Walked thence, and saw all the towne burned, and a miserable sight of Paul's church, with all the roofs fallen, and the body of the quire fallen into St. Fayth's; Paul's school also, Ludgate, and Fleet-street, my father's house, and the church, and a good part of the Temple the like. This day our Merchants first met at Gresham College, which, by proclamation, is to be their Exchange. Strange to hear what is bid for houses all up and down here; a friend of Sir W. Rider's having £150 for what he used to let for £40 per annum. Much dispute where the Custom-house shall be; thereby the growth of the City again to be foreseen. I home late to Sir W. Pen's, who did give me a bed; but without curtains or hanging, all being down. So here I went the first time into a naked bed, only my drawers on; and did sleep pretty well: but still both sleep and waking had a fear of fire in my heart, that I took little rest. People do all the world over cry out of the simplicity of my Lord Mayor in generall, and more particularly in this business of the fire, laying it all upon him.

8TH. I met with many people undone, and more that have extraordinary great losses. People speaking their thoughts variously about the beginning of the fire, and the rebuilding of the City. Then to Sir W. Batten's, and took my brother with me, and there dined with a great company of neighbours, and much good discourse; among others, of the low spirits of some rich men in the City, in sparing any encouragement to the poor people that wrought for the saving their houses. Among others, Alderman Starling, a very rich man, without children, the fire at next door to him in our lane, after our men had saved his house, did give 2s. 6d. among thirty of them, and did quarrel with some that would remove the rubbish out of the way of the fire, saying that they come to steal. Sir W. Coventry told me of another this morning in Holborne, which he shewed the King: that when it was offered to stop the fire near his house for such a reward that came but to 2s. 6d. a man among the neighbours he would give but 18d.

13TH. And so home, having this day also got my wine out of the ground again, and set in my cellar; but with great pain to keep the porters that carried it in from observing the money-chests there.

15TH. I to finish my letters, and home to bed; and find to my infinite joy many rooms clean; and myself and wife lie in our own chamber again. But much terrified in the nights now-a-days with dreams of fire, and falling down of houses.

17TH. Up betimes, and shaved myself after a week's growth: but, Lord! how ugly I was yesterday and how fine to-day! By water, seeing the City all the way, a sad sight indeed, much fire being still in.

2OTH. In the afternoon, out by coach, my wife with me, which we have not done several weeks now, through all the ruines, to shew her them, which frets her much, and is a sad sight indeed.

25TH. So home to bed, and all night still mightily troubled in my sleepe with fire and houses pulling down.

26TH. I to White Hall waiting all day on the Duke of Yorke, but could get nothing done, but here by Mr. Dugdale I hear the great loss of books in St. Paul's Church-yarde, and at their Hall also, which they value at about £150,000; some booksellers being wholly undone, and among others, they say, my poor Kirton. Here I had the hap to see my Lady Denham: and at night went into the dining-room and saw several fine ladies; among others, Castlemayne, but chiefly Denham again; and the Duke of Yorke taking her aside and talking to her in the sight of all the world, all alone; which was strange, and what also I did not like. Here I met with good Mr. Evelyn, who cries out against it, and calls it bitchering, for the Duke of Yorke talks a little to her, and then she goes away, and then he follows her again like a dog. He observes that none of the nobility come out of the country at all to help the King, or comfort him, or prevent commotions at this fire; but do as if the King were nobody; nor ne'er a priest comes to give the King and Court good council, or to comfort the poor people that suffer; but all is dead, nothing of good in any of their minds: he bemoans it, and says he fears more ruin hangs over our heads.

27TH. A very furious blowing night all the night; and my mind still mightily perplexed with dreams, and burning the rest of the town, and waking in much pain for the fleete. I then to the Exchequer, and there, among other things, spoke to Mr. Falconbridge about his girle I heard sing at Nonsuch, and took him and some other 'Chequer men to the Sun Taverne, and there spent 2s. 6d. upon them, and he sent for the girle, and she hath a pretty way of singing, but hath almost forgot for want of practice. She is poor in clothes, and not bred to any carriage, but will be soon taught all, and if Mercer do not come again, I think we may have her upon better terms, and breed her to what we please.

OCTOBER 2ND. So I away to the 'Chequer, and thence to an alehouse, and found Mr. Falconbridge, and agreed for his kinswoman to come to me. He says she can dress my wife, and will do anything we would have her to do, and is of a good spirit and mighty cheerful. He is much pleased therewith, and so we shall be. So agreed for her coming the next week.

5TH. This day, coming home. Mr. Kirton's kinsman, my bookseller, come in my way. He do believe there is above £150,000 of books burned; all the great booksellers almost undone: not only these, but their warehouses at their Hall, and under Christchurch, and elsewhere being all burned. A great want thereof there will be of books, specially Latin books and foreign books; and, among others, the Polyglottes and new Bible, which he believes will be presently worth £40 a-piece.

7TH (LORD'S DAY). After dinner I with Sir J. Minnes to White Hall, where met by [Sir] W. Batten and Lord Bruncker, to attend the King and Duke of York at the Cabinet; but nobody had determined what to speak of, but only in general to ask for money. So I was forced immediately to prepare in my mind a method of discoursing. And anon we were called in to the Green Room, where the King, Duke of York, Prince Rupert, Lord Chancellor, Lord Treasurer, Duke of Albemarle, [Sirs] G. Carteret, W. Coventry, Morrice. Nobody beginning, I did, and made a current, and I thought a good speech, laying open the ill state of the Navy: by the greatness of the debt; greatness of work to do against next yeare; the time and materials it would take; and our incapacity, through a total want of money. I had no sooner done, but Prince Rupert rose up and told the King in a heat, that whatever the gentleman had said, he had brought home his fleete in as good a condition as ever any fleete was brought home. I therefore did only answer, that I was sorry for his Highness's offence, but that what I said was but the report we received from those entrusted in the fleete to inform us. He muttered and repeated what he had said; and so, after a long silence on all hands, no body, not so much as the Duke of Albemarle, seconding the Prince, nor taking notice of what he said, we withdrew.

8TH. The King hath yesterday in Council declared his resolution of setting a fashion for clothes, which he will never alter. It will be a vest, I know not well how; but it is to teach the nobility thrift, and will do good.

12TH. So home, and there find my wife come home, and hath brought her new girle I have helped her to, of Mr. Falconbridge's. She is wretched poor, and but ordinary favoured; and we fain to lay out seven or eight pounds worth of clothes upon her back, which, methinks, do go against my heart; and I do not think I can ever esteem her as I could have done another that had come fine and handsome; and which is more, her voice, for want of use, is so furred, that it do not at present please me; but her manner of singing is such, that I shall, I think, take great pleasure in it. Well, she is come, and I wish us good fortune in her.

13TH. To White Hall, and there the Duke of York (who is gone over to all his pleasures again, and leaves off care of business, what with his woman, my Lady Denham, and his hunting three times a week) was just come in from hunting. So I stood and saw him dress himself, and try on his vest, which is the King's new fashion, and will be in it for good and all on Monday next, and the whole Court: it is a fashion, the King says, he will never change.

15TH. This day the King begins to put on his vest, and I did see several persons of the House of Lords and Commons too, great courtiers, who are in it; being a long cassocke close to the body, of black cloth, and pinked with white silke under it, and a coat over it, and the legs ruffled with black riband like a pigeon's leg; and, upon the whole, I wish the King may keep it, for it is a very fine and handsome garment.

26TH. Dined at home, and busy again after dinner, and then abroad by water to Westminster Hall, where I walked till the evening, and then out, the first time I ever was abroad with Doll Lane, to the Dog tavern, and there drank with her, a bad face, but good bodied girle. Did nothing but salute and play with her and talk, and thence away by coach, home, and so to do a little more in my accounts, and then to supper and to bed.

27TH. Towards evening I took them out to the New Exchange, and there my wife bought things, and I did give each of them a pair of Jesimy plain gloves, and another of white. Here Knipp and I walked up and down to see handsome faces, and did see several.

31ST. The seamen grow very rude, and every thing out of order; commanders having no power over their seamen, but the seamen do what they please. Few stay on board, but all coming running up hither to towne and nobody can with justice blame them, we owing them so much money; and their familys must starve if we do not give them money, or they procure upon their tickets from some people that will trust them.

NOVEMBER 2ND. Up betimes, and with Sir W. Batten to Woolwich, where first we went on board the Ruby, French prize, the only ship of war we have taken from any of our enemies this year. It seems a very good ship, but with galleries quite round the sterne to walk in as a balcone, which will be taken down. She had also about forty good brass guns, but will make little amends to our loss in The Prince.

5TH. Sir Thomas Crew, from what he hath heard at the Committee for examining the burning of the City, do conclude it as a thing certain that it was done by plots; it being proved by many witnesses that endeavours were made in several places to encrease the fire, and that both in City and country it was bragged by several Papists that upon such a day or in such a time we should find the hottest weather that ever was in England, and words of plainer sense.

12TH. This afternoon going towards Westminster, Creed and I did stop, the Duke of York being just going away from seeing of it, at Paul's, and in the Convocation House Yard did there see the body of Robert Braybrooke, Bishop of London, that died in 1404. He fell down in his tomb out of the great church into St. Fayth's this late fire, and is here seen his skeleton with the flesh on; but all tough and dry like a spongy dry leather, or touchwood all upon his bones. His head turned aside. A great man in his time, and Lord Chancellor; and [his skeleton] now exposed to be handled and derided by some, though admired for its duration by others. Many flocking to see it.

14TH. To the Exchange for some things for my wife, and then to Knipp's again, and there staid reading of Waller's verses, while she finished dressing, her husband being by. I had no other pastime. Her lodging very mean, and the condition she lives in; yet makes a shew without doors, God bless us!

15TH. I took coach and to Mrs. Pierce's, where I find her as fine as possible, and himself going to the ball at night at Court, it being the Queen's birth-day, and so I carried them in my coach. I also to the ball, and with much ado got up to the loft, where with much trouble I could see very well. Anon the house grew full, and the candles light, and the King and Queen and all the ladies set: and it was, indeed, a glorious sight to see Mrs. Stewart in black and white lace, and her head and shoulders dressed with dyamonds, and the like a great many great ladies more, only the Queen none; and the King in his rich vest of some rich silke and silver trimming, as the Duke of York and all the dancers were, some of cloth of silver, and others of other sorts, exceeding rich. Presently after the King was come in, he took the Queene, and about fourteen more couple there was, and begun the Bransles. After the Bransles, then to a Corant, and now and then a French dance; but that so rare that the Corants grew tiresome, that I wished it done. Only Mrs. Stewart danced mighty finely, and many French dances, specially one the King called the New Dance, which was very pretty; but upon the whole matter, the business of the dancing of itself was not extraordinary pleasing. But the clothes and sight of the persons was indeed very pleasing, and worth my coming, being never likely to see more gallantry while I live, if I should come twenty times. My Lady Castlemayne, without whom all is nothing, being there, very rich, though not dancing. And so after supper, it being very cold, to bed.

21ST. So home to dinner, and then to the office, where busy all the afternoon till night, and then home to supper, and after supper an hour reading to my wife and brother something in Chaucer with great pleasure, and so to bed.

22ND. At noon home to dinner, where my wife and I fell out, I being displeased with her cutting away a lace handkercher sewed about her neck down to her breasts almost, out of a belief, but without reason, that it is the fashion. Mr. Batelier tells me the newes how the King of France hath, in defiance to the King of England, caused all his footmen to be put into vests, and that the noblemen of France will do the like; which, if true, is the greatest indignity ever done by one Prince to another, and would incite a stone to be revenged.

28TH. At noon comes my Lord Hinchingbroke, Sir Thomas Crew, Mr. John Crew, Mr. Carteret, and Brisband. I had six noble dishes for them, dressed by a man-cook, and commended, as indeed they deserved, for exceeding well done. We eat with great pleasure, and I enjoyed myself in it with reflections upon the pleasures which I at best can expect, yet not to exceed this; eating in silver plates, and all things mighty rich and handsome about me. A great deal of fine discourse, sitting almost till dark at dinner, and then broke up with great pleasure, especially to myself.

DECEMBER 8TH. Mr. Pierce did also tell me as a great truth, as being told it by Mr. Cowly, who was by, and heard it, that Tom Killigrew should publiquely tell the King that his matters were coming into a very ill state; but that yet there was a way to help all, which is, says he, "There is a good, honest, able man, that I could name, that if your Majesty would employ, and command to see all things well executed, all things would soon be mended; and this is one Charles Stuart, who now spends his time in employing his lips . . . about the Court, and hath no other employment; but if you would give him this employment, he were the fittest man in the world to perform it."

12TH. Up, and to the office, where some accounts of Mr. Gawden's were examined, but I home most of the morning. He tells me how the King hath lately paid about £30,000 to clear debts of my Lady Castlemayne's; and that she and her husband are parted for ever, upon good terms, never to trouble one another more. He says that he hears £400,000 hath gone into the Privy purse since this warr; and that that hath consumed so much of our money, and makes the King and Court so mad to be brought to discover it.

16TH (LORD'S DAY). This afternoon I walked with Lord Bruncker into the Park and there talked of the times. He tells me he do not believe the Duke of York will go to sea again, though there are a great many about the King that would be glad of any occasion to take him out of the world, he standing in their ways; and seemed to mean the Duke of Monmouth, who spends his time the most viciously and idly of any man, nor will be fit for any thing; yet he speaks as if it were not impossible but the King would own him for his son, and that there was a marriage between his mother and him; which God forbid should be if it be not true, nor will the Duke of York easily be gulled in it.

19TH. Met Mr. Hingston the organist (my old acquaintance) in the Court, and I took him to the Dog Taverne and got him to set me a bass to my "It is decreed," which I think will go well, but he commends the song not knowing the words, but says the ayre is good, and believes the words are plainly expressed. He is of my mind against having of 8ths unnecessarily in composition. This did all please me mightily. Then to talk of the King's family. He says many of the musique are ready to starve, they being five years behind-hand for their wages; nay, Evens, the famous man upon the Harp, having not his equal in the world, did the other day die for mere want, and was fain to be buried at the almes of the parish, and carried to his grave in the dark at night without one linke, but that Mr. Hingston met it by chance, and did give 12d. to buy two or three links. He says all must come to ruin at this rate, and I believe him. Thence I up to the Lords' House to enquire for Lord Bellasses; and there hear how at a conference this morning between the two Houses about the business of the Canary Company, my Lord Buckingham leaning rudely over my Lord Marquis Dorchester, my Lord Dorchester removed his elbow. Duke of Buckingham asked him whether he was uneasy; Dorchester replied, yes, and that he durst not do this were he any where else: Buckingham replied, yes he would, and that he was a better man than himself; Dorchester answered that he lyed. With this Buckingham struck off his hat, and took him by his periwigg, and pulled it aside, and held him. My Lord Chamberlain and others interposed, and, upon coming into the House, the Lords did order them both to the Tower, whither they are to go this afternoon. And coming home do hear of 1,000 seamen said in the streets to be in armes. So in great fear home, expecting to find a tumult about my house, and was doubtful of my riches there. But I thank God I found all well. But by and by Sir W. Batten and Sir R. Ford do tell me, that the seamen have been at some prisons, to release some seamen, and the Duke of Albemarle is in armes, and all the Guards at the other end of the town; and the Duke of Albemarle is gone with some forces to Wapping, to quell the seamen; which is a thing of infinite disgrace to us.

2OTH. Here dined with me also Mrs. Batters, poor woman! now left a sad widow by the drowning of her husband the other day. I pity her, and will do her what kindness I can; yet I observe something of ill-nature in myself more than should be, that I am colder towards her in my charity than I should be to one so painful as he and she have been and full of kindness to their power to my wife and I.

25TH (CHRISTMAS DAY). Lay pretty long in bed, and then rose, leaving my wife desirous to sleep, having sat up till four this morning seeing her mayds make mince-pies. I to church, where our parson Mills made a good sermon. Then home, and dined well on some good ribs of beef roasted and mince pies; only my wife, brother, and Barker, and plenty of good wine of my owne, and my heart full of true joy; and thanks to God Almighty for the goodness of my condition at this day. After dinner, I begun to teach my wife and Barker my song, "It is decreed," which pleases me mightily as now I have Mr. Hinxton's base.

27TH. Up; and called up by the King's trumpets, which cost me 10s. So to the office, where we sat all the morning. From hence to the Duke's house, and there saw "Macbeth" most excellently acted, and a most excellent play for variety.

31ST. Rising this day with a full design to mind nothing else but to make up my accounts for the year past, I did take money, and walk forth to several places in the towne as far as the New Exchange, to pay all my debts, it being still a very great frost and good walking. Our enemies, French and Dutch, great, and grow more by our poverty. The Parliament backward in raising, because jealous of the spending of the money; the City less and less likely to be built again, every body settling elsewhere, and nobody encouraged to trade. A sad, vicious, negligent Court, and all sober men there fearful of the ruin of the whole kingdom this next year; from which, good God deliver us! One thing I reckon remarkable in my owne condition is, that I am come to abound in good plate, so as at all entertainments to be served wholly with silver plates, having two dozen and a half.

1667

JANUARY 1ST. Lay long, being a bitter, cold, frosty day, the frost being now grown old, and the Thames covered with ice. Up, and to the office, where all the morning busy.

7TH. To the Duke's house, and saw "Macbeth," which, though I saw it lately, yet appears a most excellent play in all respects, but especially in divertisement, though it be a deep tragedy; which is a strange perfection in a tragedy, it being most proper here, and suitable. So home, it being the last play now I am to see till a fortnight hence, I being from the last night entered into my vowes for the year coming on.

14TH. Up, and to the office, where busy getting before hand with my business as fast as I can. Busy till night, pleasing myself mightily to see what a deal of business goes off of a man's hands when he stays by it.

15TH. At night home to supper and to bed with my mind mighty light to see the fruits of my diligence in having my business go off my hand so merrily.

20TH (LORD'S DAY). Up betimes and down to the Old Swan, there called on Michell and his wife, which in her night linen appeared as pretty almost as ever to my thinking I saw woman. Here I drank some burnt brandy. They shewed me their house, which, poor people, they have built, and is very pretty. I invited them to dine with me, and so away to White Hall to Sir W. Coventry. I home, and there Michell and his wife, and we dined and mighty merry, I mightily taken more and more with her.

22ND. Up, and there come to me Darnell the fiddler, one of the Duke's house, and brought me a set of lessons, all three parts, I heard them play to the Duke of York after Christmas at his lodgings, and bid him to get me them. I did give him a crowne for them, and did enquire after the musique of the "Siege of Rhodes," which, he tells me, he can get me, which I am mighty glad of.

23RD. My Lord and I walking into the Park back again, I did observe the new buildings: and my Lord, seeing I had a desire to see them, they being the place for the priests and fryers, he took me back to my Lord Almoner; and he took us quite through the whole house and chapel, and the new monastery, showing me most excellent pieces in wax-worke: a crucifix given by a Pope to Mary Queen of Scotts, where a piece of the Cross is; two bits set in the manner of a cross in the foot of the crucifix: several fine pictures, but especially very good prints of holy pictures. I saw the *dortoire* and the cells of the priests, and we went into one; a very pretty little room, very clean, hung with pictures, set with books. The Priest was in his cell, with his hair clothes to his skin, bare-legged, with a sandall only on, and his little bed without sheets, and no feather bed; but yet, I thought, soft enough. His cord about his middle; but in so good company, living with ease, I thought it a very good life. A pretty library they have. And I was in the *refectoire,* where every man his napkin, knife, cup of earth, and basin of the same; and a place for one to sit and read while the rest are at meals. And into the kitchen I went, where a good neck of mutton at the fire, and other victuals boiling. I do not think they fared very hard. Their windows all looking into a fine garden and the Park; and mighty pretty rooms all. I wished myself one of the Capuchins. Having seen what we could here, and all with mighty pleasure, so away with the Almoner in his coach, talking merrily about the difference in our religions, to White Hall, and there we left him. To the King's house and there saw "The Humerous Lieutenant." Here, in a box above, we spied Mrs. Pierce; and, going out, they called us, and so we staid for them; and Knipp took us all in, and brought to us Nelly, a most pretty woman, who acted the great part of Cœlia to-day very fine, and did it pretty well: I kissed her, and so did my wife; and a mighty pretty soul she is. We also saw Mrs. Hall, which is my little Roman-nose black girl, that is mighty pretty: she is usually called Betty. Knipp made us stay in a box and see the dancing preparatory to to-morrow for "The Goblins," a play of Suckling's, not acted these twenty-five years; which was pretty; and so away thence, pleased with this sight also, and specially kissing of Nell.

27TH (LORD'S DAY). I through the garden into the Park, and there met with Roger Pepys, and he and I to walk in the Pell Mell. So walked to White Hall, and there I shewed my cozen Roger the Duchesse of York sitting in state, while her own mother stands by her; he had a desire, and I shew him my Lady Castlemayne, whom he approves to be very handsome, and wonders that she cannot be as good within as she is fair without. Her little black boy came by him; and a dog being in his way, the little boy called to the dog: "Pox of this dog!" "Now," says he, blessing himself, "would I whip this child till the blood come, if it were my child!" and I believe he would. But he do by no means like the liberty of the Court, and did come with expectation of finding them playing at cards to-night, though Sunday; for such stories he is told, but how true I know not.

29TH. Busy till late at night at the office, and Sir W. Batten come to me, and tells me that there is newes upon the Exchange to-day, that my Lord Sandwich's coach and the French

Embassador's at Madrid, meeting and contending for the way, they shot my Lord's postilion and another man dead; and that we have killed 25 of theirs, and that my Lord is well.

FEBRUARY 2ND. I am very well pleased this night with reading a poem I brought home with me last night from Westminster Hall, of Dryden's upon the present war; a very good poem.

3RD (LORD'S DAY). By and by to dinner, where very good company. Among other discourse, we talked much of Nostradamus his prophecy of these times, and the burning of the City of London, some of whose verses are put into Booker's Almanack this year; and Sir G. Carteret did tell a story, how at his death he did make the town swear that he should never be dug up, or his tomb opened, after he was buried; but they did after sixty years do it, and upon his breast they found a plate of brasse, saying what a wicked and unfaithful people the people of that place were, who after so many vows should disturb and open him such a day and year and hour; which, if true, is very strange.

4TH. Soon as dined, my wife and I out to the Duke's playhouse, and there saw "Heraclius," an excellent play, to my extraordinary content; and the more from the house being very dull, and great company; among others, Mrs. Stewart, very fine, with her locks done up with puffs, as my wife calls them: and several other great ladies had their hair so, though I do not like it; but my wife do mightily—but it is only because she sees it is the fashion.

5TH. This morning, before I went to the office, there come to me Mr. Young and Whistler, flagg-makers, and with mighty earnestness did present me with, and press me to take a box, wherein I could not guess there was less than £100 in gold: but I do wholly refuse it, and did not at last take it. The truth is, not thinking them safe men to receive such a gratuity from, nor knowing any considerable courtesy that ever I did do them, but desirous to keep myself free from their reports, and to have it in my power to say I had refused their offer.

8TH. At noon Lord Bruncker, Sir W. Batten, [Sir] W. Pen, and myself to the Swan in Leadenhall Street to dinner, where an exceedingly good dinner and good discourse. At dinner we talked much of Cromwell; all saying he was a brave fellow, and did owe his crowne he got to himself as much as any man that ever got one.

9TH. To the office, where we sat all the morning busy. At noon home to dinner, and then to my office again, where also busy, very busy late, and then went home and read a piece of a play, "Every Man in his Humour," wherein is the greatest propriety of speech that ever I read in my life: and so to bed.

10TH (LORD'S DAY). Up and with my wife to church, where Mr. Mills made an unnecessary sermon upon Original Sin, neither understood by himself nor the people.

12TH. T. Killigrew and I to talk: and he tells me how the audience at his house is not above half so much as it used to be before the late fire. That Knipp is like to make the best actor that ever come upon the stage, she understanding so well: that they are going to give her £30 a-year more. That the stage is now by his pains a thousand times better and more glorious than ever heretofore. Now, wax-candles, and many of them; then, not above 3 lbs. of tallow; now, all things civil, no rudeness anywhere; then, as in a bear-garden: then, two or three fiddlers; now, nine or ten of the best: then, nothing but rushes upon the ground, and every thing else mean; and now, all otherwise: then, the Queen seldom and the King never would come; now, not the King only for state, but all civil people do think they may come as well as any. He tells me that he hath gone several times, eight or ten times, he tells me, hence to Rome to hear good musique; so much he loves it, though he never did sing or play a note. That he hath endeavoured in the late King's time, and in this, to introduce good musique, but he never could do it, there never having been any musique here better than ballads. Nay, says, "Hermitt poore" and "Chevy Chese" was all the musique we had.

14TH. Home through the dark over the ruins by coach, with my sword drawn, to the office, where dispatched some business; and so home to my chamber and to supper and to bed. This morning come up to my wife's bedside, I being up dressing myself, little Will Mercer to be her Valentine; and brought her name writ upon blue paper in gold letters, done by himself, very pretty; and we were both well pleased with it. But I am also this year my wife's Valentine, and it will cost me £5; but that I must have laid out if we had not been Valentines. So to bed.

17TH (LORD'S DAY). This evening, going to the Queen's side to see the ladies, I did find the Queene, the Duchesse of York, and another or two, at cards, with the room full of great ladies and men; which I was amazed at to see on a Sunday, having not believed it; but, contrarily, flatly denied the same a little while since to my cozen Roger Pepys.

18TH. Thence away, and with my wife by coach to the Duke of York's play-house, expecting a new play, and so stayed not no more than other people, but to the King's house, to "The Mayd's Tragedy;" but vexed all the while with two talking ladies and Sir Charles Sedley; yet pleased to hear their discourse, he being a stranger. And one of the ladies would, and did sit with her mask on, all the play, and, being exceeding witty as ever I heard woman, did talk most pleasantly with him; but was, I believe, a virtuous woman, and of quality. He would fain know who she was, but she would not tell; yet did give him many pleasant hints of her knowledge of him, by that means setting his brains at work to find out who she was, and did give him leave to use all means to find out who she was, but pulling off her mask. He was mighty witty, and she also making sport with him very inoffensively, that a more pleasant *rencontre* I never heard. But by that means lost the pleasure of the play wholly, to which now and then Sir Charles Sedley's exceptions against both words and pronouncing were very pretty. So home and to the office, did much business, then home, to supper, and to bed.

23RD. This day I am, by the blessing of God, 34 years old, in very good health and mind's content, and in condition of estate much beyond whatever my friends could expect of a child of their's, this day 34 years. The Lord's name be praised! and may I be ever thankful for it.

24TH (LORD'S DAY). I enquired about the Frenchman that was said to fire the City and was hanged for it, by his own confession, that he was hired for it by a Frenchman of Roane, and that he did with a stick reach in a fire-ball in at a window of the house: whereas the master of the house, who is the King's baker, and his son, and daughter, do all swear there was no such window, and that the fire did not begin thereabouts. Yet the fellow, who, though a mopish besotted fellow, did not speak like a madman, did swear that he did fire it: and did not this like a madman; for, being tried on purpose, and landed with his speaker at the Tower Wharf, he could carry the keeper to the very house. Asking Sir R. Viner what he thought was the cause of the fire, he tells me, that the baker, son, and his daughter, did all swear again and again, that their oven was drawn by ten o'clock at night; that, having occasion to light a candle about twelve, there was not so much fire in the bakehouse as to light a match for a candle, so that they were fain to go into another place to light it; that about two in the morning they felt themselves almost choked with smoke, and rising, did find the fire coming upstairs; so they rose to save themselves; but that, at that time, the bavins were not on fire in the yard. So that they are, as they swear, in absolute ignorance how this fire should come; which is a strange thing, that so horrid an effect should have so mean and uncertain a beginning.

25TH. Lay long in bed, talking with pleasure with my poor wife, how she used to make coal fires, and wash my foul clothes with her own hand for me, poor wretch! in our little room at my

Lord Sandwich's; for which I ought for ever to love and admire her, and do; and persuade myself she would do the same thing again, if God should reduce us to it. At my goldsmith's did observe the King's new medall, where, in little, there is Mrs. Steward's face as well done as ever I saw anything in my whole life, I think: and a pretty thing it is, that he should choose her face to represent Britannia by.

MARCH 2ND. After dinner, with my wife, to the King's house to see "The Mayden Queene," a new play of Dryden's, mightily commended for the regularity of it, and the strain and wit; and, the truth is, there is a comical part done by Nell, which is Florimell, that I never can hope ever to see the like done again, by man or woman. The King and Duke of York were at the play. But so great performance of a comical part was never, I believe, in the world before as Nell do this, both as a mad girle, then most and best of all when she comes in like a young gallant; and hath the motions and carriage of a spark the most that ever I saw any man have. It makes me, I confess, admire her.

5TH. Up, and to the office, where met and sat all the morning, doing little for want of money, but only bear the countenance of an office.

7TH. This day was reckoned by all people the coldest day that ever was remembered in England; and, God knows! coals at a very great price.

8TH. Up, and to the Old Swan, where drank at Michell's, but not seeing her whom I love I by water to White Hall.

9TH. Captain Cocke, who was here to-night, did tell us that he is certain that yesterday a proclamation was voted at the Council, touching the proclaiming of my Lord Duke of Buckingham a traytor, and that it will be out on Monday. So home late, and drank some buttered ale, and so to bed and to sleep. This cold did most certainly come by my staying a little too long bare-legged yesterday morning when I rose while I looked out fresh socks and thread stockings, yesterday's having in the night, lying near the window, been covered with snow within the window, which made me I durst not put them on.

12TH. This day a poor seaman, almost starved for want of food, lay in our yard a-dying. I sent him a half-a-crown, and we ordered his ticket to be paid.

22ND. So home to dinner, where my wife having dressed herself in a silly dress of a blue petticoat uppermost, and a white satin waistcoat and white hood, though I think she did it because her gown is gone to the tailor's, did, together with my being hungry, which always makes me peevish, make me angry, but when my belly was full were friends again.

23RD. At the office all the morning, where Sir W. Pen come, being returned from Chatham, from considering the means of fortifying the river Medway, by a chain at the stakes, and ships laid there with guns to keep the enemy from coming up to burn our ships all our cares now being to fortify ourselves against their invading us.

26TH. Sir W. Pen and I to the Castle Tavern hard by and got a lobster, and he and I staid and eat it, and drank good wine; I only burnt wine, as my whole custom of late hath been, as an evasion, God knows, for my drinking of wine (but it is an evasion which will not serve me now hot weather is coming, that I cannot pretend, as indeed I really have done, that I drank it for cold), but I will leave it off, and it is but seldom, as when I am in women's company, that I must call for wine, for I must be forced to drink to them.

27TH. So I home, and there up to my wife in our chamber, and there received from my brother the newes of my mother's dying on Monday, about five or six o'clock in the afternoon, and that the last time she spoke of her children was on Friday last, and her last words were, "God bless my poor Sam!" The reading hereof did set me a-weeping heartily, and so weeping to myself awhile, and my wife also to herself, I then spoke to my wife respecting myself, and indeed, having some thoughts how much better both for her and us it is than it might have been had she outlived my father and me or my happy present condition in the world, she being helpless, I was the sooner at ease in my mind.

APRIL 4TH. Up, and going down found Jervas the barber with a periwigg which I had the other day cheapened at Westminster, but it being full of nits, as heretofore his work used to be, I did now refuse it, having bought elsewhere. I find the Duke of Albemarle at dinner with sorry company, some of his officers of the Army; dirty dishes, and a nasty wife at table, and bad meat, of which I made but an ill dinner.

6TH. Up, and betimes in the morning down to the Tower wharfe, there to attend the shipping of soldiers, to go down to man some ships going out, and pretty to see how merrily some, and most go, and how sad others—the leave they take of their friends, and the terms that some wives, and other wenches asked to part with them: a pretty mixture.

8TH. Up, and having dressed myself, to the office a little, and out, expecting to have seen the pretty daughter of the Ship taverne at the hither end of Billiter Lane (whom I never yet have opportunity to speak to). I in there to drink my morning draught of half a pint of Rhenish wine; but *a ma doleur elle* and their family are going away thence, and a new man come to the house. So I away to the Temple, to my new bookseller's; and there I did agree for Rycaut's late History of the Turkish Policy, which costs me 55s.

10TH. So away, and by coach going home saw Sir G. Carteret going towards White Hall. So 'light and by water met him, and with him to the King's little chapel; and afterwards to see the King heal the King's Evil, wherein no pleasure, I having seen it before.

12TH. Up, and when ready, and to my office, to do a little business and coming homeward again, saw my door and hatch open, left so by Luce, our cookmayde which so vexed me that I did give her a kick in our entry and offered a blow at her, and was seen doing so by Sir W. Pen's footboy, which did vex me to the heart, because I know he will be telling their family of it; though I did put on presently a very pleasant face to the boy, and spoke kindly to him, as one without passion, so as it may be he might not think I was angry, but yet I was troubled at it. So away by water to White Hall, and there did our usual business before the Duke of York.

MAY 3RD. I to Westminster Hall, and there took a turn with my old acquaintance Mr. Pechell, whose red nose makes me ashamed to be seen with him, though otherwise a good-natured man. Then to the office, and did some business, and then my wife being pretty well, by coach to little Michell's, and there saw my poor Betty and her little child, which slept so soundly we could hardly wake it in an hour's time, without hurting it, and they tell me what I did not know that a child (as this do) will hunt up and down with its mouth if you touch the cheek of it with your finger's end for a nipple, and fit its mouth for sucking, but this hath not sucked yet, she having no nipples. This day the newes is come that the fleete of the Dutch, of about 20 ships, which come upon our coast upon design to have intercepted our colliers, but by good luck failed, is gone to the Frith, and there lies, perhaps to trouble the Scotch privateers, which have galled them of late very much, it may be more than all our last year's fleete.

6TH. Up and angry with my mayds for letting in water men, and I know not who, anybody that they are acquainted with, into my kitchen to talk and prate with them, which I will not endure.

8TH. Home to dinner, where I find my wife's flageolette master, and I am so pleased with her proceeding, though she hath lost time by not practising, that I am resolved for the encouragement of the man to learn myself a little for a month or so, for I do foresee if God send my wife and I to live, she will become very good company for me.

10TH. To my Lord Treasurer's, but missed Sir Ph. Warwicke, and so back again, and drove hard towards Clerkenwell, thinking to have overtaken my Lady Newcastle, whom I saw before us in her coach, with 100 boys and girls running looking upon her: but I could not: and so she got home before I could come up to her. But I will get a time to see her.

12TH (LORD'S DAY). Up, and to my chamber, to settle some accounts there, and by and by down comes my wife to me in her night-gown, and we begun calmly, that upon having money to lace her gown for second mourning, she would promise to wear white locks no more in my sight, which I, like a severe fool, thinking not enough, begun to except against, and made her fly out to very high terms and cry, and in her heat told me of keeping company with Mrs. Knipp, saying, that if I would promise never to see her more—of whom she hath more reason to suspect than I had heretofore of Pembleton—she would never wear white locks more. This vexed me, but I restrained myself from saying anything, but do think never to see this woman—at least, to have her here more, but by and by I did give her money to buy lace, and she promised to wear no more white locks while I lived, and so all very good friends as ever, and I to my business, and she to dress herself.

16TH. We to my Lord Treasurer's where I find the porter crying, and suspected it was that my Lord is dead; and, poor Lord! we did find that he was dead just now; and the crying of the fellow did so trouble me, that considering I was not likely to trouble him any more, nor have occasion to give any more anything, I did give him 3s.; but it may be, poor man, he hath lost a considerable hope by the death of his Lord, whose house will be no more frequented as before, and perhaps I may never come thither again about any business.

18TH. I to the office, finished my letters, and then to walk an hour in the garden talking with my wife, whose growth in musique do begin to please me mightily, and by and by home and there find our Luce drunk, and when her mistress told her of it would be gone, and so put up some of her things and did go away of her accord, nobody pressing her to it. But that which did a little trouble me was that I did hear her tell her mistress that she would tell her master something before she was aware of her that she would be sorry to have him know.

21ST. Thence I home; but, Lord! how it went against my heart to go away from the very door of the Duke's play-house, and my Lady Castlemayne's coach, and many great coaches there, to see "The Siege of Rhodes." I was very near making a forfeit, but I did command myself, and so home to my office, and there did much business to my good content, much better than going to a play, and then home to my wife, who is not well with her cold, and sat and read a piece of Grand Cyrus in English by her, and then to my chamber and to supper, and so to bed.

27TH. Up, and there comes Greeting my flagelette master, and I practised with him. There comes also Richardson, the bookbinder, with one of Ogilby's Bibles in quires for me to see and buy. So to my chamber, and there did some little business, and then abroad, and stopped at the Bear-garden-stairs, there to see a prize fought. But the house was so full there was no getting in there, so forced to go through an alehouse into the pit, where the bears are baited; and upon a stool did see them fight, which they did very furiously, a butcher and a waterman. The former had the better all along, till by and by the latter dropped his sword out of his hand, and the butcher, whether not seeing his sword dropped I know not, but did give him a cut over the wrist, so as he was disabled to fight any longer. But, Lord! to see how in a minute the whole stage was full of watermen to revenge the foul play, and the butchers to defend their fellow, though most blamed him; and there they all fell to it knocking down and cutting many on each side. It was pleasant to see, but that I stood in the pit, and feared that in the tumult I might get some hurt. At last the rabble broke up, and so I away to White Hall and so to St. James's.

28TH. After dinner my wife away down with Jane and W. Hewer to Woolwich, in order to get a little ayre and to lie there to-night, and so to gather May-dew to-morrow morning, which Mrs. Turner hath taught her as the only thing in the world to wash her face with; and I am contented with it. Presently comes Creed, and he and I by water to Fox-hall, and there walked in Spring Garden. A great deal of company, and the weather and garden pleasant: that it is very pleasant and cheap going thither, for a man may go to spend what he will, or nothing, all is one. But to hear the nightingale and other birds, and here fiddles, and there a harp, and here a Jew's trump, and here laughing, and there fine people walking, is mighty divertising. Among others, there were two pretty women alone, that walked a great while, which being discovered by some idle gentlemen, they would needs take them up; but to see the poor ladies how they were put to it to run from them, and they after them and some-times the ladies put themselves along with other company, then the other drew back; at last, the last did get off out of the house, and took boat and away. I was troubled to see them abused so; and could have found in my heart, as little desire of fighting as I have, to have protected the ladies.

JUNE 1ST. Up; and there comes to me Mr. Commander, whom I employ about hiring of some ground behind the office, for the building of me a stable and coach-house; for I do find it necessary for me, both in respect to honour and the profit of it also, my expense in hackney-coaches being now so great, to keep a coach, and therefore will do it.

2ND (LORD'S DAY). Up betimes, and down to my chamber without trimming myself, or putting on clean linen, thinking only to keep to my chamber and do business to-day, but when I come there I find that without being shaved I am not fully awake, nor ready to settle to business, and so was fain to go up again and dress myself, which I did, and so down to my chamber, and fell roundly to business, and did to my satisfaction by dinner go far in the drawing up a state of my accounts of Tangier for the new Lords Commissioners.

3RD. Down by water to Deptford, it being Trinity Monday, when the Master is chosen.

4TH. To the office all the afternoon, where I dispatched much business to my great content, and then home in the evening, and there to sing and pipe with my wife, and that being done, she fell all of a sudden to discourse about her clothes and my humours in not suffering her to wear them as she pleases, and grew to high words between us, but I fell to read a book (Boyle's Hydrostatiques) aloud in my chamber and let her talk, till she was tired and vexed that I would not hear her, and so become friends, and to bed together the first night after 4 or 5 that she hath lain from me by reason of a great cold she had got.

8TH. Up, and to the office, where all the news this morning is, that the Dutch are come with a fleete of eighty sail to Harwich, and that guns were heard plain by Sir W. Rider's people at Bednall-greene, all yesterday even. The King hath sent down my Lord of Oxford to raise the countries there; and all the Westerne barges are taken up to make a bridge over the River, about the Hope, for horse to cross the River, if there be occasion.

9TH (LORD'S DAY). Up, and by water to White Hall, and so walked to St. James's. In comes my Lord Barkeley, who is going down to Harwich also to look after the militia there: and there is also the Duke of Monmouth, and with him a great many young Hectors, the Lord Chesterfield, my Lord Mandeville, and others; but to little purpose, I fear, but to debauch the country women thereabouts. Being come home I find an order come for the getting some fire-ships presently to annoy the Dutch, who are in the King's Channel and expected up higher.

10TH. Up; and news brought us that the Dutch are come up as high as the Nore; and more pressing orders for fire-ships. W. Batten, W. Pen, and I to St. James's; where the Duke of York gone this morning betimes, to send away some men down to Chatham. So we three to White Hall, and met Sir W. Coventry, who presses all that is possible for fire-ships. So we three to the office presently; and thither comes Sir Fretcheville Hollis, who is to command them all in some exploits he is to do with them on the enemy in the River. So we all down to Deptford, and pitched upon ships and set men at work: but, Lord! to see how backwardly things move at this pinch. I find the Duke of Albe-marle just come, with a great many idle lords and gentlemen, with their pistols and fooleries; and the bulwarke not able to have stood half an hour had they come up; but the Dutch are fallen down from the Hope and Shell-haven as low as Sheer-nesse, and we do plainly at this time hear the guns play.

11TH. Up, and more letters still from Sir W. Coventry about more fire-ships, and so Sir W. Batten and I to the office, where Bruncker come to us, who is just now going to Chatham upon a desire of Commissioner Pett's, who is in a very fearful stink for fear of the Dutch, and desires help for God and the King and kingdom's sake. So Bruncker goes down, and Sir J. Minnes also, from Gravesend. This morning Pett writes us word that Sheer-nesse is lost last night, after two or three hours' dispute. The enemy hath possessed himself of that place; which is very sad, and puts us into great fears of Chatham. Thence I meeting Mr. Moore went toward the other end of the town by coach, and spying Mercer in the street, I took leave of Moore and 'light and followed her, and at Paul's overtook her and walked with her through the dusty street almost to home.

12TH. Find that the Dutch had made no motion since their taking Sheernesse; and the Duke of Albemarle writes that all is safe as to the great ships against any assault, the boom and chaine being so fortified; which put my heart into great joy. When I come to Sir W. Coventry's chamber, I find him abroad; but his clerk, Powell, do tell me that ill newes is come to Court of the Dutch breaking the Chaine at Chatham; which struck me to the heart. And to White Hall to hear the truth of it; and there, going up the backstairs, I did hear some lacquies speaking of sad newes come to Court, saying, that hardly anybody in the Court but do look as if he cried, for the newes is true, that the Dutch have broken the chaine and burned our ships, and particularly "The Royal Charles:" other particulars I know not, but most sad to be sure. And, the truth is, I do fear so much that the whole kingdom is undone, that I do this night resolve to study with my father and wife what to do with the little that I have in money by me, for I give [up] all the rest that I have in the King's hands, for Tangier, for lost. So God help us! I have in my own person, done my full duty, I am sure.

13TH. No sooner up but hear the sad newes confirmed of the Royall Charles being taken by them, and now in fitting by them—and turning several others; and that another fleete is come up into the Hope. Upon which newes the King and Duke of York have been below since four o'clock in the morning, to command the sinking of ships at Barking-Creeke, and other places, to stop their coming up higher: which put me into such a fear, that I presently resolved of my father's and wife's going into the country; and, at two hours' warning, they did go by the coach this day, with about £1,300 in gold in their night-bag. Pray God give them good passage, and good care to hide it when they come home! but my heart is full of fear. They gone, I continued in fright and fear what to do with the rest. W. Hewer hath been at the banker's, and hath got £500 out of Backewell's hands of his own money; but they are so called upon that they will be all broke, hundreds coming to them for money: and their answer is, "It is payable at twenty days—when the days are out, we will pay you." In the evening, I sent for my cousin Sarah [Gyles] and her husband, who come; and I did deliver them my chest of writings about Brampton, and my brother Tom's papers, and my journalls, which I value much; and did send my two silver flaggons to Kate Joyce's: that so, being scattered what I have, something might be saved. I have also made a girdle, by which, with some trouble, I do carry about me £300 in gold about my body, that I may not be without something in case I should be surprised: for I think, in any nation but our's, people that appear (for we are not indeed so) so faulty as we, would have their throats cut. Late at night comes Mr. Hudson, the cooper, my neighbour, and tells me that he come from Chatham this evening at five o'clock, and saw this afternoon "The Royal James," "Oake," and "London" burnt by the enemy with their fire-ships: that two or three men-of-war come up with them, and made no more of Upnor Castle's shooting, than of a fly. I made my will also this day, and did give all I had equally between my father and wife, and left copies of it in each of Mr. Hater and W. Hewer's hands, who both witnessed the will, and so to supper and then to bed, and slept pretty well, but yet often waking.

14TH. The hearts as well as affections of the seamen are turned away; and in the open streets in Wapping, and up and down, the wives have cried publickly, "This comes of your not paying our husbands; and now your work is undone, or done by hands that understand it not." And Sir W. Batten told me that he was himself affronted with a woman, in language of this kind, on Tower Hill publickly yesterday; and we are fain to bear it, and to keep one at the office door to let no idle people in, for fear of firing of the office and doing us mischief. Mr. Hater tells me at noon that some rude people have been, as he hears, at my Lord Chancellor's, where they have cut down the trees before his house and broke his windows; and a gibbet either set up before or painted upon his gate, and these three words writ: "Three sights to be seen; Dunkirke, Tangier, and a barren Queene." Most people that I speak with are in doubt how we shall do to secure our seamen from running over to the Dutch; which is a sad but very true consideration at this day.

16TH (LORD'S DAY). I staid at home busy, and did show some dalliance to my maid Nell, speaking to her of her sweetheart which she had, silly girle. After sermon Roger Pepys comes again. I spent the evening with him much troubled with the thoughts of the evils of our time, whereupon we discoursed. Roger Pepys gone, I to the garden, and there dallied a while all alone with Mrs. Markham, and then home to my chamber and to read and write, and then to supper and to bed.

17TH. I to my business again, and then home to supper and to bed. I have lately played the fool much with our Nell, in playing with her breasts.

20TH. Here dined Mercer with us, and after dinner she cut my hair, and then I into my closet and there slept a little, as I do now almost every day after dinner; and then, after dallying a little with Nell, which I am ashamed to think of, away to the office.

21ST. This day comes news from Harwich that the Dutch fleete are all in sight, near 100 sail great and small, they think, coming towards them; where, they think, they shall be able to oppose them, but do cry out of the falling back of the seamen, few standing by them, and those with much faintness. The like they write from Portsmouth, and their letters this post are worth reading. Sir H. Cholmly come to me this day, and tells me the Court is as mad as ever; and that the night the Dutch burned our ships the King did sup with my Lady Castlemayne, at the Duchess of Monmouth's and they were all mad in hunting of a poor moth.

22ND. In the evening come Captain Hart and Haywood to me about the six merchant-ships now taken up for men-of-war; and in talk they told me about the taking of "The Royal Charles;" that nothing but carelessness lost the ship, for they might have saved her the very tide that the Dutch come up, if they would have but used means and had had but boats; and that the want of boats plainly lost all the other ships. That the Dutch did take her with a boat of nine men, who found not a man on board her, and her laying so near them was a main temptation to them to come on; and presently a man went up and struck her flag and jacke, and a trumpeter sounded upon her "Joan's placket is torn:" that they did carry her down at a time, both for tides and wind, when the best pilot in Chatham would not have undertaken it, they heeling her on one side to make her draw little water: and so carried her away safe.

23RD (LORD'S DAY). After dinner they all to church, and I by water alone to Woolwich, and there called on Mr. Bodham. It is a sad sight to see so many good ships there sunk in the River, while we would be thought to be masters of the sea.

24TH. Povy tells me, speaking of the horrid effeminacy of the King, that the King hath taken ten times more care and pains in making friends between my Lady Castlemayne and Mrs. Stewart, when they have fallen out, than ever he did to save his kingdom; nay, that upon any falling out between my Lady Castlemayne's nurse and her woman, my Lady hath often said she would make the King to make them friends, and they would be friends and be quiet; which the King hath been fain to do: that the King is, at this day, every night in Hyde Park with the Duchesse of Monmouth, or with my Lady Castlemaine.

27TH. Pierce tells me that all the town do cry out of our office, for a pack of fools and knaves; but says that everybody speaks either well, or at least the best of me, which is my great comfort, and I think I do deserve it, and shall shew I have; but yet do think, and he also, that the Parliament will send us all going; and I shall be well contented with it, God knows! News this tide, that about 80 sail of the Dutch, great and small, were seen coming up the river this morning; and this tide some of them to the upper end of the Hope.

28TH. They do here tell me that the Duke of Buckingham hath surrendered himself to Secretary Morrice, and is going to the Tower. Mr. Fenn, at the table, says that he hath been taken by the watch two or three times of late, at unseasonable hours, but so disguised that they could not know him: and when I come home, by and by, Mr. Lowther tells me that the Duke of Buckingham do dine publickly this day at Wadlow's, at the Sun Tavern; and is mighty merry, and sent word to the Lieutenant of the Tower, that he would come to him as soon as he had dined. Now, how sad a thing it is, when we come to make sport of proclaiming men traitors, and banishing them, and putting them out of their offices, and Privy Council, and of sending to and going to the Tower: God have mercy on us! At table, my Lady and Sir Philip Carteret have great and good discourse of the greatness of the present King of France. It is said that he do make a sport of us now; and says, that he knows no reason why his cozen, the King of England, should not be as willing to let him have his kingdom, as that the Dutch should take it from him, which is a most wretched thing that ever we should live to be in this most contemptible condition.

29TH. Up, and by coach to St. James's, and there find Sir W. Coventry and Sir W. Pen above stairs. Then we to talk of the loss of all affection and obedience now in the seamen, so that all power is lost. He told us that he do concur in thinking that want of money to do the most of it, but that that is not all, but the having of gentlemen Captains, who discourage all Tarpaulins, and have given out that they would in a little time bring it to that pass that a Tarpaulin should not dare to aspire to more than to be a Boatswain or a gunner.

30TH (LORD'S DAY). Up about three o'clock, and Creed and I got ourselves ready, and took coach at our gate, it being very fine weather, and the cool of the morning, and with much pleasure, without any stop, go to Rochester about ten of the clock, all the way having mighty pleasant talk of the fate that is over all we do, that it seems as if we were designed in every thing, by land by sea, to undo ourselves. Thence by barge, it raining hard, down to the chaine; and in our way did see the sad wrackes of the poor "Royall Oake," "James," and "London;" and several other of our ships by us sunk, and several of the enemy's, whereof three men-of-war that they could not get off, and so burned. We did also see several dead bodies lie by the side of the water. I do not see that Upnor Castle hath received any hurt by them, though they played long against it; and they themselves shot till they had hardly a gun left upon the carriages, so badly provided they were: they have now made two batteries on that side, which will be very good, and do good service. So to the chaine, and there saw it fast at the end on Upnor side of the River; very fast, and borne up upon the several stages across the River; and where it is broke nobody can tell me. I went on shore on Upnor side to look upon the end of the chaine; and caused the link to be measured, and it was six inches and one-fourth in circumference. They have burned the Crane House that was to hawl it taught. It seems very remarkable to me, and of great honour to the Dutch, that those of them that did go on shore to Gillingham, thought they went in fear of their lives, and were some of them killed; and, notwithstanding their provocation at Schelling, yet killed none of our people nor plundered their houses, but did take some things of easy carriage, and left the rest, and not a house burned; and, which is to our eternal disgrace, that what my Lord Douglas's men, who come after them, found there, they plundered and took all away; and the watermen that carried us did further tell us, that our own soldiers are far more terrible to those people of the country-towns than the Dutch themselves. Back again to Rochester, and there walked to the Cathedral as they were beginning of the service. Then into the fields, a fine walk, and there saw Sir Francis Clerke's house, which is a pretty seat, and then back to our inne and bespoke supper, and so back to the fields and into the Cherry garden, where we had them fresh gathered, and here met with a young, plain, silly shopkeeper, and his wife, a pretty young woman, the man's name Hawkins, and I did kiss her, and we talked (and the woman of the house is a very talking bawdy jade), and eat cherries together, and then to walk in the fields till it was late, and did kiss her. Walked back and left them at their house near our inne, and then to our inne, where, I hear, my Lord Bruncker hath sent for me to speak with me before I go: so I took his coach, which stands there with two horses, and to him and to his bedside, where he was in bed, and hath a watchman with a halbert at his door.

JULY 1ST. Up betimes, about 4 o'clock, waked by a damned noise between a sow gelder and a cow and a dog, nobody after we were up being able to tell us what it was. After being ready we took coach, and, being very sleepy, droused most part of the way to Gravesend, and there 'light, and down to the new batterys, which are like to be very fine, and there did hear a plain fellow cry out upon the folly of the King's officers above, to spend so much money in works at Woolwich and Deptford, and sinking of good ships loaden with goods, when, if half the charge had been laid out here, it would have secured all that, and this place too, before now. And I think it is not only true in this, but that the best of the actions of us all are so silly, that the meanest people begin to see through them, and contemn them. Besides, says he, they spoil the river by it.

7TH (LORD'S DAY). I to my office busy till the evening, and then with my wife and Jane over to Half-way house, a very good walk; and there drank, and in the cool of the evening back again and sang with pleasure upon the water, and were mightily pleased in hearing a boatfull of Spaniards sing, and so home to supper and to bed. Jane of late mighty fine, by reason of a laced whiske her mistress hath given her, which makes her a very graceful servant. But, above all, my wife and I were the most surprised in the beauty of a plain girle, which we met in the little lane going from Redriffe-stairs into the fields, one of the prettiest faces that we think we ever saw in our lives.

12TH. It is strange how he (Sir H. Cholmly) and every body do now-a-days reflect upon Oliver, and commend him, what brave things he did, and made all the neighbour princes fear him; while here a prince, come in with all the love and prayers and good liking of his people, who have given greater signs of loyalty and willingness to serve him with their estates than ever was done by any people, hath lost all so soon, that it is a miracle what way a man could devise to lose so much in so little time. Thence, after dinner, to St. James's, but missed Sir W. Coventry, and so home, and there find my wife in a dogged humour for my not dining at home and I did give her a pull by the nose and some ill words, which she provoked me to by something she spoke, that we fell extraordinarily out, insomuch, that I going to the office to avoid further anger, she followed me in a devilish manner thither, and with much ado I got her into the garden out of hearing to prevent shame, and so home, and by degrees I found it necessary to calme her, and did, and then to the office, where pretty late, and then to walk with her in the garden, and so to supper, and pretty good friends, and so to bed with my mind very quiet.

14TH (LORD'S DAY). Up, and my wife, a little before four, and to make us ready; and by and by Mrs. Turner come to us, by agreement, and she and I staid talking below, while my wife dressed herself, which vexed me that she was so long about it keeping us till past five o'clock before she was ready. She ready; and, taking some bottles of wine, and beer, and some cold fowle with us into the coach, we took coach and four horses, which I had provided last night, and so away. A very fine day, and so towards Epsum, talking all the way pleasantly, and particularly of the pride and ignorance of Mrs. Lowther, in having of her train carried up. The country very fine, only the way very dusty. We got to Epsum by eight o'clock, to the well; where much company, and there we 'light, and I drank the water: they did not, but do go about and walk a little among the women, but I did drink four pints. So we took coach again and to the towne, to the King's Head, where our coachman carried us, and there had an ill room for us to go into, but the best in the house that was not taken up. Here we called for drink, and bespoke dinner; and hear that my Lord Buckhurst and Nelly are lodged at the next house, and Sir Charles Sidly with them: and keep a merry house. Poor girl! I pity her; but more the loss of her at the King's house. Then I carried them to see my cozen Pepys's house, and 'light, and walk round about it, and they like it, as indeed it deserves, very well, and is a pretty place; and then I walked them to the wood hard by, and there got them in the thickets till they had lost themselves, and I could not find the way into any of the walks in the wood, which indeed are very pleasant, if I could have found them. At last got out of the wood again; and I, by leaping down the little bank, coming out of the wood, did sprain my right foot, which brought me great present pain, but presently, with walking, it went away for the present, and so the women and W. Hewer and I walked upon the Downes, where a flock of sheep was; and the most pleasant and innocent sight that ever I saw in my life—we find a shepherd and his little boy reading, far from any houses or sight of people, the Bible to him; so I made the boy read to me, which he did, with the forced tone that children do usually read, that was mighty pretty, and then I did give him something, and went to the father, and talked with him; and I find he had been a servant in my cozen Pepys's house, and told me what was become of their old servants. He did content himself mightily in my liking his boy's reading, and did bless God for him, the most like one of the old patriarchs that ever I saw in my life, and it brought those thoughts of the old age of the world in my mind for two or three days after. So to our inne, and there had a dish of creame, but it was sour, and so had no pleasure in it; and so paid our reckoning, and took coach, it being about seven at night, and passed and saw the people walking with their wives and children to take the ayre, and we set out for home, the sun by and by going down, and we in the cool of the evening all the way with much pleasure home, talking and pleasing ourselves with the pleasure of this day's work. Anon it grew dark, and as it grew dark we had the pleasure to see several glow-wormes, which was mighty pretty, but my foot begins more and more to pain me, which Mrs. Turner, by keeping her warm hand upon it, did much ease.

16TH. In the morning I was able to put on a wide shoe on the foot, and to the office without much pain, and there sat all the morning.

17TH. The Duke of Buckingham is, it seems, set at liberty, without any further charge against him or other clearing of him, but let to go out; which is one of the strangest instances of the fool's play with which all publick things are done in this age, that is to be apprehended.

19TH. Up and comes the flageolet master, and brings me two new great Ivory pipes which cost me 32s., and so to play.

22ND. Creed tells me of the fray between the Duke of Buckingham at the Duke's playhouse the last Saturday (and it is the first day I have heard that they have acted at either the King's or Duke's houses this month or six weeks) and Henry Killigrew, whom the Duke of Buckingham did soundly beat and take away his sword, and make a fool of, till the fellow prayed him to spare his life; and I am glad of it; for it seems in this business the Duke of Buckingham did carry himself very innocently and well, and I wish he had paid this fellow's coat well. I heard something of this at the 'Change to-day: and it is pretty to hear how people do speak kindly of the Duke of Buckingham, as one that will en-quire into faults; and therefore they do mightily favour him. And it puts me in mind that, this afternoon, Billing, the Quaker, meeting me in the Hall, come to me, and after a little discourse, did say, "Well," says he, "now you will be all called to an ac-count," meaning the Parliament is drawing near.

24TH. At noon home to dinner, where my wife mighty musty, but I took no notice of it, but after dinner to the office.

27TH. At the office all the morning; and at noon to the 'Change, where I met Fenn. He tells me that the King and my Lady Castlemayne are quite broke off, and she is going away, and is with child, and swears the King shall own it; and she will have it christened in the Chapel at White Hall so, and owned for the King's, as other Kings have done; or she will bring it into White Hall gallery, and dash the brains of it out before the King's face. He tells me that the King and Court were never in the world so bad as they are now for gaming, swearing, whoring, and drinking, and the most abominable vices that ever were in the world; so that all must come to nought. He [Sir George Carteret] do say that the Court is in a way to ruin all for their pleasures; and says that he himself hath once taken the liberty to tell the King the necessity of having, at least, a show of reli-gion in the Government, and sobriety; and that it was that, that did set up and keep up Oliver, though he was the greatest rogue in the world, and that it is so fixed in the nature of the common Englishman that it will not out of him.

29TH. To Westminster Hall, where the Hall full of people to see the issue of the day, the King being come to speak to the House to-day. One thing extraordinary was, this day a man, a Quaker, came naked through the Hall, only very civilly tied about the privities to avoid scandal, and with a chafing-dish of fire and brimstone burning upon his head, did pass through the Hall, crying, "Repent! repent!" Many guns were heard this afternoon, it seems, at White Hall and in the Temple garden very plain; but what it should be nobody knows, unless the Dutch be driving our ships up the river. To-morrow we shall know.

AUGUST 2ND. Up, but before I rose my wife fell into angry discourse of my kindness yesterday to Mrs. Knipp, and leading her, and sitting in the coach hand in hand, and my arm about her middle, and in some bad words reproached me with it. I was troubled, but having much business in my head and desirous of peace rose and did not provoke her. So she up and come to me and added more, and spoke basely of my father, who I perceive did do something in the country, at her last being there, that did not like her, but I would not enquire into anything, but let her talk, and when ready away to the Office I went. So at 12 at night home to supper and to bed, my wife being gone in an ill humour to bed before me.

5TH. After done with the Duke of York, and coming out through his dressing-room, I there spied Signor Francisco tuning his gittar, and Monsieur de Puy with him, who did make him play to me, which he did most admirably—so well as I was mightily troubled that all that pains should have been taken upon so bad an instrument.

8TH. After dinner to the office a while, and then with my wife to the Temple, where I 'light and sent her to her tailor's. I to my bookseller's; where, by and by, I met Mr. Evelyn, and talked of several things, but particuly of the times; and he tells me that wise men do prepare to remove abroad what they have, for that we must be ruined, our case being past relief, the kingdom so much in debt, and the King minding nothing but his lust, going two days a-week to see my Lady Castlemayne at Sir D. Harvy's.

10TH. After dinner I to the office, and there wrote as long as my eyes would give me leave, and then abroad and to the New Exchange, to the bookseller's there, where I hear of several new books coming out—Mr. Spratt's History of the Royal Society, and Mrs. Phillips's poems. Sir John Denham's poems are going to be all printed together; and, among others, some new things; and among them he showed me a copy of verses of his upon Sir John Minnes's going heretofore to Bullogne to eat a pig. Cowley, he tells me, is dead; who, it seems, was a mighty civil, serious man; which I did not know before.

12TH. My wife waked betimes to call up her maids to washing, and so to bed again, whom I then hugged, it being cold now in the mornings.

16TH. Up, and at the office all the morning, and so at noon to dinner, and after dinner my wife and I to the Duke's playhouse, where we saw the new play acted yesterday, "The Feign Innocence, or Sir Martin Marr-all;" a play made by my Lord Duke of Newcastle, but, as every body says, corrected by Dryden. It is the most entire piece of mirth, a complete farce from one end to the other, that certainly was ever writ. I never laughed so in all my life. I laughed till my head [ached] all the evening and night with the laughing; and at very good wit therein, not fooling. The house full, and in all things of mighty content to me.

17TH. At noon home to dinner, and presently my wife and I and Sir W. Pen to the King's playhouse, where the house extraordinary full; and there was the King and Duke of York to see the new play, "Queen Elizabeth's Troubles, and the History of Eighty Eight." I confess I have sucked in so much of the sad story of Queen Elizabeth, from my cradle, that I was ready to weep for her sometimes; but the play is the most ridiculous that sure ever come upon the stage; and, indeed, is merely a shew, only shews the true garbe of the Queen in those days, just as we see Queen Mary and Queen Elizabeth painted; but the play is merely a puppet play, acted by living puppets. Neither the design nor language better; and one stands by and tells us the meaning of things: only I was pleased to see Knipp dance among the milkmaids, and to hear her sing a song to Queen Elizabeth; and to see her come out in her night-gowne with no lockes on, but her bare face and hair only tied up in a knot behind; which is the comeliest dress that ever I saw her in to her advantage.

18TH (LORD'S DAY). I walked towards White Hall, but, being wearied, turned into St. Dunstan's Church, where I heard an able sermon of the minister of the place; and stood by a pretty, modest maid, whom I did labour to take by the hand and the body; but she would not, but got further and further from me; and, at last, I could perceive her to take pins out of her pocket to prick me if I should touch her again—which seeing I did forbear, and was glad I did spy her design. And then I fell to gaze upon another pretty maid in a pew close to me, and she on me; and I did go about to take her hand, which she suffered a little and then withdrew. So the sermon ended, and the church broke up, and my amours ended also, and so took coach and home, and there took my wife, and to Islington with her.

24TH (ST. BARTHOLOMEW'S DAY). This morning was proclaimed the peace between us and the States of the United Provinces, and also of the King of France and Denmarke; and in the afternoon the Proclamations were printed and come out; and at night the bells rung, but no bonfires that I hear of any where, partly from the dearness of firing, but principally from the little content most people have in the peace.

26TH. I walked to the King's playhouse, there to meet Sir W. Pen, and saw "The Surprizall," a very mean play, I thought: or else it was because I was out of humour, and but very little company in the house. But there Sir W. Pen and I had a great deal of discourse with Moll; who tells us that Nell is already left by my Lord Buckhurst, and that he makes sport of her, and swears she hath had all she could get of him; and Hart, her great admirer, now hates her; and that she is very poor, and hath lost my Lady Castlemayne, who was her great friend also: but she is come to the House, but is neglected by them all.

27TH. This day Mr. Pierce, the surgeon, was with me; and tells me how this business of my Lord Chancellor's was certainly designed in my Lady Castlemayne's chamber; and that, when he went from the King on Monday morning, she was in bed, though about twelve o'clock, and ran out in her smock into her aviary looking into White Hall garden; and thither her woman brought her her nightgown; and stood there joying herself at the old man's going away; and several of the gallants of White Hall, of which there were many staying to see the Chancellor return, did talk to her in her birdcage; among others, Blancford, telling her she was the bird of paradise.

SEPTEMBER 2ND. After dinner comes in Mr. Townsend; and there I was witness of a horrid rateing, which Mr. Ashburnham, as one of the Grooms of the King's Bed-chamber, did give him for want of linen for the King's person; which he swore was not to be endured, and that the King would not endure it, and that the King his father, would have hanged his Wardrobe-man should he have been served so: the King having at this day no handkerchers, and but three bands to his neck, he swore. Mr. Townsend answered want of money, and the owing of the linen-draper £5,000. From him I went to see a great match at tennis, between Prince Rupert and one Captain Cooke, against Bab. May and the elder Chichly; where the King was, and Court; and it seems are the best players at tennis in the nation.

15TH. My wife and I to my chamber, where, through the badness of my eyes, she was forced to read to me, which she do very well, and was Mr. Boyle's discourse upon the style of the Scripture, which is a very fine piece, and so to bed.

23RD. Another pretty thing was my Lady Ashly's speaking of the bad qualities of glass-coaches; among others, the flying open of the doors upon any great shake: but another was, that my Lady Peterborough being in her glass-coach, with the glass up, and seeing a lady pass by in a coach whom she would salute, the glass was so clear, that she thought it had been open, and so ran her head through the glass, and cut all her forehead!

28TH. Up, having slept not so much to-night as I used to do, for my thoughts being so full of this pretty little girle that is coming to live with us, which pleases me mightily.

30TH. So by coach home, and there found our pretty girl Willet come, brought by Mr. Batelier, and she is very pretty, and so grave as I never saw a little thing in my life. Indeed I think her a little too good for my family, and so well carriaged as I hardly ever saw. I wish my wife may use her well.

OCTOBER 5TH. Took my wife and Willet to the Duke of York's playhouse, but the house so full, it being a new play, "The Coffee House," that we could not get in, and so to the King's house: and there, going in, met with Knepp, and she took us up into the tireing-rooms: and to the women's shift, where Nell was dressing herself, and was all unready, and is very pretty, prettier than I thought. And so walked all up and down the house above, and then below into the scene-room, and there sat down, and she gave us fruit: and here I read the questions to Knepp, while she answered me, through all her part of "Flora's Figary's" which was acted to-day. But, Lord! to see how they were both painted would make a man mad, and did make me loath them; and what base company of men comes among them, and how lewdly they talk! and how poor the men are in clothes, and yet what a shew they make on the stage by candle-light, is very observable. But to see how Nell cursed, for having so few people in the pit, was pretty; the other house carrying away all the people at the new play, and is said, now-a-days, to have generally most company, as being better players. By and by into the pit, and there saw the play, which is pretty good, but my belly was full of what I had seen in the house, and so, after the play done, away home, and there to the writing my letters, and so home to supper and to bed.

7TH. Up betimes, and so, about nine o'clock, I, and my wife, and Willet, set out in a coach I have hired, with four horses; and W. Hewer and Murford rode by us on horseback; and so my wife and she in their morning gowns, very handsome and pretty, and to my great liking. We set out, and so out at Allgate, and so to the Green Man, and so on to Enfield, in our way seeing Mr. Lowther and his lady in a coach, going to Waltham-stow; and he told us that he would overtake us at night, he being to go that way. So we to Enfield, and there bayted, it being but a foul, bad day, and there Lowther and Mr. Burford, an acquaintance of his, did overtake us, and there drank and eat together; and, by and by, we parted, we going before them, and very merry, my wife and girle and I talking, and telling tales, and singing, and before night come to Bishop Stafford, where Lowther and his friend did meet us again, and carried us to the Raynedeere; where Mrs. Aynsworth, who lived heretofore at Cambridge, and whom I knew better than they think for, do live. It was the woman that, among other things, was great with my cozen Barnston, of Cottenham, and did use to sing to him, and did teach me "Full forty times over," a very lewd song: a woman they are very well acquainted with, and is here what she was at Cambridge, and all the good fellows of the country come hither. Lowther and his friend stayed and drank, and then went further this night; but here we stayed, and supped, and lodged. And so to bed, my wife and I in one bed, and the girl in another, in the same room, and lay very well, but there was so much tearing company in the house, that we could not see my landlady; so I had no opportunity of renewing my old acquaintance with her, but here we slept very well.

9TH. Up, and got ready, and eat our breakfast; and then took coach. And so away for Huntingdon mightily pleased all along the road to remember old stories; and come to Brampton at about noon, and there find my father and sister and brother all well: and here laid up our things, and up and down to see the garden with my father, and the house, and do altogether find it very pretty; especially the little parlour and the summerhouses in the garden. But altogether is very pretty; and I bless God that I am like to have such a pretty place to retire to: and I did walk with my father without doors, and do find a very convenient way of laying out money there in building, which will make a very good seat, and the place deserves it, I think, very well. By and by to dinner, and after dinner I walked up to Hinchingbroke, where my Lady expected me; and there spent all the afternoon with her: the same most excellent, good, discreet lady that ever she was; and, among other things, is mightily pleased with the lady that is like to be her son Hinchingbroke's wife, which I am mightily glad of. By and by my wife comes with Willet, my wife in her velvett vest, which is mighty fine, and becomes her exceedingly. I am pleased with my Lady Paulina and Anne, who both are grown very proper ladies, and handsome enough. So all to bed. My wife and I in the high bed in our chamber, and Willet in the trundle bed, which she desired to lie in, by us.

10TH. Waked in the morning with great pain of the collique, by cold taken yesterday, I believe, with going up and down in my shirt, but with rubbing my belly, keeping of it warm, I did at last come to some ease, and rose, and up to walk up and down the garden with my father, to talk of all our concernments: about a husband for my sister, whereof there is at present no appearance; but we must endeavour to find her one now, for she grows old and ugly: then for my brother; and resolve he shall stay here this winter, and then I will either send him to Cambridge for a year, till I get him some church promotion, or send him to sea as a chaplain, where he may study, and earn his living. My father and I, with a dark lantern, it being now night, into the garden with my wife, and there went about our great work to dig up my gold. But, Lord! what a tosse I was for some time in, that they could not justly tell where it was; that I begun heartily to sweat, and be angry, that they should not agree better upon the place, and at last to fear that it was gone: but by and by poking with a spit, we found it, and then begun with a spudd to lift up the ground. But, good God! to see how silly they did it, not half a foot under ground, and in the sight of the world from a hundred places, if any body by accident were near hand, and within sight of a neighbour's window, and their hearing also, being close by: only my father says that he saw them all gone to church before he begun the work, when he laid the money, but that do not excuse it to me. But I was out of my wits almost, and the more from that, upon lifting up the earth with the spudd, I did discern that I had scattered the pieces of gold round about the ground among the grass and loose earth; and taking up the iron head-pieces wherein they were put, I perceive the earth was got among the gold, and wet, so that the bags were all rotten, and all the notes, that I could not tell what in the world to say to it, not knowing how to judge what was wanting, or what had been lost by Gibson in his coming down: which, all put together, did make me mad; and at last was forced to take up the head-pieces, dirt and all, and as many of the scattered pieces as I could with the dirt discern by the candle-light, and carry them up into my brother's chamber, and there locke them up till I had eat a little supper: and then, all people going to bed, W. Hewer and I did all alone, with several pails of water and basins, at last wash the dirt off of the pieces, and parted the pieces and the dirt, and then begun to tell [them]; and by a note which I had of the value of the whole in my pocket, do find that there was short above a hundred pieces, which did make me mad; so W. Hewer and I out again about midnight, for it was now grown so late, and there by candle-light did make shift to gather forty-five pieces more. And so in, and to cleanse them: and by this time it was past two in the morning; and so to bed, with my mind pretty quiet to think that I have recovered so many.

11TH. Rose and called W. Hewer, and he and I, with pails and a sieve, did lock ourselves into the garden, and there gather all the earth about the place into pails, and then sift those pails in one of the summer-houses, just as they do for dyamonds in other parts of the world; and there, to our great content, did with much trouble by nine o'clock (and by the time we emptied

several pails and could not find one), we did make the last
night's forty-five up seventy-nine: so that we are come to about
twenty or thirty of what I think the true number should be; and
perhaps within less; and of them I may reasonably think that
Mr. Gibson might lose some: so I am pretty well satisfied that
my loss is not great, and do bless God that it is so well, and do
leave my father to make a second examination of the dirt,
which he promises he will do, and, poor man, is mightily troubled for this accident, but I declared myself well satisfied, and
so indeed I am. Here I took leave of my father, and did give my
sister 20s. She cried at my going; but whether it was at her unwillingness for my going, or any unkindness of my wife's, or no,
I know not; but, God forgive me! I take her to be so cunning and
ill-natured, that I have no great love for her; but only [she] is
my sister, and must be provided for. My gold I put into a basket,
and set under one of the seats; and so my work every quarter of
an hour was to look to see whether all was well; and I did ride
in great fear all the day, but it was a pleasant day, and good
company, and I mightily contented.

12TH. Up, and eat our breakfast, and set out about nine o'-
clock, and so to Barnett, where we staid and baited, the weather
very good all day and yesterday, and by five o'clock got home,
where I find all well; and did bring my gold, to my heart's content, very safe home, having not this day carried it in a basket,
but in our hands: the girl took care of one, and my wife another
bag, and I the rest, I being afraid of the bottom of the coach,
lest it should break, and therefore was at more ease in my mind
than I was yesterday.

13TH (LORD'S DAY). Up, and by water to White Hall, and
thence walked to Sir W. Coventry's lodgings, but he was gone
out, so I to St. James's, and there to the Duke of York's chamber:
and there he was dressing; and many Lords and Parliament-
men come to kiss his hands, they being newly come to town.
And there the Duke of York did of himself call me to him, and
tell me that he had spoke to the King, and that the King had
granted me the ship I asked for; and did, moreover, say that he

was mightily satisfied with my service, and that he would be willing to do anything that was in his power for me: which he said with mighty kindness; which I did return him thanks for, and departed with mighty joy, more than I did expect.

20TH (LORD'S DAY). This morning is brought to me an order for the presenting the Committee of Parliament to-morrow with a list of the commanders and ships' names of all the fleetes sent out since the war, and particularly of those ships which were divided from the fleete with Prince Rupert; which gives me occasion to see that they are busy after that business, and I am glad of it.

22ND. Slept but ill all the last part of the night, for fear of this day's success in Parliament: therefore up, and all of us all the morning close, till almost two o'clock, collecting all we had to say and had done from the beginning touching the safety of the River Medway and Chatham. And, having done this, and put it into order, we away, I not having time to eat my dinner; and so all in my Lord Bruncker's coach, that is to say, Bruncker, W. Pen, T. Harvy, and myself. We come to the Parliament-door, and there, after a little waiting till the Committee was sat, we were, the House being very full, called in: Sir W. Pen went in and sat as a Member; and my Lord Bruncker would not at first go in, expecting to have a chair set for him, and his brother bid him not go in, till he was called for; but, after a few words, I had occasion to mention him, and so he was called in, but without any more chair or respect paid him than myself: and so Bruncker, and T. Harvy, and I, were there to answer: and I had a chair brought me to lean my books upon: and so did give them such an account, in a series of the whole business that had passed the Office touching the matter, and so answered all questions given me about it, that I did not perceive but they were fully satisfied with me and the business as to our Office: and then Commissioner Pett (who was by at all my discourse, and this held till within an hour after candle-light, for I had candles brought in to read my papers by) was to answer for himself, we having lodged all matters with him for execution.

But, Lord! what a tumultuous thing this Committee is, for all the reputation they have of a great council, is a strange consideration; there being as impertinent questions, and as disorderly proposed, as any man could make. At last, the House dismissed us, and shortly after did adjourne the debate till Friday next: and my cozen Pepys did come out and joy me in my acquitting myself so well, and so did several others, and my fellow-officers all very brisk to see themselves so well acquitted; which makes me a little proud, but yet not secure but we may yet meet with a back-blow which we see not.

23RD. Up, and Sir W. Pen and I in his coach to White Hall, there to attend the Duke of York. Thence Sir W. Pen and I back into London; and there saw the King, with his kettle-drums and trumpets, going to the Exchange, to lay the first stone of the first pillar of the new building of the Exchange. They did vote this day thanks to be given to the Prince and Duke of Albemarle, for their care and conduct in the last year's war, which is a strange act; but, I know not how, the blockhead Albemarle hath strange luck to be loved, though he be, and every man must know it, the heaviest man in the world, but stout and honest to his country.

NOVEMBER 2ND. Up, and to the office, where busy all the morning; at noon home, and after dinner my wife and Willett and I to the King's playhouse, and there saw "Henry the Fourth:" and contrary to expectation, was pleased in nothing more than in Cartwright's speaking of Falstaffe's speech about "What is Honour?" The house full of Parliament-men, it being holyday with them: and it was observable how a gentleman of good habit, sitting just before us, eating of some fruit in the midst of the play, did drop down as dead, being choked; but with much ado Orange Moll did thrust her finger down his throat, and brought him to life again. After the play, we home, and I busy at the office late, and then home to supper and to bed.

11TH. To Captain Cocke's (he out of doors), and there drank their morning draught, and thence [Sir] G. Carteret and I toward the Temple in coach together; and there he did tell me how the King do all he can in the world to overthrow my Lord Chancellor, and that notice is taken of every man about the King that is not seen to promote the ruine of the Chancellor; and that this being another great day in his business, he dares not but be there. He tells me that as soon as Secretary Morrice brought the Great Seale from my Lord Chancellor, Bab. May fell upon his knees, and catched the King about the legs, and joyed him, and said that this was the first time that ever he could call him King of England, being freed from this great man: which was a most ridiculous saying. And he told me that, when first my Lord Gerard, a great while ago, come to the King, and told him that the Chancellor did say openly that the King was a lazy person and not fit to govern, which is now made one of the things in the people's mouths against the Chancellor, "Why," says the King, "that is no news, for he hath told me so twenty times, and but the other day he told me so;" and made matter of mirth at it; but yet this light discourse is likely to prove bad to him.

12TH. Up, and to the Office, where sat all the morning; and there hear the Duke of York do yet do very well with his small-pox: pray God he may continue to do so!

19TH. My father did also this week, by Shepley, return me up a guinny, which, it seems, upon searching the ground, they have found since I was there.

DECEMBER 3RD. Sir Richard Ford told us this evening that this day hath been made appear to them that the Keeper of Newgate, at this day, hath made his house the only nursery of rogues, and whores, and pickpockets, and thieves in the world; where they were bred and entertained, and the whole society met.

4TH. Into the House, and there spied a pretty woman with spots on her face, well clad, who was enquiring for the guard chamber; I followed her, and there she went up, and turned into the turning towards the chapel, and I after her, and upon the stairs there met her coming up again, and there kissed her twice, and her business was to enquire for Sir Edward Bishop, one of the serjeants at armes. I believe she was a woman of pleasure, but was shy enough to me, and so I saw her go out afterwards, and I took a hackney coach, and away.

6TH. Up, and with Sir J. Minnes to the Duke of York, the first time that I have seen him, or we waited on him, since his sickness; and, blessed be God! he is not at all the worse for the smallpox, but is only a little weak yet. We did much business with him, and so parted.

7TH. All the morning at the office, and at noon home to dinner with my clerks, and while we were at dinner comes Willet's aunt to see her and my wife; she is a very fine widow and pretty handsome but extraordinary well carriaged and speaks very handsomely and with extraordinary understanding, so as I spent the whole afternoon in her company with my wife, she understanding all the things of note touching plays and fashions and Court and everything and speaks rarely, which pleases me mightily, and seems to love her niece very well, and was so glad (which was pretty odde) that since she came hither her breasts begin to swell, she being afeard before that she would have none, which was a pretty kind of content she gave herself.

19TH. At the office all the afternoon, and at night by coach to Westminster. Here I hear how the House of Lords, with great severity, if not tyranny, have ordered poor Carr to stand in the pillory two or three times, and his eares cut, and be imprisoned I know not how long. But it is believed that the Commons, when they meet, will not be well pleased with it; and they have no reason, I think.

21ST. At the office all the morning, and at noon home to dinner with my Clerks and Creed, who among other things all alone, after dinner, talking of the times, he tells me that the Nonconformists are mighty high, and their meetings frequented and connived at; and they do expect to have their day now soon; for my Lord of Buckingham is a declared friend to them, and even to the Quakers, who had very good words the other day from the King himself.

22ND (LORD'S DAY). Up, and my wife, poor wretch, still in pain, and then to dress myself and down to my chamber to settle some papers, and thither come to me Willet with an errand from her mistress, and this time I first did give her a little kiss, she being a very pretty humoured girle, and so one that I do love mightily.

23RD. Meeting there with Creed, he and I to the Exchange, and there I saw Carr stand in the pillory for the business of my Lord Gerard, which is supposed will make a hot business in the House of Commons, when they shall come to sit again, the Lords having ordered this with great injustice, as all people think. This day, at the 'Change, Creed shewed me Mr. Coleman, of whom my wife hath so good an opinion, and says that he is as very a rogue for women as any in the world; which did disquiet me, like a fool, and run in my mind a great while.

24TH. So to White Hall, and sent my coach round, I through the Park to chapel, where I got in up almost to the rail, and with a great deal of patience staid from nine at night to two in the morning, in a very great crowd; and there expected, but found nothing extraordinary, there being nothing but a high masse. The Queen was there, and some ladies. But, Lord! what an odde thing it was for me to be in a crowd of people, here a footman, there a beggar, here a fine lady, there a zealous poor papist, and here a Protestant, two or three together, come to see the shew. I was afeared of my pocket being picked very much. . . . Their musique very good indeed, but their service I confess too frivolous, that there can be no zeal go along with it, and I do find by them themselves that they do run over their beads with one hand, and point and play and talk and make signs with the other in the midst of their masse. But all things very rich and beautiful; and I see the papists have the wit, most of them, to bring cushions to kneel on, which I wanted, and was mightily troubled to kneel. All being done, there I left people receiving the Sacrament: and the Queen gone, and ladies; only my Lady Castlemayne, who looked prettily in her night-clothes, and so took my coach, which waited, and away through Covent Garden, to set down two gentlemen and a lady, who come thither to see also, and did make mighty mirth in their talk of the folly of this religion. And so I stopped, having set them down and drank some burnt wine at the Rose Tavern door, while the constables come, and two or three Bellmen went by.

25TH. It being a fine, light, moonshine morning, and so home round the city, and stopped and dropped money at five or six places, which I was the willinger to do, it being Christmas-day, and so home, and there find my wife in bed, and Jane and the maids making pyes, and so I to bed, and slept well, and rose about nine, and to church.

28TH. Up, and to the office, where busy all the morning. With my wife and girle to the King's house, and there saw "The Mad Couple," which is but an ordinary play; but only Nell's and Hart's mad parts are most excellently done, but especially her's: which makes it a miracle to me to think how ill she do any serious part, as, the other day, just like a fool or changeling; and, in a mad part, do beyond all imitation almost.

30TH. I met with Cooling at the Temple-gate, after I had been at both my booksellers—and there laid out several pounds in books now against the new year. From the 'Change (where I met with Captain Cocke, who would have borrowed money of me, but I had the grace to deny him, he would have had 3 or £400).

1668

JANUARY 1ST. Thence I after dinner to the Duke of York's playhouse, and there saw "Sir Martin Mar-all;" which I have seen so often, and yet am mightily pleased with it, and think it mighty witty, and the fullest of proper matter for mirth that ever was writ; and I do clearly see that they do improve in their acting of it. Here a mighty company of citizens, 'prentices, and others; and it makes me observe, that when I begun first to be able to bestow a play on myself, I do not remember that I saw so many by half of the ordinary 'prentices and mean people in the pit at 2s. 6d. a-piece as now; I going for several years no higher than the 12d. and then the 18d. places, though I strained hard to go in then when I did: so much the vanity and prodigality of the age is to be observed in this particular. By and by I met with Mr. Brisband; and having it in my mind this Christmas to (do what I never can remember that I did) go to see the manner of the gaming at the Groome-Porter's, I having in my coming from the playhouse stepped into the two Temple-halls, and there saw the dirty 'prentices and idle people playing. I did tell Brisband of it, and he did lead me thither, where, after staying an hour, they begun to play at about eight at night, where to see how differently one man took his losing from another, one cursing and swearing, and another only muttering and grumbling to himself, a third without any apparent discontent at all: to see how the dice will run good luck in one hand, for half an hour together, and another have no good luck at all: to see how easily here, where they play nothing but guinnys, a £100 is won or lost: to see two or three gentlemen come in there drunk, and putting their stock of gold together, one 22 pieces, the second 4, and the third 5 pieces; and these to play one with another, and forget how much each of them brought, but he that brought the 22 thinks that he brought no more than the rest: to see the different humours of gamesters to change their luck, when it is bad, how ceremonious they are as to call for new dice, to shift their places, to alter their manner of throwing, and that with great industry, as if there was anything in it: to see how some old gamesters, that have no money now to spend as formerly, do come and sit and look on, as among others, Sir Lewis Dives, who was here, and hath been a great gamester in his time: to hear their cursing and damning to no purpose, as one man being to throw a seven if he could, and, failing to do it after a great many throws, cried he would be damned if ever he flung seven more while he lived, his despair of throwing it being so great, while others did it as their luck served almost every throw: to see how persons of the best quality do here sit down, and play with people of any, though meaner; and to see how people in ordinary clothes shall come hither, and play away 100, or 2 or 300 guinnys, without any kind of difficulty: and lastly, to see the formality of the groome-porter, who is their judge of all disputes in play and all quarrels that may arise therein, and how his under-officers are there to observe true play at each table, and to give new dice, is a consideration I never could have thought had been in the world, had I not now seen it. And another pretty observation of a man, that did win mighty fast when I was there. I think he won £100 at single pieces in a little time. While all the rest envied him his good fortune, he cursed it, saying, "A pox on it, that it should come so early upon me, for this fortune two hours hence would be worth something to me, but then, God damn me, I shall have no such luck." This kind of prophane, mad entertainment they give themselves. And so I, having enough for once, refusing to venture, though Brisband pressed me hard, and tempted me with saying that no man was ever known to lose the first time, the devil being too cunning to discourage a gamester; and he offered me also to lend me ten pieces to venture; but I did refuse, and so went away, and took coach and home about 9 or 10 at night.

2ND. Up, and with Sir J. Minnes by coach to White Hall, and there attended the King and the Duke of York in the Duke of York's lodgings, with the rest of the Officers and many of the Commanders of the fleete, and some of our master ship-wrights. Mr. Wren whispered me in the eare, and said that the Duke of Albemarle had put it into his Narrative for the House, that not above twenty-five ships fought in the engagement wherein he was, and that another was brought into his ship that had been turned out of his place when he was a boatswain, not long before, for being a drunkard. And the Prince said to me, standing by me, "God damn me, if they will turn out every man that will be drunk, they must turn out all the commanders in the fleete. What is the matter if he be drunk, so when he comes to fight he do his work? At least, let him be punished for his drunkenness, and not put out of his command presently." This he spoke, very much concerned for this idle fellow, one Greene.

6TH. Up, leaving my wife to get her ready, and the maids to get a supper ready against night for our company; and I by coach to White Hall. Home, where we find my house with good fires and candles ready, and our Office the like, and the two Mercers, and Betty Turner, Pendleton, and W. Batelier. And so with much pleasure we into the house, and there fell to danc-ing, having extraordinary musick, two viollins, and a base viollin, and theorbo, four hands, the Duke of Buckingham's musique, the best in towne, sent me by Greeting, and there we set in to dancing. By and by to my house, to a very good supper, and mighty merry, and good musick playing; and after supper to dancing and singing till about twelve at night; and then we had a good sack posset for them, and an excellent cake, cost me near 20s., of our Jane's making, which was cut into twenty pieces, there being by this time so many of our company, by the coming in of young Goodyer and some others of our neighbours, young men that could dance, hearing of our dancing; and anon comes in Mrs. Turner, the mother, and brings with her Mrs. Hollworthy, which pleased me mightily. And so to dancing again, and singing, with extraordinary great pleasure, till about two in the morning, and then broke up. I paid the fiddlers £3 among the four, and so away to bed, weary and mightily pleased, and have the happiness to reflect upon it as I do sometimes on other things, as going to a play or the like, to be the greatest real comfort that I am to expect in the world, and that it is that that we do really labour in the hopes of; and so I do really enjoy myself, and understand that if I do not do it now I shall not hereafter, it may be, be able to pay for it, or have health to take pleasure in it, and so fill myself with vain expectation of pleasure and go without it.

10TH. Up, and with Sir Denis Gawden, who called me, to White Hall, and there to wait on the Duke of York with the rest of my brethren, which we did a little in the King's Greenroom, while the King was in Council. This morning there was a Persian in that country dress, with a turban, waiting to kiss the King's hand in the Vane-room, against he come out: it was a comely man as to features, and his dress, methinks, very comely. Thence to my new bookseller's, Martin's. The truth is, I have bought a great many books lately to a great value; but I think to buy no more till Christmas next, and those that I have will so fill my two presses that I must be forced to give away some to make room for them, it being my design to have no more at any time for my proper library than to fill them. So home to dinner, and then with my wife and Deb. to the King's house, to see "Aglaura," which hath been always mightily cried up; and so I went with mighty expectation, but do find nothing extraordinary in it at all, and but hardly good in any degree.

11TH. So up, and to the office, where all the morning busy, and thence home to dinner, and from dinner with Mercer, who dined with us, and wife and Deb. to the King's house, there to see "The Wild-goose Chase," which I never saw, but have long longed to see it, being a famous play, but as it was yesterday I do find that where I expect most I find least satisfaction, for in this play I met with nothing extraordinary at all, but very dull inventions and designs. Knepp come and sat by us, and her talk pleased me a little, she telling me how Mis Davis is for certain going away from the Duke's house, the King being in love with her; and a house is taken for her, and furnishing; and she hath a ring given her already worth £600: that the King did send several times for Nelly, and she was with him, but what he did she knows not; this was a good while ago, and she says that the King first spoiled Mrs. Weaver, which is very mean, methinks, in a prince, and I am sorry for it, and can hope for no good to the State from having a Prince so devoted to his pleasure. And then home to supper, and so by the fireside to have my head combed, as I do now often do, by Deb., whom I love should be fiddling about me, and so to bed.

16TH. At noon home to dinner with my gang of clerks, in whose society I am mightily pleased, and mightily with Mr. Gibson's talking; he telling me so many good stories relating to the war and practices of commanders, which I will find a time to recollect; and he will be an admirable help to my writing a history of the Navy, if ever I do. So little care there has been to this day to know or keep any history of the Navy.

17TH. Up, and by coach to White Hall to attend the Council there, and here I met first by Mr. Castle the shipwright, whom I met there, and then from the whole house the discourse of the duell yesterday between the Duke of Buckingham, Holmes, and one Jenkins, on one side, and my Lord of Shrewsbury, Sir John Talbot, and one Bernard Howard, on the other side: and all about my Lady Shrewsbury, who is a whore, and is at this time, and hath for a great while been, a whore to the Duke of Buckingham. And so her husband challenged him, and they met yesterday in a close near Barne-Elmes, and there fought: and my Lord Shrewsbury is run through the body, from the right breast through the shoulder: and Sir John Talbot all along up one of his armes; and Jenkins killed upon the place, and the rest all, in a little measure, wounded. This will make the world think that the King hath good councillors about him, when the Duke of Buckingham, the greatest man about him, is a fellow of no more sobriety than to fight about a whore. And this may prove a very bad accident to the Duke of Buckingham, but that my Lady Castlemayne do rule all at this time as much as ever she did, and she will, it is believed, keep all matters well with the Duke of Buckingham: though this is a time that the King will be very backward, I suppose, to appear in such a business.

18TH. At the office all the morning busy sitting. At noon home to dinner, where Betty Turner dined with us, and after dinner carried my wife, her and Deb. to the 'Change, where they bought some things, while I bought "The Mayden Queene," a play newly printed, which I like at the King's house so well, of Mr. Dryden's, which he himself, in his preface, seems to brag of, and indeed is a good play.

21ST. Up, and while at the office comes news from Kate Joyce that if I would see her husband alive, I must come presently. So, after the office was up, I to him, and W. Hewer with me, and find him in his sick bed (I never was at their house, this Inne, before) very sensible in discourse and thankful for my kindness to him, and his breath rattled in his throate, and they did lay pigeons to his feet while I was in the house, and all despair of him, and with good reason. But the story is that it seems on Thursday last he went sober and quiet out of doors in the morning to Islington, and behind one of the inns, the White Lion, did fling himself into a pond, was spied by a poor woman and got out by some people binding up hay in a barn there, and set on his head and got to life, and known by a woman coming that way; and so his wife and friends sent for. He confessed his

doing the thing, being led by the Devil; and do declare his reason to be, his trouble that he found in having forgot to serve
God as he ought, since he come to this new employment: and I
believe that, and the sense of his great loss by the fire, did bring
him to it, and so everybody concludes. He stayed there all that
night, and come home by coach next morning, and there grew
sick, and worse and worse to this day. I stayed awhile among the
friends that were there, and they being now in fear that the
goods and estate would be seized on, though he lived all this
while, because of his endeavouring to drown himself, my cozen
did endeavour to remove what she could of plate out of the
house, and desired me to take my flagons; which I was glad of,
and did take them away with me in great fear all the way of
being seized; though there was no reason for it, he not being
dead, but yet so fearful I was. So home, and there eat my dinner,
and busy all the afternoon, and troubled at this business. In the
evening with Sir D. Gawden, to Guild Hall, to advise with the
Towne-Clerke about the practice of the City and nation in this
case: and he thinks that it cannot be found selfe-murder; but if
it be, it will fall, all the estate, to the King. So we parted, and I
to my cozen's again; where I no sooner come but news was
brought down from his chamber that he was departed. So, at
their entreaty, I presently took coach to White Hall, and there
find Sir W. Coventry; and he carried me to the King, the Duke
of York being with him, and there told my story which I had
told him: and the King, without more ado, granted that, if it was
found, the estate should be to the widow and children.

22ND. This day come the first demand from the Commissioners of Accounts to us, and it contains more than we shall
ever be able to answer while we live, and I do foresee we shall
be put to much trouble and some shame, at least some of us.
Thence stole away after dinner to my cozen Kate's, and there
find the Crowner's jury sitting, but they could not end it, but
put off the business to Shrove Tuesday next, and so do give way
to the burying of him, and that is all; but they all incline to find
it a natural death, though there are mighty busy people to have
it go otherwise, thinking to get his estate, but are mistaken.

Thence, after sitting with her and company a while, comforting her: though I can find she can, as all other women, cry, and yet talk of other things all in a breath.

24TH. After dinner carried my wife to the Temple, and thence she to a play, and I to St. Andrew's church, in Holburne, at the 'Quest House, where the company meets to the burial of my cozen Joyce; and here I staid with a very great rabble of four or five hundred people of mean condition, and I staid in the room with the kindred till ready to go to church, where there is to be a sermon of Dr. Stillingfleete, and thence they carried him to St. Sepulchre's. But it being late, and, indeed, not having a black coat to lead her [Kate Joyce] with, or follow the corps, I away, and saw, indeed, a very great press of people follow the corps. I to the King's playhouse, to fetch my wife, and there saw the best part of "The Mayden Queene," which, the more I see, the more I love, and think one of the best plays I ever saw, and is certainly the best acted of any thing ever the House did, and particularly Becke Marshall, to admiration. Found my wife and Deb., and saw many fine ladies, and sat by Colonell Reames, who understands and loves a play as well as I, and I love him for it.

27TH. Here Mr. Povy do tell me how he is like to lose his £400 a-year pension of the Duke of York, which he took in consideration of his place which was taken from him. He tells me the Duchesse is a devil against him, and do now come like Queen Elizabeth, and sits with the Duke of York's Council, and sees what they do; and she crosses out this man's wages and prices, as she sees fit, for saving money; but yet, he tells me, she reserves £5,000 a-year for her own spending; and my Lady Peterborough, by and by, tells me that the Duchesse do lay up, mightily, jewels. Thence to my Lady Peterborough's, she desiring to speak with me. She loves to be taken dressing herself, as I always find her.

28TH. Coming home, my wife and I went and saw Kate Joyce, who is still in mighty sorrow, and the more from something that Dr. Stillingfleete should simply say in his sermon, of her husband's manner of dying, as killing himself.

29TH. So home, and there to dinner, and after dinner all the afternoon and till 12 o'clock at night with Mr. Gibson at home upon my Tangier accounts, and did end them fit to be given the last of them to the Auditor tomorrow, to my great content. This evening come Betty Turner and the two Mercers, and W. Batelier, and they had fiddlers, and danced, and kept a quarter, which pleased me, though it disturbed me; but I could not be with them all.

31ST. Up; and by coach, with W. Griffin with me, and our Contract-books, to Durham Yard, to the Commissioners for Accounts; the first time I ever was there; and staid awhile before I was admitted to them. Presently I was called in, where I found the whole number of Commissioners, and was there received with great respect and kindness; and did give them great satisfaction, making it my endeavour to inform them what it was they were to expect from me, and what was the duty of other people; this being my only way to preserve myself, after all my pains and trouble. They did ask many questions, and demanded other books of me, which I did give them very ready and acceptable answers to; and, upon the whole, I observe they do go about their business like men resolved to go through with it, and in a very good method, like men of understanding. They have Mr. Jessop, their secretary; and it is pretty to see that they are fain to find out an old-fashioned man of Cromwell's to do their business for them, as well as the Parliament to pitch upon such, for the most part, in the list of people that were brought into the House, for Commissioners. I went away, with giving and receiving great satisfaction.

FEBRUARY 2ND (LORD'S DAY). Wife took physick this day, I all day at home, and all the morning setting my books in order in my presses, for the following year, their number being much increased since the last, so as I am fain to lay by several books to make room for better, being resolved to keep no more than just my presses will contain. At noon to dinner, my wife coming down to me, and a very good dinner we had, of a powdered leg of pork and a loin of lamb roasted, and with much content she and I and Deb. After dinner my head combed an hour, and then to work again.

5TH. Up, and I to Captain Cocke's, where he and I did discourse of our business that we are to go about to the Commissioners of Accounts about our prizes, and having resolved to conceal nothing but to confess the truth, the truth being likely to do us most good, we parted, and I to White Hall, where missing of the Commissioners of the Treasury, I to the Commissioners of Accounts, where I was forced to stay two hours before I was called in, and when come in did take an oath to declare the truth to what they should ask me, which is a great power, I doubt more than the Act do, or as some say can, give them, to force a man to swear against himself; and so they fell to enquire about the business of prize-goods, wherein I did answer them as well as I could, answer them in everything the just truth, keeping myself to that. They were inquisitive into the minutest particulars, and had had great information; but I think that they can do me no hurt—at the worst, more than to make me refund, if it must be known, what profit I did make of my agreement with Captain Cocke. After they had done with me, they called in Captain Cocke, with whom they were shorter; and I do fear he may answer foolishly, for he did speak to me foolishly before he went in; but I hope to preserve myself, and let him shift for himself as well as he can.

7TH. Up, and to the office, to the getting of my books in order, to carry to the Commissioners of Accounts this morning. Thence to the Commissioners of Accounts, and there presented my books, and was made to sit down, and used with much respect, otherwise than the other day, when I come to them as a criminal about the business of the prizes. I sat here with them a great while, while my books were inventoried. I find these gentlemen to sit all day, and only eat a bit of bread at noon, and a glass of wine; and are resolved to go through their business with great severity and method.

8TH. Away to the Strand to my bookseller's and there staid an hour, and bought the idle, rogueish book, *"L'escholle des filles;"* which I have bought in plain binding, avoiding the buying of it better bound, because I resolved, as soon as I have read it, to burn it, that it may not stand in the list of books, nor among them, to disgrace them if it should be found.

9TH (LORD'S DAY). Up, and at my chamber all the morning and the office doing business, and also reading a little of *"L'escholle des filles;"* which is a mighty lewd book, but yet not amiss for a sober man once to read over to inform himself in the villainy of the world. At noon home to dinner, where by appointment Mr. Pelling come and with him three friends, Wallington, that sings the good base, and one Rogers, and a gentleman, a young man, his name Tempest, who sings very well indeed, and understands anything in the world at first sight. After dinner we into our dining-room, and there to singing all the afternoon. We sang until almost night, and drank mighty good store of wine, and then they parted, and I to my chamber, where I did read through *"L'escholle des filles;"* a lewd book. And after I had done it I burned it, that it might not be among my books to my shame, and so at night to supper and to bed.

11TH. This morning my wife in bed told me the story of our Tom and Jane; how the rogue did first demand her consent to love and marry him, and then, with pretence of displeasing me, did slight her; but both he and she have confessed the matter to her, and she hath charged him to go on with his love to her, and be true to her, and so I think the business will go on, which, for my love to her, because she is in love with him, I am pleased with; but otherwise I think she will have no good bargain of it, at least if I should not do well in my place. But if I do stand, I do intend to give her £50 in money, and do them all the good I can in my way.

13TH. Up, and to the office, where all the morning. At noon home to dinner, and thence with my wife and Deb. to White Hall. Waiting here some time without, I did meet with several people, among others Mr. Brisband, who tells me in discourse that Tom Killigrew hath a fee out of the Wardrobe for cap and bells, under the title of the King's Foole or Jester; and may with privilege revile or jeere any body, the greatest person, without offence by the privilege of his place.

14TH (VALENTINE'S DAY). Up, being called up by Mercer, who come to be my Valentine, and so I rose and my wife, and were merry a little, I staying to talk, and did give her a guinny in gold for her Valentine's gift. There comes also my cozen Roger Pepys betimes, and comes to my wife, for her to be his Valentine, whose Valentine I was also, by agreement to be so to her every year; and this year I find it is likely to cost £4 or £5 in a ring for her, which she desires. I to my Office, to perfect my Narrative about prize-goods; and did carry it to the Commissioners of Accounts, who did receive it with great kindness, and express great value of, and respect to me: and my heart is at rest that it is lodged there, in so full truth and plainness, though it may hereafter prove some loss to me.

16TH (LORD'S DAY). Up, and to my chamber, where all the morning making a catalogue of my books, which did find me work, but with great pleasure, my chamber and books being now set in very good order, and my chamber washed and cleaned, which it had not been in some months before, my business and trouble having been so much.

17TH. Some mutterings I did hear of a design of dissolving the Parliament; but I think there is no ground for it yet, though Oliver would have dissolved them for half the trouble and contempt these have put upon the King and his councils. I did spend a little time at the Swan, and there did kiss the maid, Sarah.

18TH. Up by break of day, and walked down to the old Swan. I drank, but did not see Betty, and so to Charing Cross stairs, and thence walked to Sir W. Coventry's, and talked with him, who tells me how he hath been persecuted. I will remember what, in mirth, he said to me this morning, when upon this discourse he said, if ever there was another Dutch war, they should not find a Secretary; "Nor," said I, "a Clerk of the Acts, for I see the reward of it; and, thanked God! I have enough of my own to buy me a good book and a good fiddle, and I have a good wife." I stepped to the Dog Taverne, and thither come to me Doll Lane, and there we did drink together, and she tells me she is my valentine.... Home, and up to my wife, not owning my being at a play, and there she shews me her ring of a Turky-stone set with little sparks of dyamonds, which I am to give her, as my Valentine, and I am not much troubled at it. It will cost me near £5—she costing me but little compared with other wives, and I have not many occasions to spend on her.

20TH. So down to the Hall, where my wife by agreement stayed for me at Mrs. Michell's, and thence by one o'clock to the King's house: a new play, "The Duke of Lerma," of Sir Robert Howard's: where the King and Court was; and Knepp and Nell spoke the prologue most excellently, especially Knepp, who spoke beyond any creature I ever heard. The play designed to reproach our King with his mistresses, that I was troubled for it, and expected it should be interrupted; but it ended all well, which salved all.

21ST. At the office all the morning to get a little business done. Hither comes to me young Captain Beckford, the slopseller, and there presents me a little purse with gold in it, it being, as he told me, for his present to me, at the end of the last year. I told him I had not done him any service I knew of. He persisted, and I refused, but did at several denials; and telling him that it was not an age to take presents in, he told me he had reason to present me with something, and desired me to accept of it, which, at his so urging me, I did, and so fell to talk of his business, and so parted. I do not know of any manner of kindness I have done him this last year, nor did expect anything. It

was therefore very welcome to me, but yet I was not fully satisfied in my taking it.

23RD. This evening, my wife did with great pleasure shew
me her stock of jewells, encreased by the ring she hath made
lately as my Valentine's gift this year, a Turky stone set with diamonds: and, with this and what she had, she reckons that she
hath above £150 worth of jewells, of one kind or other; and I
am glad of it, for it is fit the wretch should have something to
content herself with.

24TH. I was prettily served this day at the playhouse-door,
where, giving six shillings into the fellow's hand for us three,
the fellow by legerdemain did convey one away, and with so
much grace faced me down that I did give him but five, that,
though I knew the contrary, yet I was overpowered by his so
grave and serious demanding the other shilling, that I could not
deny him, but was forced by myself to give it him.

27TH. All the morning at the office, and at noon home to
dinner, and thence with my wife and Deb. to the King's House,
to see "The Virgin Martyr," the first time it hath been acted a
great while: and it is mighty pleasant; not that the play is worth
much, but it is finely acted by Becke Marshal. But that which
did please me beyond any thing in the whole world was the
wind-musique when the angel comes down, which is so sweet
that it ravished me, and indeed, in a word, did wrap up my soul
so that it made me really sick, just as I have formerly been when
in love with my wife; that neither then, nor all the evening
going home, and at home, I was able to think of any thing, but
remained all night transported, so as I could not believe that
ever any musick hath real command over the soul of a man as
this did upon me: and makes me resolve to practice wind-
musique, and to make my wife do the like.

28TH. Comes in Mr. Wren from the House, where, he tells
us, another storm hath been all this day almost against the Of-

ficers of the Navy: and so they have at last ordered that we shall be heard at the bar of the House upon this business on Thursday next. This did mightily trouble me and us all; but me particularly, who am at least able to bear these troubles, though I have the least cause to be concerned in it. He tells me that that made them so mad to-day first was, several letters in the House about the Fanatickes, in several places, coming in great bodies, and turning people out of the churches, and there preaching themselves, and pulling the surplice over the Parsons' heads: this was confirmed from several places; which makes them stark mad, especially the hectors and bravadoes of the House, who shew all the zeal on this occasion.

MARCH 1ST (LORD'S DAY). Up very betimes, and by coach to Sir W. Coventry's; and there, largely carrying with me all my notes and papers, did run over our whole defence in order to the answering the House on Thursday next; and I do think, unless they be set without reason to ruin us, we shall make a good defence. So that my head is full of care and weariness in my employment. Thence home, and there my mind being a little lightened by my morning's work in the arguments I have now laid together in better method for our defence to the Parliament, I to talk with my wife; and in lieu of a coach this year, I have got my wife to be contented with her closet being made up this summer, and going into the country this summer for a month or two, to my father's, and there Mercer and Deb. and Jane shall go with her, which I the rather do for the entertaining my wife, and preventing of fallings out between her and my father or Deb., which used to be the fate of her going into the country.

2ND. This day I have the news that my sister was married on Thursday last to Mr. Jackson; so that work is, I hope, well over.

3RD. Up betimes to work again, and then met at the Office, where to our great business of this answer to the Parliament;

where to my great vexation I find my Lord Brouncker prepared only to excuse himself, while I, that have least reason to trouble myself, am preparing with great pains to defend them all.

4TH. I come home fell to my work at the office, shutting the doors, that we, I and my clerks, might not be interrupted, and so, only with room for a little dinner, we very busy all the day till night that the officers met for me to give them the heads of what I intended to say, which I did with great discontent to see them all rely on me that have no reason at all to trouble myself about it, nor have any thanks from them for my labour, but contrarily Brouncker looked mighty dogged, as thinking that I did not intend to do it so as to save him. This troubled me so much as, together with the shortness of the time and muchness of the business, did let me be at it till but about ten at night, and then quite weary, and dull, and vexed, I could go no further, but resolved to leave the rest to to-morrow morning, and so in full discontent and weariness did give over and went home, with[out] supper vexed and sickish to bed, and there slept about three hours, but then waked, and never in so much trouble in all my life of mind, thinking of the task I have upon me, and upon what dissatisfactory grounds, and what the issue of it may be to me.

5TH. With these thoughts I lay troubling myself till six o'clock, restless, and at last getting my wife to talk to me to comfort me, which she at last did, and made me resolve to quit my hands of this Office, and endure the trouble of it no longer than till I can clear myself of it. So with great trouble, but yet with some ease, from this discourse with my wife, I up, and to my Office, whither come my clerks, and so I did huddle the best I could some more notes for my discourse to-day, and by nine o'clock was ready, and did go down to the Old Swan, and there by boate, with T. H[ater] and W. H[ewer] with me, to Westminster, where I found myself come time enough, and my brethren all ready. But I full of thoughts and trouble touching the issue of this day; and, to comfort myself, did go to the Dog and drink half-a-pint of mulled sack, and in the Hall [Westminster] did drink a dram of brandy at Mrs. Hewlett's; and with the warmth of this did find myself in better order as to courage, truly. So we all up to the lobby; and between eleven and twelve o'clock, we were called in, with the mace before us, into the House, where a mighty full House; and we stood at the bar, namely, Brouncker, Sir J. Minnes, Sir T. Harvey, and myself, W. Pen being in the House, as a Member. I perceive the whole House was full, and full of expectation of our defence what it would be, and with great prejudice. After the Speaker had told us the dissatisfaction of the House, and read the Report of the Committee, I began our defence most acceptably and smoothly, and continued at it without any hesitation or losse, but with full scope, and all my reason free about me, as if it had been at my own table, from that time till past three in the afternoon; and so ended, without any interruption from the Speaker; but we withdrew. And there all my Fellow-Officers, and all the world that was within hearing, did congratulate me, and cry up my speech as the best thing they ever heard; and my Fellow-Officers overjoyed in it; and we were in hopes to have had a vote this day in our favour, and so the generality of the House was; but my speech, being so long, many had gone out to dinner and come in again half drunk; and this prevented it, so that they put it off to to-morrow come se'nnight. However, it is plain we have got great ground; and everybody says I have got the most honour that any could have had opportunity of getting; and so with our hearts mightily overjoyed at this success, we all to dinner to Lord Brouncker's.

6TH. Up betimes, and with Sir D. Gawden to Sir W. Coventry's chamber: where the first word he said to me was, "Good-morrow, Mr. Pepys, that must be Speaker of the Parliament-house:" and did protest I had got honour for ever in Parliament. He said that his brother, that sat by him, admires me; and another gentleman said that I could not get less than £1,000 a-year if I would put on a gown and plead at the Chancery-bar; but, what pleases me most, he tells me that the Sollicitor-Generall did protest that he thought I spoke the best of any man in England. After several talks with him alone, touching his own businesses, he carried me to White Hall, and there parted; and I to the Duke of York's lodgings, and find him going to the Park, it being a very fine morning, and I after him; and, as soon as he saw me, he told me, with great satisfaction, that I had converted a great many yesterday, and did, with great praise of me, go on with the discourse with me. And, by and by, overtaking the King, the King and Duke of York come to me both; and he said, "Mr. Pepys, I am very glad of your success yesterday;" and fell to talk of my well speaking, and many of the Lords there. My Lord Barkeley did cry me up for what they had heard of it; and others, Parliament-men there, about the King, did say that they never heard such a speech in their lives delivered in that manner. Progers, of the Bedchamber, swore to me afterwards before Brouncker, in the afternoon, that he did tell the King that he thought I might teach the Sollicitor-Generall. Everybody that saw me almost come to me, as Joseph Williamson and others, with such eulogys as cannot be expressed. From thence I went to Westminster Hall, where I met Mr. G. Montagu, who come to me and kissed me, and told me that he had often heretofore kissed my hands, but now he would kiss my lips: protesting that I was another Cicero, and said, all the world said the same of me. Mr. Ashburnham, and every creature I met there of the Parliament, or that knew anything of the Parliament's actings, did salute me with this honour:—Mr. Godolphin;—Mr. Sands, who swore he would go twenty mile, at any time, to hear the like again, and that he never saw so many sit four hours together to hear any man in his life, as there did to hear me; Mr. Chichly,—Sir John Duncomb,—and everybody do say that the kingdom will ring of my abilities, and that I have done myself right for my whole life: and so Captain Cocke, and others of my friends, say that no man had ever such an opportunity of making his abilities known; and, that I may cite all at once, Mr. Lieutenant of the Tower did tell me that Mr. Vaughan did protest to him, and that, in his hearing it, said so to the Duke of Albemarle, and afterwards to W. Coventry, that he had sat twenty-six years in Parliament and never heard such a speech there before: for which the Lord God make me thankful! and that I may make

use of it not to pride and vain-glory, but that, now I have this
esteem, I may do nothing that may lessen it! I spent the morning thus walking in the Hall, being complimented by everybody with admiration.

8TH (LORD'S DAY). At my sending to desire it, Sir J. Robinson, Lieutenant of the Tower, did call me with his coach, and
carried me to White Hall, where met with very many people
still that did congratulate my speech the other day in the
House of Commons, and I find all the world almost rings of it.

12TH. Up, and to the office, where all the morning, at noon
home, and after dinner with wife and Deb., took my wife up
and left her at the 'Change while I to Gresham College, there
to shew myself; and was there greeted by Dr. Wilkins, Whistler,
and others, as the patron of the Navy Office, and one that got
great fame by my late speech to the Parliament. Here I saw a
great trial of the goodness of a burning glass, made of a new
figure, not spherical (by one Smithys, I think, they call him),
that did burn a glove of my Lord Brouncker's from the heat of
a very little fire, which a burning glass of the old form, or much
bigger, could not do, which was mighty pretty.

13TH. Up betimes to my office, where to fit myself for attending the Parliament again, not to make any more speech,
which, while my fame is good, I will avoid, for fear of losing it;
but only to answer what objections will be made against us.

18TH. Up betimes to Westminster. I spent most of the
morning walking with one or other, and anon met Doll Lane at
the Dog tavern, ... and I did give her as being my valentine 20s.
to buy what she would. Thence away by coach to my bookseller's, and to several places to pay my debts, and to Ducke
Lane, and there bought Montaigne's Essays, in English, and so
away home to dinner, and after dinner with W. Pen to White
Hall, where we and my Lord Brouncker attended the Council,
to discourse about the fitness of entering of men presently for
the manning of the fleete, before one ship is in condition to re-

ceive them. W. Coventry did argue against it: I was wholly silent, because I saw the King, upon the earnestness of the Prince, was willing to it, crying very sillily, "If ever you intend to man the fleete, without being cheated by the captains and pursers, you may go to bed, and resolve never to have it manned;" and so it was, like other things, over-ruled that all volunteers should be presently entered. Then there was another great business about our signing of certificates to the Exchequer for [prize] goods, which the Commissioners of the Treasury did all oppose, and to the laying fault upon us. But I did then speak to the justifying what we had done, even to the angering of Duncomb and Clifford, which I was vexed at: but, for all that, I did set the Office and myself right, and went away with the victory. But, before I began to say anything in this matter, the King and the Duke of York talking at the Council-table, before all the Lords; "Why," says the King, "it is then but Mr. Pepys making of another speech to them;" which made all the Lords, and there were by also the Atturny and Sollicitor-Generall, look upon me.

19TH. Up, and betimes to the Old Swan, and by water to White Hall. Back to the Old Swan, and drank at Michell's, whose house goes up apace, but I could not see Betty, and thence walked all along Thames Street, which I had not done since it was burned, as far as Billingsgate; and there do see a brave street likely to be, many brave houses being built.

24TH. To White Hall, where great talk of the tumult at the other end of the town, about Moore-fields, among the 'prentices, taking the liberty of these holydays to pull down bawdy-houses. And Lord! to see the apprehensions which this did give to all people at Court, that presently order was given for all the soldiers, horse and foot, to be in armes! and forthwith alarmes were beat by drum and trumpet through Westminster, and all to their colours, and to horse, as if the French were coming into the town! So Creed, whom I met here, and I to Lincolne's Inn-fields, thinking to have gone into the fields to have seen the 'prentices; but here we found these fields full of soldiers all in a body, and my Lord Craven commanding of them, and riding up and down to give orders, like a madman. And some young men we saw brought by soldiers to the Guard at White Hall, and overheard others that stood by say, that it was only for pulling down the bawdy-houses; and none of the bystanders finding fault with them, but rather of the soldiers for hindering them. And we heard a Justice of the Peace this morning say to the King, that he had been endeavouring to suppress this tumult, but could not; and that, imprisoning some [of them] in the new prison at Clerkenwell, the rest did come and break open the prison and release them; and that they do give out that they are for pulling down the bawdy-houses, which is one of the greatest grievances of the nation. To which the King made a very poor, cold, insipid answer: "Why, why do they go to them, then?" and that was all, and had no mind to go on with the discourse. So home and there to my chamber, to prick out my song, "It is Decreed," intending to have it ready to give Mr. Harris on Thursday, when we meet, for him to sing, believing that he will do it more right than a woman that sings better, unless it were Knepp, which I cannot have opportunity to teach it to.

25TH. Up, and walked to White Hall, there to wait on the Duke of York, which I did. The Duke of York and all with him this morning were full of the talk of the 'prentices, who are not yet [put] down, though all the guards and militia of the town have been in armes all this night and the night before; and the 'prentices have made fools of them, sometimes by running from them and flinging stones at them. Some blood hath been spilt, but a great many houses pulled down; and, among others, the Duke of York was mighty merry at that of Damaris Page's, the great bawd of the seamen; and the Duke of York complained merrily that he hath lost two tenants, by their houses being pulled down, who paid him for their wine licenses £15 a year. But here it was said how these idle fellows have had the confidence to say that they did ill in contenting themselves in pulling down the little bawdy-houses, and did not go and pull down the great bawdy-house at White Hall. And some of them have the last night had a word among them, and it was "Reformation and Reducement." This do make the courtiers ill at ease to see this spirit among people, though they think this matter will not come to much: but it speaks people's minds; and then they do say that there are men of understanding among them, that have been of Cromwell's army: but how true that is, I know not.

26TH. Up betimes to the office, thence I alone to the Duke of York's house, to see the new play called, "The Man is the Master," where the house was, it being not above one o'clock, very full. But my wife and Deb. being there before, with Mrs. Pierce and Corbet and Betty Turner, whom my wife carried with her, they made me room; and there I sat, it costing me 8s. upon them in oranges, at 6d. a-piece. By and by the King come; and we sat just under him, so that I durst not turn my back all the play. Thence, by agreement, we all of us to the Blue Balls, hard by, whither Mr. Pierce also goes with us, who met us at the play, and anon comes Manuel, and his wife, and Knepp, and Harris, who brings with him Mr. Banister, the great master of musique; and after much difficulty in getting of musique, we to dancing, and then to a supper of some French dishes, which yet did not please me, and then to dance and sing; and mighty merry we were till about eleven or twelve at night, with mighty great content in all my company, and I did, as I love to do, enjoy myself in my pleasure as being the height of what we take pains for and can hope for in this world, and therefore to be enjoyed while we are young and capable of these joys. My wife extraordinary fine to-day, in her flower tabby suit, bought a year and more ago, before my mother's death put her into mourning, and so not worn till this day: and everybody in love with it; and indeed she is very fine and handsome in it. I having paid the reckoning, which come to almost £4, we parted: my company and William Batelier, who was also with us, home in a coach, round by the Wall, where we met so many stops by the Watches, that it cost us much time and some trouble, and more money, to every Watch, to them to drink; this being encreased by the trouble the 'prentices did lately give the City, so that the

Militia and Watches are very strict at this time: and we had like to have met with a stop for all night at the Constable's watch, at Mooregate, by a pragmatical Constable; but we come well home at about two in the morning, and so to bed. This noon, from Mrs. Williams's, my Lord Brouncker sent to Somersett House to hear how the Duchess of Richmond do; and word was brought him that she is pretty well, but mighty full of the smallpox, by which all do conclude she will be wholly spoiled, which is the greatest instance of the uncertainty of beauty that could be in this age; but then she hath had the benefit of it to be first married, and to have kept it so long, under the greatest temptations in the world from a King, and yet without the least imputation.

27TH. Home to dinner, where my wife and I had a small squabble, but I first this day tried the effect of my silence and not provoking her when she is in an ill humour, and do find it very good, for it prevents its coming to that height on both sides which used to exceed what was fit between us. So she became calm by and by and fond.

31ST. I called Deb. to take pen, ink, and paper and write down what things come into my head for my wife to do in order to her going into the country, and the girl, writing not so well as she would do, cried, and her mistress construed it to be sullenness, and so away angry with her too, but going to bed she undressed me, and there I did give her good advice and *baiser la, elle* weeping still.

APRIL 1ST. Up, and to dress myself, and call as I use Deb. to brush and dress me . . . , and I to my office, where busy till noon, and then out to bespeak some things against my wife's going into the country to-morrow.

2ND. Up, after much pleasant talk with my wife, and upon some alterations I will make in my house in her absence, and I do intend to lay out some money thereon. So she and I up, and she got her ready to be gone, and by and by comes Betty

Turner and her mother, and W. Batelier, and they and Deb., to whom I did give 10s. this morning, to oblige her to please her mistress (and *ego* did *basier* her *mouche*), and also Jane, and so in two coaches set out about eight o'clock towards the carrier, there for to take coach for my father's, that is to say, my wife and Betty Turner, Deb., and Jane; but I meeting my Lord Anglesey going to the Office, was forced to 'light in Cheapside, and there took my leave of them (not *baisado* Deb., which *je* had a great mind to), left them to go to their coach, and I to the office, where all the morning busy. Thence with Lord Brouncker to the Royall Society, where they were just done; but there I was forced to subscribe to the building of a College, and did give £40; and several others did subscribe, some greater and some less sums; but several I saw hang off: and I doubt it will spoil the Society, for it breeds faction and ill-will, and becomes burdensome to some that cannot, or would not, do it. Here, to my great content, I did try the use of the Otacousticon, which was only a great glass bottle, broke at the bottom, putting the neck to my eare, and there I did plainly hear the dashing of the oares of the boats in the Thames to Arundell gallery window, which, without it, I could not in the least do, and may, I believe, be improved to a great height, which I am mighty glad of.

4TH. Up betimes, and by coach towards White Hall, and took Aldgate Street in my way, and there called upon one Hayward, that makes virginalls, and did there like of a little espinette, and will have him finish it for me: for I had a mind to a small harpsichon, but this takes up less room, and will do my business as to finding out of chords, and I am very well pleased that I have found it. And after dinner Sir W. Pen and I away by water to White Hall, and there did attend the Duke of York, and he did carry us to the King's lodgings: but he was asleep in his closet; so we stayed in the Green-Roome, where the Duke of York did tell us what rules he had, of knowing the weather, and did now tell us we should have rain before to-morrow, it having been a dry season for some time, and so it did rain all night almost; and pretty rules he hath, and told Brouncker and me some of them, which were such as no reason seems ready to be given. By and by the King comes out, and he did easily agree to what we moved, and would have the Commissioners of the Navy to meet us with him to-morrow morning: and then to talk of other things; about the Quakers not swearing, and how they do swear in the business of a late election of a Knight of the Shire of Hartfordshire in behalf of one they have a mind to have; and how my Lord of Pembroke says he hath heard him (the Quaker) at the tennis-court swear to himself when he loses: and told us what pretty notions my Lord Pembroke hath of the first chapter of Genesis, how Adam's sin was not the sucking (which he did before) but the swallowing of the apple, by which the contrary elements begun to work in him, and to stir up these passions, and a great deal of such fooleries, which the King made mighty mockery at. Thence my Lord Brouncker and I into the Park in his coach, and there took a great deal of ayre, saving that it was mighty dusty, and so a little unpleasant.

5TH (LORD'S DAY). Up, and to my chamber, and there to the writing fair some of my late musique notions, and so to church, where I have not been a good while. I to my musique again, and to read a little, and to sing with Mr. Pelling, who come to see me, and so spent the evening, and then to supper and to bed. I hear that eight of the ringleaders in the late tumults of the 'prentices at Easter are condemned to die.

6TH. I thence to Westminster, and walked in the Hall and up and down, and at noon with Sir Herbert Price to Mr. George Montagu's to dinner, being invited by him in the hall, and there mightily made of, even to great trouble to me to be so commended before my face, with that flattery and importunity, that I was quite troubled with it. Yet he is a fine gentleman, truly, and his lady a fine woman; and, among many sons that I saw there, there was a little daughter that is mighty pretty, of which he is infinite fond: and, after dinner, did make her play on the gittar and sing, which she did mighty prettily, and seems to have a mighty musical soul, keeping time with most excellent spirit.

7TH. Up, and at the office all the morning, where great hurry to be made in the fitting forth of this present little fleete, but so many rubs by reason of want of money. I by coach to the King's playhouse, and there saw "The English Monsieur;" sitting for privacy sake in an upper box: the play hath much mirth in it as to that particular humour. After the play done, I down to Knipp, and did stay her undressing herself; and there saw the several players, men and women go by; and pretty to see how strange they are all, one to another, after the play is done. Here I saw a wonderful pretty maid of her own, that come to undress her, and one so pretty that she says she intends not to keep her, for fear of her being undone in her service, by coming to the playhouse. Here I hear Sir W. Davenant is just now dead; and so who will succeed him in the mastership of the house is not yet known. She tells me mighty news, that my Lady Castlemayne is mightily in love with Hart of their house: and he is much with her in private, and she goes to him, and do give him many presents; and that the thing is most certain, and Becke Marshall only privy to it, and the means of bringing them together, which is a very odd thing; and by this means she is even with the King's love to Mrs. Davis.

8TH. Up, and at my office all the morning, doing business, and then at noon home to dinner all alone. Then I to Drumbleby's, and there did talk a great deal about pipes; and did buy a recorder, which I do intend to learn to play on, the sound of it being, of all sounds in the world, most pleasing to me. So home to my chamber, to be fingering of my Recorder, and getting of the scale of musique without book, which I at last see is necessary for a man that would understand musique, as it is now taught to understand, though it be a ridiculous and troublesome way, and I know I shall be able hereafter to show the world a simpler way; but, like the old hypotheses in philosophy, it must be learned, though a man knows a better.

9TH. Up, and to the office, where all the morning sitting, and then abroad to my bookseller's, and up and down to the Duke of York's playhouse, there to see, which I did, Sir W. Davenant's corpse carried out towards Westminster, there to be buried. Here were many coaches and six horses, and many hacknies, that make it look, methought, as if it were the buriall of a poor poet.

1OTH (FRIDAY). All the morning at Office. At noon with W. Pen to Duke of York, and attended Council. So to piper and Duck Lane, and there kissed bookseller's wife, and bought Legend. So home, coach. Sailor. Mrs. Hannan dead. News of Peace. Conning my gamut.

12TH (SUNDAY). Dined at Brouncker's, and saw the new book. Peace. Cutting away sails.

13TH (MONDAY). Spent at Michel's 6d.; in the Folly, 1s.; oysters 1s.; coach to W. Coventry about Mrs. Pett, 1s.; thence to Commissioners of Treasury, and so to Westminster Hall by water, 6d. So with Creed to a play. Little laugh, 4s. Thence towards the Park by coach, 2s. 6d.

14TH (TUESDAY). Up betimes by water to the Temple. In the way read the Narrative about prizes. Thence to Commissioners of Accounts and there examined, and so back to Westminster Hall, where all the talk of committing all to the Tower, and Creed and I to the Quaker's, dined together. Thence to the House, where rose about four o'clock; and, with much ado, Pen got to Thursday, to bring in his answer; so my Lord escapes today. Water, 1s. Porter, 6d. Water, 6d. Dinner, 3s. 6d. Play part, 2s, Oranges, 1s. Home coach, 1s. 6d.

15TH. After playing a little upon my new little flageolet, that is so soft that pleases me mightily, betimes to my office, where most of the morning. Then by coach, 1s., and meeting Lord Brouncker, 'light at the Exchange, and thence by water to White Hall, 1s., and there to the Chapel, expecting wind musick: and to the Harp-and-Ball, and drank all alone, 2d. Back, and to the fiddling concert, and heard a practice mighty good of Grebus, and thence to Westminster. Thence I left

Creed, and to the King's playhouse, into a corner of the 18d. box, and there saw "The Maid's Tragedy," a good play. Coach, 1s.: play and oranges, 2s. 6d. Creed come, dropping presently here, but he did not see me, and come to the same place, nor would I be seen by him. Thence with Creed to the Cock alehouse, and there spent 6d., and so by coach home, 2s. 6d., and so to bed.

16TH. TH[URSDAY]. Greeting's book, 1s. Begun this day to learn the Recorder. To the office, where all the morning.

20TH. Thence took coach and I all alone to Hyde Park (passing through Duck Lane among the booksellers, only to get a sight of the pretty little woman I did salute the other night, and did in passing), and so all the evening in the Park, being a little unwilling to be seen there, and at night home.

22ND. Up, and all the morning at my office busy. At noon, it being washing day, I toward White Hall, and stopped and dined all alone at Hercules Pillars. I by water from the Privy-stairs to Westminster Hall; and, taking water, the King and the Duke of York were in the new buildings; and the Duke of York called to me whither I was going? and I answered aloud, "To wait on our maisters at Westminster;" at which he and all the company laughed; but I was sorry and troubled for it afterwards, for fear any Parliament-man should have been there; and will be a caution to me for the time to come. So to the fishmonger's, and bought a couple of lobsters, and over to the 'sparagus garden, thinking to have met Mr. Pierce, and his wife and Knepp; but met their servant coming to bring me to Chatelin's, the French house, in Covent Garden, and there with musick and good company, Manuel and his wife, and one Swaddle, a clerk of Lord Arlington's, who dances, and speaks French well, but got drunk, and was then troublesome, and here mighty merry till ten at night, and then I away, and got a coach, and so home. This night the Duke of Monmouth and a great many blades were at Chatelin's, and I left them there, with a hackney-coach attending him.

24TH. Up betimes, and by water to White Hall, to the Duke of York. Thence to Ducke Lane, and there did overlook a great many of Monsieur Fouquet's library, that a bookseller hath bought, and I did buy one Spanish [work], *"Los Illustres Varones."* Here did I endeavour to see my pretty woman that I did *baiser in las tenebras* a little while *depuis.* And did find her *sola* in the book [shop], but had not *la confidence para aller à elle.* So lost my pains. But will another time, and so home and to my office, and then to dinner. After dinner down to the Old Swan, and by the way called at Michell's, and there did see Betty, and that was all, for either she is shy or foolish, and *su mardi* hath no mind *para laiser* me see *su moher.*

30TH. Thus ends this month; my wife in the country, myself full of pleasure and expense; and some trouble for my friends, my Lord Sandwich, by the Parliament, and more for my eyes, which are daily worse and worse, that I dare not write or read almost anything. The Parliament going in a few days to rise. The kingdom in an ill state through poverty; a fleete going out, and no money to maintain it, or set it out; seamen yet unpaid, and mutinous when pressed to go out again. So we are all poor, and in pieces—God help us! while the peace is like to go on between Spain and France; and then the French may be apprehended able to attack us. So God help us!

MAY 1ST. Up, and to the office, where all the morning busy. Then to Westminster Hall. Here met my cozen Thomas Pepys of Deptford, and took some turns with him; who is mightily troubled for this Act now passed against Conventicles, and in few words, and sober, do lament the condition we are in, by a negligent Prince and a mad Parliament. Then to the King's playhouse, and there saw "The Surprizall:" and a disorder in the pit by its raining in, from the cupola at top, it being a very foul day, and cold.

5TH. Up, and all the morning at the office. At noon home to dinner and Creed with me, and after dinner he and I to the Duke of York's playhouse; and there coming late, he and I up to the balcony-box, where we find my Lady Castlemayne and several great ladies. My Lady [Castlemayne] pretty well pleased with it; but here I sat close to her fine woman, Wilson, who indeed is very handsome, but, they say, with child by the King. I asked, and she told me this was the first time her Lady had seen it, I having a mind to say something to her. One thing of familiarity I observed in my Lady Castlemayne: she called to one of her women, another that sat by this, for a little patch off her face, and put it into her mouth and wetted it, and so clapped it upon her own by the side of her mouth, I suppose she feeling a pimple rising there.

7TH. Up, and to the office, where all the morning. Thence called Knepp from the King's house, where going in for her, the play being done, I did see Beck Marshall come dressed, off of the stage, and looks mighty fine, and pretty, and noble: and also Nell, in her boy's clothes, mighty pretty. But, Lord! their confidence! and how many men do hover about them as soon as they come off the stage, and how confident they are in their talk! Here I did kiss the pretty woman newly come, called Pegg, that was Sir Charles Sidly's mistress, a mighty pretty woman, and seems, but is not, modest.

15TH. I am told also that the Countess of Shrewsbury is brought home by the Duke of Buckingham to his house, where his Duchess saying that it was not for her and the other to live together in a house, he answered, "Why, Madam, I did think so, and, therefore, have ordered your coach to be ready, to carry you to your father's," which was a devilish speech, but, they say, true; and my Lady Shrewsbury is there, it seems.

21ST. All the morning at the office, and at noon my clerks dined with me, and there do hear from them how all the town is full of the talk of a meteor, or some fire, that did on Saturday last fly over the City at night, many clusters of people talking of it, and many people of the towns about the city did see it, and the world do make much discourse of it, their apprehensions being mighty full of the rest of the City to be burned, and the Papists to cut our throats. Which God prevent!

23RD. Up by four o'clock; and, getting my things ready, and recommending the care of my house to W. Hewer, I with my boy Tom, whom I take with me, to the Bull, in Bishopsgate Street, and there, about six, took coach, he and I, and a gentleman and his man, there being another coach also, with as many more, I think, in it; and so away to Bishop's Stafford, and there dined, and changed horses and coach, at Mrs. Aynsworth's; but I took no knowledge of her. After dinner away again and come to Cambridge, after much bad way, about nine at night; and there, at the Rose, I met my father's horses, with a man, staying for me. But it is so late, and the waters so deep, that I durst not go to-night; but after supper to bed; and there lay very ill, by reason of some drunken scholars making a noise all night, and vexed for fear that the horses should not be taken up from grass, time enough for the morning.

24TH (LORD'S DAY). I up, at between two and three in the morning, and, calling up my boy, and father's boy, we set out by three o'clock, it being high day; and so through the waters with very good success, though very deep almost all the way, and got to Brampton, where most of them in bed, and so I weary up to my wife's chamber, whom I find in bed, and pretended a little not well, but fell to talk and mightily pleased both of us, and up got the rest, Betty Turner and Willet and Jane, all whom I was glad to see, and very merry, and got me ready in my new stuff clothes that I sent down before me, and so my wife and they got ready too, while I to my father, poor man, and walked with him up and down the house—it raining a little, and the waters all over Portholme and the meadows, so as no pleasure abroad. At noon comes Mr. Phillips and dines with us, and a pretty odd-humoured man he seems to be; but good withal, but of mighty great methods in his eating and drinking, and will not kiss a woman since his wife's death. After dinner my Lady Sandwich sending to see whether I was come, I presently took horse, and find her and her family at chapel; and thither I went in to them, and sat out the sermon, where I heard Jervas Fullword, now their chaplain, preach a very good and seraphic kind of sermon, too good for an ordinary congregation.

25TH. Waked betimes. At noon to dinner, where Mr. Shepley come and we merry, all being in good humour between my wife and her people about her, and after dinner took horse, I promising to fetch her away about fourteen days hence, and so calling all of us, we men on horseback, and the women and my father, at Goody Gorum's, and there in a frolic drinking I took leave, there going with me and my boy, my two brothers, and so we away and got well to Cambridge, about seven to the Rose, the waters being now so high as before. And here 'lighting, I took my boy and two brothers, and walked to Magdalene College: and there into the butterys, as a stranger, and there drank my bellyfull of their beer, which pleased me, as the best I ever drank: and hear by the butler's man, who was son to Goody Mulliner over against the College, that we used to buy stewed prunes of, concerning the College and persons in it; and find very few, only Mr. Hollins and Pechell, I think, that were of my time. But I was mightily pleased to come in this condition to see and ask, and thence, giving the fellow something, away walked to Chesterton, to see our old walk, and there into the Church, the bells ringing, and saw the place I used to sit in, and so to the ferry, and ferried over to the other side, and walked with great pleasure, the river being mighty high by Barnewell Abbey: and so by Jesus College to the town, and so to our quarters, and to supper, and then to bed, being very weary and sleepy, and mightily pleased with this night's walk.

26TH. Up by four o'clock; and by the time we were ready, and had eat, we were called to the coach, where about six o'clock we set out, there being a man and two women of one company, ordinary people, and one lady alone, that is tolerably handsome, but mighty well spoken, whom I took great pleasure in talking to, and did get her to read aloud in a book she was reading, in the coach, being the King's meditations; and then the boy and I to sing, and so about noon come to Bishop's Stafford, to another house than what we were at the other day, and better used. And here I paid for the reckoning 11s., we dining together, and pretty merry; and then set out again, sleeping most part of the way; and got to Bishopsgate Street before eight o'clock, the waters being now most of them down, and we avoiding the bad way in the forest by a privy way, which brought us to Hodsden; and so to Tibalds, that road, which was mighty pleasant. So home, where we find all well, and brother Balty and his wife looking to the house, she mighty fine, in a new gold-laced *just à cour.*

30TH. Up, and put on a new summer black bombazin suit, and so to the office; and being come now to an agreement with my barber, to keep my perriwig in good order at 20s. a-year, I am like to go very spruce, more than I used to do. All the morning at the office and at noon home to dinner, and so to the King's playhouse, and there saw "Philaster;" where it is pretty to see how I could remember almost all along, ever since I was a boy, Arethusa, the part which I was to have acted at Sir Robert Cooke's; and it was very pleasant to me, but more to think what a ridiculous thing it would have been for me to have acted a beautiful woman. Thence to Mr. Pierce's, and there saw Knepp also, and were merry; and here saw my little Lady Katherine Montagu come to town, about her eyes, which are sore, and they think the King's evil, poor, pretty lady.

JUNE 2ND. Up, and to the office, where all the morning. At noon home to dinner, and there dined with me, besides my own people, W. Batelier and Mercer, and we were very merry. After dinner, they gone, only Mercer and I to sing a while, and then parted, and I out and took a coach, and called Mercer at their back-door, and she brought with her Mrs. Knightly, a little pretty sober girl, and I carried them to Old Ford, a town by Bow, where I never was before, and there walked in the fields very pleasant, and sang: and so back again, and stopped and drank at the Gun, at Mile End, and so to the Old Exchange door, and did buy them a pound of cherries, cost me 2s., and so set them down again; and I to my little mercer's Finch, that lives now in the Minories, where I have left my cloak, and did here *baiser su moher, a belle femme,* and there took my cloak which I had left there, and so by water, it being now about nine o'clock, down to Deptford, where I have not been many a day, and there it being dark I did by agreement *aller a la* house *de* Bagwell, and there after a little playing and *baisando* we did go up in the dark a *su camera* . . . and to my boat again, and against the tide home. Got there by twelve o'clock, taking into my boat, for company, a man that desired a passage—a certain western bargeman, with whom I had good sport, talking of the old woman of Woolwich, and telling him the whole story.

18TH. Up betimes and to the office. At noon home to dinner, where my wife still in a melancholy, fusty humour, and crying, and do not tell me plainly what it is; but I by little words find that she hath heard of my going to plays, and carrying people abroad every day, in her absence; and that I cannot help but the storm will break out, I think, in a little time. After dinner carried her by coach to St. James's.

19TH. I home, and there we to bed again, and slept pretty well, and about nine rose, and then my wife fell into her blubbering again, and at length had a request to make of me, which was, that she might go into France, and live there, out of trouble; and then all come out, that I loved pleasure and denied her any, and a deal of do; and I find that there have been great fallings out between my father and her, whom, for ever hereafter, I must keep asunder, for they cannot possibly agree. And I said nothing, but, with very mild words and few, suffered her humour to spend, till we begun to be very quiet, and I think all will be over, and friends, and so I to the office, where all the morning doing business.

23RD. Up, and all the morning at the office. At noon home to dinner, and so to the office again all the afternoon, and then to Westminster to Dr. Turberville about my eyes, whom I met with: and he did discourse, I thought, learnedly about them;

and takes time before he did prescribe me any thing, to think of it.

30TH. Up, and at the Office all the morning: then home to dinner, where a stinking leg of mutton, the weather being very wet and hot to keep meat in. I very melancholy under the fear of my eyes being spoiled, and not to be recovered; for I am come that I am not able to read out a small letter, and yet my sight good for the little while I can read, as ever they were, I think.

JULY 3RD. Betimes to the office. So abroad by water to Eagle Court in the Strand, and there to an alehouse: met Mr. Pierce, the Surgeon, and Dr. Clerke, Waldron, Turberville, my physician for the eyes, and Lowre, to dissect several eyes of sheep and oxen, with great pleasure, and to my great information. But strange that this Turberville should be so great a man, and yet, to this day, had seen no eyes dissected, or but once, but desired this Dr. Lowre to give him the opportunity to dissect some.

12TH. Busy all the morning upon some accounts with W. Hewer. This last night Betty Michell about midnight cries out, and my wife goes to her, and she brings forth a girl, and this afternoon the child is christened, and my wife godmother again to a Betty.

13TH. This morning I was let blood, and did bleed about fourteen ounces, towards curing my eyes.

14TH. Up, and to my office, where sat all the morning. This afternoon my Lady Pickering come to see us: I busy, saw her not. But how natural it is for us to slight people out of power, and for people out of power to stoop to see those that while in power they contemned!

16TH. I by water with my Lord Brouncker to Arundell House, to the Royall Society, and there saw an experiment of a dog's being tied through the back, about the spinal artery, and thereby made void of all motion; and the artery being loosened again, the dog recovers.

17TH. The weather excessive hot, so as we were forced to lie in two beds, and I only with a sheet and rug, which is colder than ever I remember I could bear.

18TH. At the office all the morning. At noon dined at home and Creed with me, who I do really begin to hate, and do use him with some reservedness. Here was also my old acquaintance, Will Swan, to see me, who continues a factious fanatick still, and I do use him civilly, in expectation that those fellows may grow great again. Creed told me this day how when the King was at my Lord Cornwallis's, when he went last to Newmarket, that being there on a Sunday, the Duke of Buckingham did in the afternoon to please the King make a bawdy sermon to him out of Canticles, and that my Lord Cornwallis did endeavour to get the King a whore, and that must be a pretty girl the daughter of the parson of the place, but that she did get away, and leaped off of some place and killed herself, which if true is very sad.

19TH (LORD'S DAY). Up, and to my chamber, and there I up and down in the house spent the morning getting things ready against noon, when come Mr. Cooper, Hales, Harris, Mr. Butler, that wrote Hudibras, and Mr. Cooper's cozen Jacke; and by and by comes Mr. Reeves and his wife, whom I never saw before: and there we dined: a good dinner, and company that pleased me mightily, being all eminent men in their way.

23RD. Up, and all day long, but at dinner, at the Office, at work, till I was almost blind, which makes my heart sad.

27TH. Busy all the morning at my office. At noon dined, and then I out of doors to my bookseller in Duck Lane, but *su moher* not at home, and it was pretty here to see a pretty woman pass by with a little wanton look, and *je* did *sequi* her round about the street from Duck Lane to Newgate Market, and then *elle* did turn back, and *je* did lose her. So over the water with my wife, and Deb., and Mercer, to Spring-Garden, and there eat and walked; and observe how rude some of the young gallants of the town are become, to go into people's arbours where there are not men, and almost force the women; which troubled me, to see the confidence of the vice of the age: and so we away by water, with much pleasure home.

AUGUST 11TH. This day I hear that, to the great joy of the Non-conformists, the time is out of the Act against them, so that they may meet: and they have declared that they will have a morning lecture up again, which is pretty strange; and they are connived at by the King every where, I hear, in City and country. This afternoon my wife, and Mercer, and Deb., went with Pelling to see the gypsies at Lambeth, and have their fortunes told; but what they did, I did not enquire.

22ND. Going through Leaden-Hall, it being market-day, I did see a woman catched, that had stolen a shoulder of mutton off of a butcher's stall, and carrying it wrapt up in a cloth, in a basket. The jade was surprised, and did not deny it, and the women so silly, as to let her go that took it, only taking the meat.

23RD (LORD'S DAY). After dinner to the Office. Mr. Gibson and I, to examine my letter to the Duke of York, which, to my great joy, I did very well by my paper tube, without pain to my eyes. And I do mightily like what I have therein done; and did, according to the Duke of York's order, make haste to St. James's, and about four o'clock got thither: and there the Duke of York was ready, to expect me, and did hear it all over with extraordinary content; and did give me many and hearty thanks, and in words the most expressive tell me his sense of my good endeavours, and that he would have a care of me on all occasions.

26TH. Up, and to the office, where all the morning almost. Thence to White Hall, and it is strange to say with what speed the people employed do pull down Paul's steeple, and with what ease: it is said that it, and the choir are to be taken down this year, and another church begun in the room thereof, the next.

29TH. Up, and all the morning at the Office, where the Duke of York's long letter was read, to their great trouble, and their suspecting me to have been the writer of it.

SEPTEMBER 1ST. Up, and all the morning at the office busy. So to the Fair, and there saw several sights; among others, the mare that tells money, and many things to admiration; and, among others, come to me, when she was bid to go to him of the company that most loved a pretty wench in a corner. And this did cost me 12d. to the horse, which I had flung him before, and did give me occasion to *baiser* a mighty *belle fille* that was in the house that was exceeding plain, but *fort belle*. At night took coach home, and taking coach was set on by a wench that was naught, and would have gone along with me to her lodging in Shoe Lane, but *ego* did *donner* her a shilling and left her, and home.

2ND. Fast-day for the burning of London, strictly observed.

3RD. Exchequer and several places, calling on several businesses, and particularly my bookseller's among others, for "Hobbs's Leviathan," which is now mightily called for; and what was heretofore sold for 8s. I now give 24s. for, at the second hand, and is sold for 30s., it being a book the Bishops will not let be printed again.

4TH. Up, and met at the Office all the morning; and at noon my wife, and Deb., and Mercer, and W. Hewer and I to the Fair, and there, at the old house, did eat a pig, and was pretty merry, but saw no sights, my wife having a mind to see the play "Bartholomew-Fayre," with puppets. Which we did, and it is an excellent play; the more I see it, the more I love the wit of it; only the business of abusing the Puritans begins to grow stale, and of no use, they being the people that, at last, will be found the wisest.

9TH. To Westminster, to Sir R. Long's office; and, going, met Mr. George Montagu, who talked and complimented me mightily. He tells me that now Buckingham does rule all; and the other day, in the King's journey he is now on, at Bagshot, and that way, he caused Prince Rupert's horses to be turned out of an inne, and caused his own to be kept there, which the Prince complained of to the King, and the Duke of York seconded the complaint: but the King did over-rule it for Buckingham, by which there are high displeasures among them; and Buckingham and Arlington rule all. So, after a little supper, vexed, and spending a little time melancholy in making a base to the Lark's song, I to bed.

10TH. To Unthanke's, and 'Change, where wife did a little business, while Mercer and I staid in the coach; and, in a quarter of an hour, I taught her the whole Larke's song perfectly, so excellent an eare she hath.

15TH. Up mighty betimes, my wife and people, Mercer lying here all night, by three o'clock, and I about five; and they before, and I after them, to the coach in Bishopsgate Street, which was not ready to set out. So took wife and Mercer and Deb. and W. Hewer (who are all to set out this day for Cambridge, to cozen Roger Pepys's, to see Sturbridge Fayre); and I shewed them the Exchange, which is very finely carried on, with good dispatch. So walked back and saw them gone, there being only one man in the coach besides them.

16TH. Up; and dressing myself I did begin *para toker* the breasts of my maid Jane, which *elle* did give way to more than usual heretofore, so I have a design to try more when I can bring it to. So to the office, and thence to St. James's to the Duke of York, walking it to the Temple, and in my way observe that the Stockes are now pulled quite down; and it will make the coming into Cornhill and Lumber Street mighty noble.

19TH. Up, and to the office, where all the morning busy, and so dined with my people at home, and then to the King's playhouse, and there saw "The Silent Woman;" the best comedy, I think, that ever was wrote; and sitting by Shadwell the poet, he was big with admiration of it.

21ST. And so out again and by water to Somerset House, but when come thither I turned back and to Southwarke-Fair, very dirty, and there saw the puppet-show of Whittington, which was pretty to see; and how that idle thing do work upon people that see it, and even myself too! And thence to Jacob Hall's dancing on the ropes, where I saw such action as I never saw before, and mightily worth seeing; and here took acquaintance with a fellow that carried me to a tavern, whither come the musick of this booth, and by and by Jacob Hall himself, with whom I had a mind to speak, to hear whether he had ever any mischief by falls in his time. He told me, "Yes, many; but never to the breaking of a limb:" he seems a mighty strong man. So giving them a bottle or two of wine, I away with Payne, the waterman. He, seeing me at the play, did get a link to light me and so light me to the Beare, where Bland, my waterman, waited for me with gold and other things he kept for me, to the value of £40 and more, which I had about me, for fear of my pockets being cut. So by link-light through the bridge, it being mighty dark, but still weather, and so home.

27TH (LORD'S DAY). I to walk all the morning in the Park, where I met Mr. Wren; and he and I walked together in the Pell-Mell, it being most summer weather that ever was seen: and, here talking of several things: of the corruption of the Court, and how unfit it is for ingenious men, and himself particularly, to live in it, where a man cannot live but he must spend, and cannot get suitably, without breach of his honour.

28TH. Up betimes, and Knepp's maid comes to me, to tell me that the women's day at the playhouse is to-day, and that therefore I must be there, to encrease their profit. I did give the pretty maid Betty that comes to me half-a-crown for coming, and had a *baiser* or two—*elle* being mighty *jolie.* And so I about my business.

OCTOBER 20TH. I walked out to several places to pay debts and among other things to look out for a coach, and saw many; and did light on one for which I bid £50, which do please me mightily, and I believe I shall have it.

21ST. I away to the New Exchange, and there staid for my wife, and she come, we to Cow Lane, and there I shewed her the coach which I pitch on, and she is out of herself for joy almost.

23RD. So away with Mr. Pierce, the surgeon, towards Tyburne, to see the people executed; but come too late, it being done; two men and a woman hanged, and so back again and to my coachmaker's, and there did come a little nearer agreement for the coach. This day Pierce do tell me, among other news, the late frolick and debauchery of Sir Charles Sidly and Buckhurst, running up and down all the night, through the streets; and at last fighting, and being beat by the watch and clapped up all night; and how the King takes their parts; and my Lord Chief Justice Keeling hath laid the constable by the heels to answer it next Sessions: which is a horrid shame. How the King and these gentlemen did make the fiddlers of Thetford, this last progress, to sing them all the bawdy songs they could think of.

24TH. This morning comes to me the coachmaker, and agreed with me for £53, and stand to the courtesy of what more I should give him upon the finishing of the coach: he is likely also to fit me with a coachman.

25TH (LORD'S DAY). So home and to dinner, and after dinner all the afternoon got my wife and boy to read to me, and at night W. Batelier comes and sups with us; and, after supper, to have my head combed by Deb., which occasioned the greatest sorrow to me that ever I knew in this world, for my wife, coming up suddenly, did find me embracing the girl. . . . I was at a wonderful loss upon it, and the girle also, and I endeavoured to put it off, but my wife was struck mute and grew angry, and so her voice come to her, grew quite out of order, and I to say little, but to bed, and my wife said little also, but could not sleep all night, but about two in the morning waked me and cried, and fell to tell me as a great secret that she was a Roman Catholique and had received the Holy Sacrament, which troubled me, but I took no notice of it, but she went on from one thing to another till at last it appeared plainly her trouble was at what she saw, but yet I did not know how much she saw, and therefore said nothing to her. But after her much crying and reproaching me with inconstancy and preferring a sorry girl before her, I did give her no provocation, but did promise all fair usage to her and love, and foreswore any hurt that I did with her, till at last she seemed to be at ease again, and so toward morning a little sleep, and so I with some little repose and rest.

26TH. Rose, and up and by water to White Hall, but with my mind mightily troubled for the poor girle, whom I fear I have undone by this, my [wife] telling me that she would turn her out of doors. However, I was obliged to attend the Duke of York. Thence by coach home and to dinner, finding my wife mightily discontented, and the girle sad, and no words from my wife to her. So after dinner they out with me about two or three things, and so home again, I all the evening busy, and my wife full of trouble in her looks, and anon to bed, where about midnight she wakes me, and there falls foul of me again, affirming that she saw me hug and kiss the girle; the latter I denied, and truly, the other I confessed and no more, and upon her pressing me did offer to give her under my hand that I would never see Mrs. Pierce more nor Knepp, but did promise her particular demonstrations of my true love to her, owning some indiscretions in what I did, but that there was no harm in it. She at last upon these promises was quiet, and very kind we were, and so to sleep.

27TH. In the morning up, but my mind troubled for the poor girle, with whom I could not get the opportunity to speak, but to the office, my mind mighty full of sorrow for her. My wife did towards bedtime begin in a mighty rage from some new matter that she had got in her head, and did most part of the night in bed rant at me in most high terms of threats of publishing my shame, and when I offered to rise would have rose too, and caused a candle to be light to burn by her all night in the chimney while she ranted, while the knowing myself to have given some grounds for it, did make it my business to appease her all I could possibly, and by good words and fair promises did make her very quiet, and so rested all night, and rose with perfect good peace, being heartily afflicted for this folly of mine that did occasion it, but was forced to be silent about the girle, which I had no mind to part with, but much less that the poor girle should be undone by my folly. So up with mighty kindness from my wife and a thorough peace, and being up did by a note advise the girle what I had done and owned, which note I was in pain for till she told me she had burned it.

NOVEMBER 3RD. So home, and there to supper, and I observed my wife to eye my eyes whether I did ever look upon Deb., which I could not but do now and then (and to my grief did see the poor wretch look on me and see me look on her, and then let drop a tear or two, which do make my heart relent at this minute that I am writing this with great trouble of mind, for she is indeed my sacrifice, poor girle); and my wife did tell me in bed by and by of my looking on other people, and that the only way is to put things out of sight, and this I know she means by Deb.

5TH. Up, and Willet come home in the morning, and, God forgive me! I could not conceal my content thereat by smiling, and my wife observed it, but I said nothing, nor she, but away to the Office.

6TH. Up, and presently my wife up with me, which she professedly now do every day to dress me, that I may not see Willet, and do eye me, whether I cast my eye upon her, or no, and do keep me from going into the room where she is among the upholsters at work in our blue chamber.

8TH (LORD'S DAY). Up, and at my chamber all the morning, setting papers to rights, with my boy; and so to dinner at noon. The girle with us, but my wife troubled thereat to see her, and do tell me so, which troubles me, for I love the girle.

9TH. Up, and I did by a little note which I flung to Deb. advise her that I did continue to deny that ever I kissed her, and so she might govern herself. The girl read, and as I bid her return me the note, flinging it to me in passing by. And so I abroad by [coach] to White Hall, and there to the Duke of York to wait on him.

10TH. Up, and my wife still every day as ill as she is all night, will rise to see me out doors, telling me plainly that she dares not let me see the girle, and so I out to the office, where all the morning, and so home to dinner, where I found my wife mightily troubled again, more than ever, and she tells me that it is from her examining the girle and getting a confession now from her of all . . . which do mightily trouble me, as not being able to foresee the consequences of it, as to our future peace together. We to talk again, and she to be troubled, reproaching me with my unkindness and perjury, I having denied my ever kissing her. As also with all her old kindnesses to me, and my ill-using of her from the beginning, and the many temptations she hath refused out of faithfulness to me, whereof several she was particular in, and especially from my Lord Sandwich, by the sollicitation of Captain Ferrers, and then afterward the courtship of my Lord Hinchingbrooke, even to the trouble of his lady. All which I did acknowledge and was troubled for, and wept, and at last pretty good friends again, and so I to my office, and there late.

11TH. To the office, and there having done, I home and to supper and to bed, where, after lying a little while, my wife starts up, and with expressions of affright and madness, as one frantick, would rise, and I would not let her, but burst out in tears myself, and so continued almost half the night, the moon shining so that it was light, and after much sorrow and re-proaches and little ravings (though I am apt to think they were counterfeit from her), and my promise again to discharge the girle myself, all was quiet again, and so to sleep.

12TH. I to my wife and to sit with her a little and then called her and Willet to my chamber, and there did, with tears in my eyes, which I could not help, discharge her and advise her to be gone as soon as she could, and never to see me, or let me see her more while she was in the house, which she took with tears too, but I believe understands me to be her friend, and I am apt to believe by what my wife hath of late told me is a cunning girle, if not a slut. Thence, parting kindly with my wife, I away by coach to my cozen Roger.

13TH. To White Hall, and there staid in Mr. Wren's cham-ber with him. He tells me that there is no way to rule the King but by brisknesse, which the Duke of Buckingham hath above all men; and that the Duke of York having it not, his best way is what he practices, that is to say, a good temper, which will support him till the Duke of Buckingham and Lord Arlington fall out, which cannot be long first. Thence I home, and there to talk, with great pleasure all the evening, with my wife, who tells me that Deb. has been abroad to-day, and is come home and says she has got a place to go to, so as she will be gone to-morrow morning. This troubled me. But she will be gone and I not know whither. Before we went to bed my wife told me she would not have me to see her or give her her wages, and so I did give my wife £10 for her year, and half a quarter's wages which she went into her chamber and paid her, and so to bed, and there, blessed be God! we did sleep well and with peace, which I had not done in now almost twenty nights to-gether.

14TH. I to the Office, with my heart sad, and find that I can-not forget the girl, and vexed I know not where to look for her.

And more troubled to see how my wife is by this means likely for ever to have her hand over me, that I shall for ever be a slave to her—that is to say, only in matters of pleasure.

15TH (LORD'S DAY). So to supper and to bed, with my mind pretty quiet, and less troubled about Deb. than I was, though yet I am troubled, I must confess, and would be glad to find her out, though I fear it would be my ruin.

16TH. Up, and by water to White Hall. This being done I away to Holborne, about Whetstone's Park, where I never was in my life before, where I understand by my wife's discourse that Deb. is gone, which do trouble me mightily that the poor girle should be in a desperate condition forced to go thereabouts, and there not hearing of any such man as Allbon, with whom my wife said she now was.

18TH. Lay long in bed talking with my wife, she being unwilling to have me go abroad, saying and declaring herself jealous of my going out for fear of my going to Deb., which I do deny, for which God forgive me, for I was no sooner out about noon but I did go by coach directly to Somerset House, and there enquired among the porters there for Dr. Allbun, and the first I spoke with told me he knew him, and that he was newly gone to Lincoln's Inn Fields, but whither he could not tell me. At last he comes back and tells me she is well, and that I may see her if I will, but no more. So I could not be commanded by my reason, but I must go this very night, and so by coach, it being now dark, I to her, close by my tailor's, and she come into the coach to me, and *je* did *baiser* her. . . . I did nevertheless give her the best council I could, to have a care of her honour, and to fear God, and suffer no man *para avoir* to do *con* her as *je* have done, which she promised. *Je* did give her 20s. and directions *para laisser* sealed in paper at any time the name of the place of her being at Herringman's, my bookseller in the 'Change, by which I might go *para* her, and so bid her good night with much content to my mind, and resolution to look after her no more till I heard from her. And so home, and there told my wife a fair tale, God knows, how I spent the whole day, with which the poor wretch was satisfied, or at least seemed so, she having been mighty busy all day in getting of her house in order against to-morrow to hang up our new hangings and furnishing our best chamber.

19TH. Up, and at the Office all the morning, with my heart full of joy to think in what a safe condition all my matters now stand between my wife and Deb. and me, and at noon running up stairs to see the upholsters, who are at work upon hanging my best room, and setting up my new bed, I find my wife sitting sad in the dining room; which enquiring into the reason of, she begun to call me all the false, rotten-hearted rogues in the world, letting me understand that I was with Deb. yesterday, which, thinking it impossible for her ever to understand, I did a while deny, but at last did, for the ease of my mind and hers, and for ever to discharge my heart of this wicked business, I did confess all, and above stairs in our bed chamber there I did endure the sorrow of her threats and vows and curses all the afternoon, and, what was worse, she swore by all that was good that she would slit the nose of this girle, and be gone herself this very night from me, and did there demand 3 or £400 of me to buy my peace, that she might be gone without making any noise, or else protested that she would make all the world know of it. So with most perfect confusion of face and heart, and sorrow and shame, in the greatest agony in the world I did pass this afternoon, fearing that it will never have an end; but at last I did call for W. Hewer, who I was forced to make privy now to all, and the poor fellow did cry like a child, [and] obtained what I could not, that she would be pacified upon condition that I would give it under my hand never to see or speak with Deb. while I live. So, before it was late, there was, beyond my hopes as well as desert, a durable peace; and so to supper, and pretty kind words, and to bed, and did this night begin to pray to God upon my knees alone in my chamber, which God knows I cannot yet do heartily; but I hope God will give me the grace more and more every day to fear Him, and to be true to my poor wife.

20TH. This morning up, with mighty kind words between my poor wife and I; and so to White Hall by water, W. Hewer with me, who is to go with me every where, until my wife be in condition to go out along with me herself; for she do plainly declare that she dares not trust me out alone, and therefore made it a piece of our league that I should always take somebody with me, or her herself, which I am mighty willing to, being, by the grace of God, resolved never to do her wrong more.

22ND (LORD'S DAY). My wife and I lay long, with mighty content; and so rose, and she spent the whole day making herself clean, after four or five weeks being in continued dirt; and I knocking up nails, and making little settlements in my house, till noon, and then eat a bit of meat in the kitchen, I all alone.

23RD. So to White Hall, where a Committee of Tangier expected, but none met. Thence with W. Hewer, who goes up and down with me like a jaylour, but yet with great love and to my great good liking, it being my desire above all things to please my wife therein.

25TH. My wife and I to the Duke of York's house, to see "The Duchesse of Malfy," a sorry play, and sat with little pleasure, for fear of my wife's seeing me look about, and so I was uneasy all the while, though I desire and resolve never to give her trouble of that kind more. So home at noon to dinner, where I find Mr. Pierce and his wife: but I was forced to shew very little pleasure in her being there because of my vow to my wife.

28TH. Up, and all the morning at the Office, where, while I was sitting, one comes and tells me that my coach is come. So I was forced to go out, and to Sir Richard Ford's, where I spoke to him, and he is very willing to have it brought in, and stand there; and so I ordered it, to my great content, it being mighty pretty, only the horses do not please me, and, therefore, resolve to have better.

29TH (LORD'S DAY). This morning my coachman's clothes come home; and I like the livery mightily.

30TH. Up betimes, and with W. Hewer, who is my guard, to White Hall, to a Committee of Tangier.

DECEMBER 2ND. Abroad with my wife, the first time that ever I rode in my own coach, which do make my heart rejoice, and praise God, and pray him to bless it to me and continue it. So she and I to the King's playhouse, and there sat to avoid seeing Knepp in a box above where Mrs. Williams happened to be, and there saw "The Usurper;" a pretty good play, in all but what is designed to resemble Cromwell and Hugh Peters, which is mighty silly. The play done, we to White Hall; where my wife staid while I up to the Duchesse's and Queen's side, to speak with the Duke of York: and here saw all the ladies, and heard the silly discourse of the King, with his people about him, telling a story of my Lord Rochester's having of his clothes stole, while he was with a wench; and his gold all gone, but his clothes found afterwards stuffed into a feather bed by the wench that stole them.

3RD. And so home, it being mighty pleasure to go alone with my poor wife, in a coach of our own, to a play, and makes us appear mighty great, I think, in the world; at least, greater than ever I could, or my friends for me, have once expected; or, I think, than ever any of my family ever yet lived, in my memory, but my cozen Pepys in Salisbury Court.

5TH. Up, after a little talk with my wife, which troubled me, she being ever since our late difference mighty watchful of sleep and dreams, and will not be persuaded but I do dream of Deb., and do tell me that I speak in my dreams and that this night I did cry, Huzzy, and it must be she, and now and then I start otherwise than I used to do, she says, which I know not, for I do not know that I dream of her more than usual, though I cannot deny that my thoughts waking do run now and then against my will and judgment upon her, for that only is wanting to undo me, being now in every other thing as to my mind most happy, and may still be so but for my own fault, if I be catched loving any body but my wife again.

7TH. This afternoon, passing through Queen's Street, I saw pass by our coach on foot Deb., which, God forgive me, did put me into some new thoughts of her, and for her, but durst not shew them, and I think my wife did not see her, but I did get my thoughts free of her soon as I could.

9TH. So took our coach and home, having now little pleasure to look about me to see the fine faces, for fear of displeasing my wife, whom I take great comfort now, more than ever, in pleasing; and it is a real joy to me.

12TH. This day was brought home my pair of black coach-horses, the first I ever was master of. They cost me £50, and are a fine pair.

18TH. And so home, where I have a new fight with my wife, who is under new trouble by some news she hath heard of Deb.'s being mighty fine, and gives out that she has a friend that gives her money, and this my wife believes to be me, and, poor wretch! I cannot blame her, and therefore she run into mighty extremes.

25TH (CHRISTMAS-DAY). Up, and continued on my waist-coat, the first day this winter, and I to church. So home, and to dinner alone with my wife, who, poor wretch! sat undressed all day, till ten at night, altering and lacing of a noble petticoat: while I by her, making the boy read to me the Life of Julius

Caesar, and Des Cartes' book of Musick—the latter of which I understand not, nor think he did well that writ it, though a most learned man. Then, after supper, I made the boy play upon his lute, and so, my mind in mighty content, we to bed.

26TH. Lay long with pleasure, prating with my wife, and then up, and a little to the Office.

27TH (LORD'S DAY). So home, my coach coming for me, and there find Balty and Mr. How, who dined with me; and there my wife and I fell out a little about the foulness of the linen of the table, but were friends presently, but she cried, poor heart! which I was troubled for, though I did not give her one hard word.

28TH. Up, called up by drums and trumpets; these things and boxes having cost me much money this Christmas already, and will do more.

1669

JANUARY 1ST. Up, and presented from Captain Beckford with a noble silver warming-pan, which I am doubtful whether to take or no.

7TH. Up, and to the office, where busy all the morning, and then at noon home to dinner, and thence my wife and I to the King's playhouse, and there saw "The Island Princesse," the first time I ever saw it; and it is a pretty good play, many good things being in it, and a good scene of a town on fire. We sat in an upper box, and the jade Nell come and sat in the next box; a bold merry slut, who lay laughing there upon people; and with a comrade of hers of the Duke's house, that come in to see the play.

11TH. Up, and with W. Hewer, my guard, to White Hall. So home; and there at home all the evening; and made Tom to prick down some little conceits and notions of mine, in musique, which do mightily encourage me to spend some more thoughts about it; for I fancy, upon good reason, that I am in the

right way of unfolding the mystery of this matter, better than
ever yet.

12TH. This evening I observed my wife mighty dull, and I
myself was not mighty fond, because of some hard words she
did give me at noon, out of a jealousy at my being abroad this
morning, which, God knows, it was upon the business of the
Office unexpectedly; but I to bed, not thinking but she would
come after me. But waking by and by out of a slumber, which I
usually fall into presently after my coming into the bed, I found
she did not prepare to come to bed, but got fresh candles, and
more wood for her fire, it being mighty cold, too. At this being
troubled, I after a while prayed her to come to bed, all my people being gone to bed; so, after an hour or two, she silent, and I
now and then praying her to come to bed, she fell out into a
fury, that I was a rogue, and false to her. At last, about one
o'clock, she come to my side of the bed, and drew my curtaine
open, and with the tongs red hot at the ends, made as if she did
design to pinch me with them, at which, in dismay, I rose up,
and with a few words she laid them down; and did by little and
little, very sillily, let all the discourse fall; and about two, but
with much seeming difficulty, come to bed, and there lay well
all night.

15TH. With Lord Brouncker to Sir R. Murray, into the
King's little elaboratory, under his closet, a pretty place; and
there saw a great many chymical glasses and things, but understood none of them.

16TH. That my Lady Castlemayne is now in a higher command over the King than ever—not as a mistress, for she scorns
him, but as a tyrant, to command him.

22ND. Up, and with W. Hewer to White Hall, and there attended the Duke of York, and thence to the Exchange, in the
way calling at several places on occasions relating to my feast
to-morrow, on which my mind is now set; and then home to

look after things against to-morrow, and among other things was mightily pleased with the fellow that come to lay the cloth, and fold the napkins, which I like so well, as that I am resolved to give him 40s. to teach my wife to do it. So to supper, with much kindness between me and my wife, which, now-a-days, is all my care, and so to bed.

23RD. Up, and again to look after the setting things right against dinner, which I did to very good content. So to the office, where all the morning till noon, when word brought me to the Board that my Lord Sandwich was come; so I presently rose, leaving the Board ready to rise, and there I found my Lord Sandwich, Peterborough, and Sir Charles Harbord; and presently after them comes my Lord Hinchingbroke, Mr. Sidney, and Sir William Godolphin. And after greeting them, and some time spent in talk, dinner was brought up, one dish after another, but a dish at a time, but all so good; but, above all things, the variety of wines, and excellent of their kind, I had for them, and all in so good order, that they were mightily pleased, and myself full of content at it: and indeed it was, of a dinner of about six or eight dishes, as noble as any man need to have, I think; at least, all was done in the noblest manner that ever I had any, and I have rarely seen in my life better anywhere else, even at the Court. After dinner, my Lords to cards, and the rest of us sitting about them and talking, and looking on my books and pictures, and my wife's drawings, which they commend mightily; and mighty merry all day long, with exceeding great content, and so till seven at night; and so took their leaves, it being dark and foul weather. Thus was this entertainment over, the best of its kind, and the fullest of honour and content to me, that ever I had in my life: and shall not easily have so good again. So to my wife's chamber, and there supped, and got her cut my hair and look my shirt, for I have itched mightily these 6 or 7 days, and when all comes to all she finds that I am lousy, having found in my head and body about twenty lice, little and great, which I wonder at, being more than I have had I believe these 20 years. I did think I might have got them from the little boy, but they did presently look him, and found none. So how they come I know not, but presently did shift myself, and so shall be rid of them, and cut my hair close to my head, and so with much content to bed.

FEBRUARY 1ST. Meeting Mr. Povy, he and I away to Dancre's. Thence set him down at Little Turnstile, and so I home, and there eat a little dinner, and away with my wife by coach to the King's playhouse, thinking to have seen "The Heyresse," first acted on Saturday last; but when we come thither, we find no play there; Kinaston, that did act a part therein, in abuse to Sir Charles Sedley, being last night exceedingly beaten with sticks, by two or three that assaulted him, so he is mightily bruised, and forced to keep his bed.

1OTH. Up, and with my wife and W. Hewer, she set us down at White Hall, where the Duke of York was gone a-hunting: and so, after I had done a little business there, I to my wife, and with her to the plaisterer's at Charing Cross, that casts heads and bodies in plaister: and there I had my whole face done; but I was vexed first to be forced to daub all my face over with pomatum: but it was pretty to feel how soft and easily it is done on the face, and by and by, by degrees, how hard it becomes, that you cannot break it, and sits so close, that you cannot pull it off, and yet so easy, that it is as soft as a pillow, so safe is everything where many parts of the body do bear alike. Thus was the mould made; but when it came off there was little pleasure in it, as it looks in the mould, nor any resemblance whatever there will be in the figure, when I come to see it cast off, which I am to call for a day or two hence, which I shall long to see.

12TH. And so home, and there Pelling hath got me W. Pen's book against the Trinity. I got my wife to read it to me; and I find it so well writ as, I think, it is too good for him ever to have writ it; and it is a serious sort of book, and not fit for every body to read.

15TH. Up, and with Tom to White Hall and then to the plaisterer's, and there saw the figure of my face taken from the mould: and it is most admirably like, and I will have another made, before I take it away.

17TH. At home comes Castle to me, to desire me to go to Mr. Pedly this night, which I, therefore, did, by hackney-coach, first going to White Hall to meet with Sir W. Coventry, but missed him. But here I had a pleasant *rencontre* of a lady in mourning, that, by the little light I had, seemed handsome. I passing by her, I did observe she looked back again and again upon me, I suffering her to go before, and it being now duske. I observed she went into the little passage towards the Privy Water-Gate, and I followed, but missed her; but coming back again, I observed she returned, and went to go out of the Court. I followed her, and took occasion, in the new passage now built, where the walke is to be, to take her by the hand, to lead her through, which she willingly accepted, and I led her to the Great Gate, and there left her, she telling me, of her own accord, that she was going as far as Charing Cross; but my boy was at the gate, and so *je* durst not go out *con* her, which vexed me, and my mind (God forgive me) did run *après* her *toute* that night, though I have reason to thank God, and so I do now, that I was not tempted to go further.

18TH. Up, and to the Office, and at noon home, expecting to have this day seen Bab. and Betty Pepys here, but they come not; and so after dinner my wife and I to the Duke of York's house, to a play, and there saw "The Mad Lover," which do not please me so well as it used to do, only Betterton's part still pleases me. But here who should we have come to us but Bab. and Betty and Talbot, the first play they were yet at; and then took Bab. and Betty to our house, where they lay and supped, and pretty merry, and very fine with their new clothes, and good comely girls they are enough, and very glad I am of their being with us, though I would very well have been contented to have been without the charge. So they to bed and we to bed.

21ST (LORD'S DAY). Here we dined with W. Batelier, and W. Hewer with us, these two girls making it necessary that they be always with us, for I am not company light enough to be always merry with them: and so sat talking all the afternoon, and then Shepley went away first, and then my cozen Roger and his wife. And so I to my Office, to write down my Journall, and so home to my chamber and to do a little business there, my papers being in mighty disorder, and likely so to continue while these girls are with us.

23RD. Up: and to the Office, where all the morning, and then home, and put a mouthfull of victuals in my mouth; and by a hackney-coach followed my wife and the girls, who are gone by eleven o'clock, thinking to have seen a new play at the Duke of York's house. But I do find them staying at my tailor's, the play not being to-day, and therefore I now took them to Westminster Abbey, and there did show them all the tombs very finely, having one with us alone, there being other company this day to see the tombs, it being Shrove Tuesday; and here we did see, by particular favour, the body of Queen Katherine of Valois; and I had the upper part of her body in my hands, and I did kiss her mouth, reflecting upon it that I did kiss a Queen, and that this was my birth-day, thirty-six years old, that I did first kiss a Queen. But here this man, who seems to understand well, tells me that the saying is not true that says she was never buried, for she was buried; only, when Henry the Seventh built his chapel, it was taken up and laid in this wooden coffin; but I did there see that, in it, the body was buried in a leaden one, which remains under the body to this day. Thence to the Duke of York's playhouse, and there, finding the play begun, we homeward to the Glass-House, and there shewed my cozens the making of glass, and had several things made with great content; and, among others, I had one or two singing-glasses made, which make an echo to the voice, the first that ever I saw; but so thin, that the very breath broke one or two of them.

26TH. Was forced to send my excuse to the Duke of York for not attending him with my fellows this day because of my cold.

MARCH 1ST. Surprised this morning by my Lord Bellassis, who, by appointment, met me at Auditor Woods, at the Temple, and tells me of a duell designed between the Duke of Buckingham and my Lord Halifax, or Sir W. Coventry; the challenge being carried by Harry Saville, but prevented by my Lord Arlington, and the King told of it; and this was all the discourse at Court this day.

4TH. Up, and a while at the office, and away to White Hall, where in the first court I did meet Sir Jeremy Smith, who did tell me that Sir W. Coventry was just now sent to the Tower, about the business of his challenging the Duke of Buckingham.

8TH. Up, and with W. Hewer by hackney coach to White Hall, where the King and the Duke of York is gone by three in the morning, and had the misfortune to be over-set with the Duke of York, the Duke of Monmouth, and the Prince at the King's Gate in Holborne; and the King all dirty, but no hurt. How it come to pass I know not, but only it was dark, and the torches did not, they say, light the coach as they should do.

9TH. Up, and to the Tower; and there find Sir W. Coventry alone, writing down his Journal, which, he tells me, he now keeps of the material things; upon which I told him, and he is the only man I ever told it to, I think, that I kept it most secretly these eight or ten years; and I am sorry almost that I told it him, it not being necessary, nor may be convenient, to have it known.

11TH. Up, and to Sir W. Coventry, to the Tower, where I walked and talked with him an hour alone, from one good thing to another.

12TH. In my coach with W. Hewer towards Westminster; and there to Nott's, the famous bookbinder, that bound for my Lord Chancellor's library; and here I did take occasion for curiosity to bespeak a book to be bound, only that I might have one of his binding. And so home, where, thinking to meet my wife with content, after my pains all this day, I find her in her closet, alone, in the dark, in a hot fit of railing against me, upon some news she has this day heard of Deb.'s living very fine, and with black spots, and speaking ill words of her mistress, which with good reason might vex her; and the baggage is to blame, but, God knows, I know nothing of her, nor what she do, nor what becomes of her, though God knows that my devil that is within me do wish that I could. But in her fit she did tell me what vexed me all the night, that this had put her upon putting off her handsome maid and hiring another that was full of the small pox, which did mightily vex me, though I said nothing, and do still.

18TH. To the Office, where we sat all the morning, and so home to dinner, where my wife mighty finely dressed, by a maid that she hath taken, and is to come to her when Jane goes; and the same she the other day told me of, to be so handsome. I therefore longed to see her, but did not till after dinner, that my wife and I going by coach, she went with us to Holborne, where we set her down. She is a mighty proper maid, and pretty comely, but so so; but hath a most pleasing tone of voice, and speaks handsomely, but hath most great hands, and I believe ugly; but very well dressed, and good clothes, and the maid I believe will please me well enough.

21ST (LORD'S DAY). News is lately come of the Algerines taking £13,000 in money, out of one of our Company's East India ships, outward bound, which will certainly make the war last; which I am sorry for, being so poor as we are, and broken in pieces.

22ND. Up, and by water, with W. Hewer, to White Hall, there to attend the Lords of the Treasury; but, before they sat, I did make a step to see Sir W. Coventry at his house, where, I bless God! he is come again; but in my way I met him, and so he took me into his coach and carried me to White Hall, and there set me down where he ought not—at least he hath not yet leave to come.

23RD. After supper, we fell to talk of spirits and apparitions, whereupon many pretty, particular stories were told, so as to make me almost afeard to lie alone, but for shame I could not help it; and so to bed; and, being sleepy, fell soon to rest, and so rested well.

25TH. Up, and by and by, about eight o'clock, come Rear-Admiral Kempthorne and seven Captains more, by the Duke of York's order, as we expected, to hold the Court-martiall about the loss of "The Defyance;" and so presently we by boat to "The Charles," which lies over against Upnor Castle, and there we fell to the business; and there I did manage the business, the Duke of York having, by special order, directed them to take the assistance of Commissioner Middleton and me, forasmuch as there might be need of advice in what relates to the government of the ships in harbour. And so I did lay the law open to them, and rattle the Master-Attendants out of their wits almost; and made the trial last till seven at night, not eating a bit all the day; only when we had done examination, and I given my thoughts that the neglect of the Gunner of the ship was as great as I thought any neglect could be, which might by the law deserve death, but Commissioner Middleton did declare that he was against giving the sentence of death, we withdrew, as not being of the Court, and so left them to do what they pleased; and, while they were debating it, the Boatswain of the ship did bring us out of the kettle a piece of hot salt beef, and some brown bread and brandy; and there we did make a little meal, but so good as I never would desire to eat better meat while I live, only I would have cleaner dishes. By and by they had done, and called us down from the quarter-deck; and there we find they do sentence that the Gunner of "The Defyance" should stand upon "The Charles" three hours with his fault writ upon his breast, and with a halter about his neck, and so be made incapable of any office. The truth is, the man do seem, and is, I believe, a good man; but his neglect, in trusting a girl to carry fire into his cabin, is not to be pardoned. This being done, we took boat and home.

31st. Up, and by water to Sir W. Coventry's, there to talk with him about business of the Navy. After much discourse with him, I walked out with him into St. James's Park, where, being afeard to be seen with him, he having not leave yet to kiss the King's hand, but notice taken, as I hear, of all that go to him, I did take the pretence of my attending the Tangier Committee, to take my leave, though to serve him I should, I think, stick at nothing.

April 2nd. Up, and by water to White Hall, and there with the Office attended the Duke of York. In the mean time, stepping to the Duchess of York's side to speak with Lady Peterborough, I did see the young Duchess, a little child in hanging sleeves, dance most finely, so as almost to ravish me, her ears were so good: taught by a Frenchman that did heretofore teach the King, and all the King's children, and the Queen-Mother herself, who do still dance well.

6th. Middleton and I did in plain terms acquaint the Duke of York what we thought and had observed in the late Court-martiall, which the Duke did give ear to; and though he thinks not fit to revoke what is already done in this case by a Court-martiall, yet it shall bring forth some good laws in the behaviour of Captains to their under Officers for the time to come.

9th. Among others to Westminster Hall, and I took occasion to make a step to Mrs. Martin's, the first time I have been with her since her husband went last to sea, which is I think a year since.

10th. After dinner comes Mr. Seymour to visit me, a talking fellow: but I hear by him that Captain Trevanion do give it out everywhere, that I did over-rule the whole Court-martiall against him, as long as I was there; and perhaps I may receive, at this time, some wrong by it: but I care not, for what I did was out of my desire of doing justice.

13TH. I away home, and there sent for W. Hewer, and he and I by water to White Hall to look, among other things, for Mr. May, to unbespeak his dining with me to-morrow. But here being in the court-yard, as God would have it, I spied Deb., which made my heart and head to work, and I presently could not refrain, but sent W. Hewer away to look for Mr. Wren (W. Hewer, I perceive, did see her, but whether he did see me see her I know not, or suspect my sending him away I know not, but my heart could not hinder me), and I run after her and two women and a man, more ordinary people, and she in her old clothes, and after hunting a little, find them in the lobby of the chapel below stairs, and there I observed she endeavoured to avoid me, but I did speak to her and she to me, and did get her *pour dire me où* she *demeurs* now, and did charge her *para* say nothing of me that I had *vu elle,* which she did promise, and so with my heart full of surprize and disorder I away. And so back to White Hall, and then back to the Park with Mr. May, but could see her no more, and so with W. Hewer, who I doubt by my countenance might see some disorder in me, we home by water, to my wife, who is come home from Deptford. But, God forgive me, I hardly know how to put on confidence enough to speak as innocent, having had this passage to-day with Deb., though only, God knows, by accident. But my great pain is lest God Almighty shall suffer me to find out this girl, whom indeed I love, and with a bad *amour,* but I will pray to God to give me grace to forbear it.

14TH. Up, and with W. Hewer to White Hall, and there I did speak with the Duke of York, the Council sitting in the morning. Thence home, and there to talk and to supper and to bed, all being very safe as to my seeing of poor Deb. yesterday.

15TH. Up, and to the office, and thence before the office sat to the Excise Office with W. Hewer, but found some occasion to go another way to the Temple upon business, and I by Deb.'s direction did know whither in Jewen Street to direct my hackney coachman. Thence I away, and through Jewen Street, my mind, God knows, running that way, but stopped not, but going down Holborne hill, by the Conduit, I did see Deb. on foot going up the hill. I saw her, and she me, but she made no stop, but seemed unwilling to speak to me; so I away on, but then stopped and 'light, and after her and overtook her at the end of Hosier lane in Smithfield, and without standing in the street desired her to follow me, and I led her into a little blind ale-house within the walls, and there she and I alone fell to talk and *baiser la* and *toker su mammailles,* but she mighty coy, and I hope modest. . . . I did give her in a paper 20s., and we did agree *para* meet again in the Hall at Westminster on Monday next; and so giving me great hopes by her carriage that she continues mod-est and honest, we did there part, she going home and I to Mrs. Turner's.

23RD. Here, by accident, we met Mr. Sheres, and yet I could not but be troubled, because my wife do so delight to talk of him, and to see him. Nevertheless, we took him with us to our mercer's, and to the Exchange, and he helped me to choose a summer-suit of coloured camelott, coat and breeches, and a flowered tabby vest very rich; and so home, where he took his leave.

24TH. Up, and to the office, where all the morning, and at noon home to dinner, Mr. Sheres dining with us by agreement; and my wife, which troubled me, mighty careful to have a handsome dinner for him; but yet I see no reason to be troubled at it, he being a very civil and worthy man, I think; but only it do seem to imply some little neglect of me. Well pleased to-night to have Lead, the vizard-maker, bring me home my vizard, with a tube fastened in it, which, I think, will do my business, at least in a great measure, for the easing of my eyes.

25TH (LORD'S DAY). Up, and to my Office awhile, and thither comes Lead with my vizard, with a tube fastened within both eyes; which, with the help he prompts me to, of a glass in the tube, do content me mightily.

26TH. Creed, coming just now to see me, my wife, and he, and I out, and I set him down at Temple Bar, and myself and wife went down the Temple upon seeming business, only to put him off, and just at the Temple gate I spied Deb. with another gentlewoman, and Deb. winked on me and smiled, but undiscovered, and I was glad to see her. So my wife and I to the 'Change, about things for her.

MAY 1ST. Up betimes. Called up by my tailor, and there first put on a summer suit this year: but it was not my fine one of flowered tabby vest, and coloured camelott tunique, because it was too fine with the gold lace at the hands, that I was afeard to be seen in it; but put on the stuff suit I made the last year, which is now repaired; and so did go to the Office in it, and sat all the morning, the day looking as if it would be fowle. At noon home to dinner, and there find my wife extraordinary fine, with her flowered tabby gown that she made two years ago, now laced exceeding pretty; and, indeed, was fine all over; and mighty earnest to go, though the day was very lowering; and she would have me put on my fine suit, which I did. And so anon we went alone through the town with our new liveries of serge, and the horses' manes and tails tied with red ribbons, and the standards there gilt with varnish, and all clean, and green reines, that people did mightily look upon us; and, the truth is, I did not see any coach more pretty, though more gay, than ours, all the day.

3RD. To White Hall, and met with Creed, and I took him to the Harp and Balls, and there drank a cup of ale, he and I alone, and discoursed of matters; and I perceive by him that he makes no doubt but that all will turn to the old religion, for these people cannot hold things in their hands, nor prevent its coming to that; and by his discourse fits himself for it, and would have my Lord Sandwich do so, too, and me.

7TH. So to the Treasury chamber, and then walked home round by the Excise Office, having by private vows last night in prayer to God Almighty cleared my mind for the present of the thoughts of going to Deb. at Greenwich, which I did long after.

I passed by Guildhall, which is almost finished, and saw a poor labourer carried by, I think, dead with a fall, as many there are, I hear. Thence with my wife abroad, with our coach, most pleasant weather; and to Hackney, and into the marshes, where I never was before, and thence round about to Old Ford and Bow; and coming through the latter home, there being some young gentlewomen at a door, and I seeming not to know who they were, my wife's jealousy told me presently that I knew well enough it was that damned place where Deb. dwelt, which made me swear very angrily that it was false, as it was, and I carried [her] back again to see the place, and it proved not so, so I continued out of humour for a good while at it, she being willing to be friends, so I was by and by, saying no more of it.

10TH. Troubled, about three in the morning, with my wife's calling her maid up, and rising herself, to go with her coach abroad, to gather May-dew, which she did, and I troubled for it, for fear of any hurt, going abroad so betimes, happening to her; but I to sleep again, and she come home about six, and to bed again all well. To White Hall, and thence walked, my boy Jacke with me, to my Lord Crew, whom I have not seen since he was sick, which is eight months ago, I think, and there dined with him: he is mightily broke. A stranger, a country gentleman, was with him: and he pleased with my discourse accidentally about the decay of gentlemen's families in the country, telling us that the old rule was, that a family might remain fifty miles from London one hundred years, one hundred miles from London two hundred years, and so farther or nearer London more or less years. He also told us that he hath heard his father say, that in his time it was so rare for a country gentleman to come to London, that, when he did come, he used to make his will before he set out. Thence I to White Hall, and there took boat to Westminster, and to Mrs. Martin's, who is not come to town from her husband at Portsmouth. So drank only at Cragg's with Doll, and so to the Swan, and there *baiser* a new maid that is there.

11TH. My wife again up by four o'clock, to gather May-dew; and so back home by seven, to bed.

16TH (LORD'S DAY). I all the afternoon drawing up a foul draught of my petition to the Duke of York, about my eyes, for leave to spend three or four months out of the Office, drawing it so as to give occasion to a voyage abroad, which I did, to my pretty good liking.

19TH. With my coach to St. James's; and there finding the Duke of York gone to muster his men, in Hyde Park, I alone with my boy thither, and there saw more, walking out of my coach as other gentlemen did, of a soldier's trade, than ever I did in my life: the men being mighty fine, and their Commanders, particularly the Duke of Monmouth; but methought their trade but very easy as to the mustering of their men, and the men but indifferently ready to perform what was commanded, in the handling of their arms. Here the news was first talked of Harry Killigrew's being wounded in nine places last night, by footmen, in the highway, going from the Park in a hackney-coach towards Hammersmith, to his house at Turnham Greene: they being supposed to be my Lady Shrewsbury's men, she being by, in her coach with six horses; upon an old grudge of his saying openly that he had lain with her. Thence by and by to White Hall, and there I waited upon the King and Queen all dinner-time, in the Queen's lodgings, she being in her white pinner and apron, like a woman with child; and she seemed handsomer plain so, than dressed. And by and by, dinner done, I out, and to walk in the Gallery, for the Duke of York's coming out; and there, meeting Mr. May, he took me down about four o'clock to Mr. Chevins's lodgings, and all alone did get me a dish of cold chickens, and good wine; and I dined like a prince, being before very hungry and empty. By and by the Duke of York comes, and readily took me to his closet, and received my petition, and discoursed about my eyes, and pitied me, and with much kindness did give me his consent to be absent, and approved of my proposition to go into Holland to observe things there, of the Navy; but would first ask the King's leave, which he anon did, and did tell me that the King would be a good master to me, these were his words, about my eyes, and do like of my going into Holland, but do advise that nobody should know of my going thither, but pretend that I did go into the country somewhere, which I liked well.

20TH. Yesterday, at my coming home, I found that my wife had, on a sudden, put away Matt upon some falling out, and I doubt my wife did call her ill names by my wife's own discourse; but I did not meddle to say anything upon it, but let her go, being not sorry, because now we may get one that speaks French, to go abroad with us.

24TH. To White Hall, where I attended the Duke of York, and was by him led to [the King], who expressed great sense of my misfortune in my eyes, and concernment for their recovery; and accordingly signified, not only his assent to my desire therein, but commanded me to give them rest this summer, according to my late petition to the Duke of York.

31ST. Up very betimes, and so continued all the morning with W. Hewer, upon examining and stating my accounts, in order to the fitting myself to go abroad beyond sea, which the ill condition of my eyes, and my neglect for a year or two, hath kept me behindhand in, and so as to render it very difficult now, and troublesome to my mind to do it; but I this day made a satisfactory entrance therein. Dined at home, and in the afternoon by water to White Hall, calling by the way at Michell's, where I have not been many a day till just the other day, and now I met her mother there and knew her husband to be out of town. And there *je* did *baiser elle*. And thence had another meeting with the Duke of York, at White Hall, on yesterday's work, and made a good advance: and so, being called by my wife, we to the Park, Mary Batelier, and a Dutch gentleman, a friend of hers, being with us. Thence to "The World's End," a drinking-house by the Park; and there merry, and so home late.

And thus ends all that I doubt I shall ever be able to do with my own eyes in the keeping of my Journal, I being not able to do it any longer, having done now so long as to undo my eyes almost every time that I take a pen in my hand; and, therefore, whatever comes of it, I must forbear: and, therefore, resolve, from this time forward, to have it kept by my people in long-hand, and must therefore be contented to set down no more than is fit for them and all the world to know; or, if there be anything, which cannot be much, now my *amours* to Deb. are past, and my eyes hindering me in almost all other pleasures, I must endeavour to keep a margin in my book open, to add, here and there, a note in short-hand with my own hand.

And so I betake myself to that course, which is almost as much as to see myself go into my grave: for which, and all the discomforts that will accompany my being blind, the good God prepare me!

S.P.

May 31, 1669.

A NOTE ON THE TYPE

The principal text of this Modern Library edition
was set in a digitized version of Janson,
a typeface that dates from about 1690 and was cut by
Nicholas Kis, a Hungarian working in Amsterdam.
The original matrices have
survived and are held by the Stempel foundry in Germany.
Hermann Zapf redesigned some of the weights and sizes for
Stempel, basing his revisions on the original design.